The Learning and Teaching of Reading and Writing

The Learning and Teaching of Reading and Writing

NAOMI FLYNN

University of Winchester

RHONA STAINTHORP

Institute of Education, University of London

WILEY

Other Wiley Editorial Offices

John Wiley & Sons Inc., 111 River Street, Hoboken, NJ 07030, USA

Jossey-Bass, 989 Market Street, San Francisco, CA 94103-1741, USA

Wiley-VCH Verlag GmbH, Boschstr. 12, D-69469 Weinheim, Germany

John Wiley & Sons Australia Ltd, 42 McDougall Street, Milton, Queensland 4064, Australia

John Wiley & Sons (Asia) Pte Ltd, 2 Clementi Loop #02-01, Jin Xing Distripark, Singapore 129809

John Wiley & Sons Canada Ltd, 22 Worcester Road, Etobicoke, Ontario, Canada M9W 1L1

Wiley also publishes its books in a variety of electronic formats. Some content that appears in print may not be available in electronic books.

Library of Congress Cataloging-in-Publication Data

Flynn, Naomi.
    The learning and teaching of reading and writing / Naomi Flynn and Rhona Stainthorp.
      p. cm.
    ISBN 0-470-01939-5
    1. Language arts (Elementary)   2. Language arts (Elementary)–England–Case studies.
      I. Stainthorp, Rhona.   II. Title.
    LB1576.F494 2006
    372.6–dc22
                                                                    2005036436

British Library Cataloguing in Publication Data

A catalogue record for this book is available from the British Library

ISBN 10 – 0-470-01939-5
ISBN 13 – 978-0-470-01939-9

Typeset by SNP Best-set Typesetter Ltd., Hong Kong
Printed and bound by TJ International, Padstow, Cornwall, UK
This book is printed on acid-free paper responsibly manufactured from sustainable forestry in which at least two trees are planted for each one used for paper production.

Dedication

We dedicate this book to the three wonderful teachers whose work is described in the following chapters and to their inspired headteachers. As I watched them I learned so much about what makes teachers extraordinary; and I truly understood the power, for tomorrow's teachers, of observing brilliance in action in the classroom.

Naomi Flynn

Contents

About the Authors

Naomi Flynn is a Senior Lecturer in Primary Education at the University of Winchester where she teaches English, Professional Studies and Early Years subject specialism on several initial teacher education programmes. She taught in inner city primary schools for 18 years; the last four serving as a Headteacher. While teaching in and leading a school she worked through the implementation of the NLS and became interested in why its prescribed pedagogy seemed to work well in some schools but not in others. More recently, her interest was further fuelled by observations of disparate interpretations of the NLS in primary schools that gave student teachers a confusing picture of how best to teach reading and writing. This book grew in part from her desire to show both trainee and qualified teachers some fundamental principles for teaching literacy, using current curriculum guidance, which might anchor them in a sea of variable approaches. She acknowledges with grateful thanks the crucial role played by Rhona Stainthorp, in teaching her to see where theory must partner practice in the classroom.

Rhona Stainthorp is a Professor of Education and Director of the Language and Literacy Research Centre in the School of Psychology and Human Development at the Institute of Education, University of London. Her research interests centre on the development and teaching of reading and writing, including spelling and handwriting. She is a psychologist who has been involved in the professional education of teachers for the last thirty years and contributes to both Initial Teacher Education and In Service advanced courses. The present book grew out of a very fruitful collaboration with Naomi Flynn when she supervised her MA work, which received a distinction.

I Learning and Teaching Reading and Writing

1 How to Read this Book

This book contains a combination of guidance relating to literacy development and research into the teaching of literacy in three effective schools. It
is intended to support trainee and newly qualified teachers in adopting a
confident, research-based rationale for their pedagogy for teaching reading
and writing. It will also be useful for more experienced teachers and for literacy coordinators and consultants because it provides a very detailed report
on literacy practice in successful schools and can thus support school improvement. It is a celebration of the work of three schools and three effective
teachers of literacy. It also supports teacher subject knowledge for literacy
both in terms of understanding the development of current classroom practice
and in understanding the significance of research related to literacy development. By using all of the chapters in this book you will be able to see how
research can inform your practice and generate a much more purposeful and
well-grounded logic to your planning and delivery for literacy teaching. You
will also develop an understanding of how knowledge about the teaching of
children with English as an additional language can provide a rich resource
even for teachers of monolingual speakers.

However, you may also use this book in parts. Chapter 2 explains in detail
how the National Literacy Strategy (NLS) became the blueprint for teaching
reading and writing in English primary schools. The text follows arguments
for and against the NLS together with documents monitoring its rise and its
strengths and weaknesses in the first seven years. Chapters 3 and 4 introduce
the reader to research-based models of reading and writing and Chapter 5
covers the general issues for children who speak English as an additional language (EAL). Each of these chapters could stand alone. Our purpose for
including them is to enhance understanding of many of the points we make in
later chapters when we discuss our three effective teachers of literacy and their
schools. They allow the reader to see how schools and teachers might use their
understanding of literacy development and individual needs to fuel their decisions for classroom practice rather than responding to printed guidance.

We refer to our research occasionally in Chapters 2 to 5 but the real heart
of this book is in its later chapters where we report on the detail of the practice
of the three Year 2 teachers observed teaching the Literacy Hour. We explain
the background to their thinking, their planning and their choices for delivery.
In describing their practice we provide fine-grained analyses of each lesson
in order to demonstrate how their chosen pedagogy matched findings related
to effective teaching and, more importantly, to research on how children

develop as readers and writers. These chapters will give food for thought to both new and experienced classroom practitioners. They include references to the research discussed in all of the earlier chapters in the book and show how the teachers' practice was a successful marriage of the NLS *Framework for Teaching* and their understanding of the theoretical basis for early literacy development.

As we introduce these teachers it will become obvious that the large number of EAL pupils in their classes influenced Aidan's and Bridget's practice in particular. Those readers teaching pupils who are all, or almost all, monolingual English speaking pupils may feel that there is little to help them in engaging with their practice. They may, for example, feel more drawn to the observations of Clare whose class was more mixed and who had had different influences on her practice in terms of school setting. Nevertheless, we would urge such readers to observe the practice of all three teachers because, although each had unique qualities that make them fascinating to study, the underlying similarities will demonstrate the richness of practice that is based on understanding how children develop as readers and writers. There is something that each teacher can show us regardless of the settings in which we teach ourselves.

When we studied the practice of these teachers in 2003 we observed the very significant role that successful teacher-talk played in scaffolding learning during their lessons. Success in any lesson was due to a combination of careful planning, effective management of pupils and support staff, secure subject knowledge and rich experiences of teaching English; but the way in which these teachers communicated with their pupils during the lesson appeared perhaps most significant. In the original research we coded the types of teacher-talk that we observed and produced a range of histograms detailing teacher–pupil interaction for each part of the lesson. Such detail is not appropriate for a book of this kind but reference in the teacher chapters to the ways in which the teachers spoke to their pupils has grown from this earlier microanalysis.

In the concluding chapter we report on interviews carried out in 2005 and explore how the schools had moved yet further way from their use of the NLS as they embraced a more creative approach to curriculum planning and delivery. We discuss implications for the practice of individual teachers and of whole-school approaches to teaching literacy.

Throughout our commentary we refer to our schools and our teachers by names. In order to give you a reference point for keeping track of them, the following table details everyone mentioned. In keeping with the ethics of research-based writing all the names are pseudonyms.

Our wish is that you draw from this book two key messages, namely:

- that truly effective pedagogy for literacy grows from a deep understanding of how children learn to be readers and writers

- that starting from the children's learning needs will always be more important in generating successful lessons, than starting with the requirements of any one curriculum framework.

This book will help you to see how you might develop both of the above in your own practice.

Table 1.1 Names used in this book

Schools	Headteachers	Year 2 teachers	EAL coordinators
Anderson Primary	Mr Abbott	Aidan	Alan
Ballard Primary	Ms Bradshaw	Bridget	Ms Bradshaw
Campbell Primary	Ms Chadwick	Clare	Caitlyn

2 Teaching Reading and Writing in English Primary Schools: an Historical Perspective

In this chapter we chart the progress of the NLS as the principal tool used for teaching English in our primary schools. We explore its successes and areas of weakness as evidenced by research and professional commentary. There is some discussion of the link between school effectiveness, school leadership and a corresponding success with the NLS. Furthermore we discuss the ways in which more recent developments in our understanding of effective pedagogy may be encouraging schools to adapt the original model for the Literacy Hour.

The NLS introduced the Literacy Hour and its corresponding *Framework for Teaching* into English primary schools in 1998. Prior to this a number of schools and local education authorities (LEAs) had been involved in a pilot year – the National Literacy Project (NLP) – which had led to modifications in the original model devised by the architects of the NLS. It was undoubtedly one of the most ambitious and large-scale reforms of teaching undertaken by any country in recent years (Fullan, 2000). It attempted to change not only the curriculum for English, by introducing a very detailed scheme of work, but it also set about changing the way in which primary school teachers organised their teaching of reading and writing; it prescribed what was to many teachers a hitherto unused pedagogy for literacy (Fisher and Lewis, 2002). In tackling both the curriculum content and its delivery simultaneously, the NLS was highly focused in its aim to drive up standards in literacy rapidly. This ambition was at times matched with success but at others met with criticism from academics and inspectors alike. The following discussion tracks the flow of comments regarding the NLS as it attempted to change the face of literacy teaching in English schools.

WHY A NATIONAL STRATEGY? MAKING A CASE FOR REFORM

For those of you who are training, who are new to the profession, or who have entered the profession since 1998, it must be difficult to imagine your teaching practice for literacy without using the NLS. Before discussing its introduction, therefore, it is valuable to look at the commentary published in the years prior to the NLS, and to develop some insight into why such a radical root-and-branch reform was considered necessary. Some of the 'evidence' used as a lever for reform was a series of HMI and OfSTED reports between 1991 and 1998, which tracked some improvement in educational standards in schools. These reports make for slightly confusing reading because sometimes they appear to be heavily critical of the teaching of English while acknowledging some improvement of educational standards generally and in the quality of teaching.

It would be disingenuous of us not to acknowledge that what should be entirely an educational issue is often led by the political agenda of the time. Prior to the onset of the National Literacy Project in 1997, the agenda of the then Conservative government included a 'back-to-basics' policy that was also championed by HMCI Woodhead who has since come to be widely associated with a right agenda for schools. The 'Aunt Sally' of this agenda was to suggest that any approach to education that was not predicated on 'back to basics' was 'loony left'.

However, it is now clear that there were concerns about the teaching of literacy that crossed the political divide and it is often very difficult to differentiate between the policies of either of the main English political parties. At the time when the back-to-basics policy was becoming more prominent and Woodhead was HMCI, the concept of regular school inspection using OfSTED was introduced for the first time. This perhaps coloured the tone of some reports because they seemed almost evangelical in their desire to rid the primary sector of what were considered 'loony-left' practices. For example, in *Curriculum Organisation and Classroom Practice in Primary Schools*, an HMI report of 1992, this statement was made:

> Over the last few decades the progress of primary pupils has been hampered by the influence of highly questionable dogmas, which have led to excessively complex classroom practices and devalued the place of subjects in the curriculum.
>
> (DES, 1992, p. 1)

Nevertheless, there was evidence of poor performance among pupils, particularly those in disadvantaged neighbourhoods and, leaving aside politics, there was perhaps a strong case for reform. This reform of literacy and mathematics teaching started under the Conservatives but was in fact implemented by the Labour government after Labour's election victory in 1997. Evidence of how the case for reform grew in strength can be seen by an analysis of commentary prior to 1997.

To begin at some sort of beginning – bearing in mind that any process of reform will draw on decades of preceding thinking and practice – we will start with an introduction to the Kingman Report (DES, 1988). In the same way that Plowden and Bullock have remained key publications long after their initial high-profile introductions, Kingman should be understood in the context of its influence on how post-1988 literacy teaching was shaped. The committee responsible for writing this report was commissioned to do so following concern from HMI, during the 1980s, that there were weaknesses in the teaching of English language in primary and secondary schools. Their concern was not only over weaknesses in teaching but in what they saw as a correlation between ineffective literacy teaching and poor teacher subject knowledge about the English language. As you read the concerns of later writers featured in this chapter you will observe that this particular worry did not appear to fade as new initiatives were introduced. Indeed, we would argue that it is precisely the acquisition and maintenance of sound subject knowledge that underpinned the success of the effective teachers we studied for this book.

The Kingman Report, written 10 years before the NLS was rolled out in English primary schools, considered spoken and written English and the relationship between the two in considerable detail. It attempted to set out a series of recommendations that might introduce more rigour into the teaching of English. For example it put forward the idea that all primary and secondary teachers should receive specific instruction in order to develop their subject knowledge for English. In particular, the committee was keen to illustrate the need for individuals – teachers and their pupils – to understand the 'forms of the English language'. To illustrate what they meant by this they identified separate parts to language – similar to the word, sentence and text level divisions we see in the NLS – but also identified how detailed knowledge of language for communication, reading for comprehension and writing for different purposes were necessary parts of English language subject knowledge. This in turn influenced the nature of the National Curriculum for English, which has as its three attainment targets speaking and listening (AT 1), reading (AT 2) and writing (AT 3).

The portrait of the English language that was drawn in this report was rich and complex. It provided the reader with a combination of observation, guidance and recommendations that now look very different from the inspection-driven professional commentary we see today. It clearly articulated a case for teaching children specific language conventions in order to enhance their use of spoken and written English but did not suggest that this would be done in the compartmentalised way we might sometimes observe with teaching using the NLS. References to the interrelationship of speaking to writing and of reading to writing are made throughout the report. In particular, the report underlines the importance of teacher confidence in supporting successful English teaching. The following extract comes from a section on reading; the italics are presented as they are in the report:

The teacher's knowledge of the tools of analysis, linguistic and literary, should be confident and comprehensive. *It is for the teacher to decide how much of that knowledge is made explicit to the pupil or class at a given moment, and how it might be done* . . . Without such developing language knowledge, the implicit gradually becoming explicit and articulated, a child's capacity for intelligent reading and for reflection upon what is read will be restricted.

(DES, 1988, p. 37, para. 15)

In the context of more recent guidance from the NLS, the italicised sentence is interesting. If in 1988 Kingman considered that teacher autonomy was worth supporting with emphasis, how, by 1998, did we reach a point where teachers were handed very precise instructions as to how they might teach both reading and writing?

By way of explanation we should point out that, in education in England, there has developed a tension between English as an academic discipline in its own right and English as the vehicle for teaching children to read and write. We would maintain that the rolling of teaching reading, writing and spelling in the early years into 'English' can be problematic because it appears to assume that reading is the province of the English curriculum rather than a discrete skill that needs to be taught in a focused way. In fact it is theoretically possible to teach reading entirely through science books but historically it has been taught through materials that sit more comfortably with the English curriculum. It may be that, because of this, the focus of the National Curriculum for English seemed to be more on developing an acquaintance with children's literature than with the teaching of reading and writing. Both of these are important in their own right and children do not have to see them as being exclusive to the English curriculum.

Throughout the 1990s, a series of reports from HMI and later OfSTED painted a picture of weakness in English teaching that did not appear to be improving despite Kingman's recommendations. There might have been several reasons for this; perhaps the report was never fully embraced and the recommendation to teacher training institutions to include specific English teaching in their courses was not taken up, or perhaps the focus on what was considered important in English teaching changed as the OfSTED inspectorate was introduced. Moreover, perhaps the tension we have described above – English as a subject versus English as teaching reading and writing as skills – was left unexplored. Furthermore, there were concerns not just about the teaching of English but about teaching in primary schools in general and how it had become unfocused in the ways described by *Curriculum Organisation and Classroom Practice in Primary Schools* (Alexander, Rose and Woodhead, 1992).

This highly influential discussion paper, referred to as that by 'the three wise men', set out a picture of unacceptable inconsistency in pedagogy and the curriculum offered in English primary schools despite the introduction of the National Curriculum in 1989. In fact, the report mentioned the National Curriculum as a possible causal link to declining standards in literacy, explaining that teaching time for the 'basics' such as English and mathematics had been squeezed by the introduction of so many subjects not previously taught at primary level. Criticism was levelled at teachers for inflexibility and for unskilled use of time and teaching techniques; there was also mention of the problems caused by teachers' devotion to topic-based planning, which combined several subjects. The paper called for a sensible approach to the use of whole-class, group and individual teaching, which should reflect the needs of the lesson objectives. The judgement of how to organise pupils for learning was stressed as necessarily 'educational and organisational, rather than, as it so often is, doctrinal' (Alexander, Rose and Woodhead, 1992, p. 30, para. 99). Yet again we see a pre-NLS reference to the teacher needing to make decisions about classroom organisation based on her professional judgement. Even in this really very critical report there was no suggestion of an imposed pedagogy for any subject. On the contrary the three wise men went on to

> endorse the common sense view that teachers need to be competent in a range of techniques in order to achieve different learning outcomes. They need for example, to be able to give precise instructions, to explain ideas clearly, to demonstrate practical activities, to pose different kinds of questions, and to help pupils understand how well they have done.
>
> (Alexander, Rose and Woodhead, 1992, p. 31, para. 103)

Through this series of points they describe the skills of the experienced and effective teacher but do not suggest that there is one method of organisation through which these might be put to best use.

So, through reports from Kingman and the three wise men (Alexander, Rose and Woodhead, 1992), we see a picture of concern for pupils' poor literacy development coupled with an understanding of the need for detailed teacher subject knowledge and the use of higher order teaching skills. A shift in emphasis occurred in 1993 when Alexander, Rose and Woodhead wrote a followup report to their discussion paper (Alexander, Rose and Woodhead, 1993). This document repeated concerns about the need for teachers to leave behind their apparent desire to teach according to topics or themes and to return to a more subject-focused day. It talked of the need for a 'climate of change' in primary classroom pedagogy. However, this paper also emphasised that change should be through a gradual process of appraisal and consideration of existing practices. Nevertheless, change was hot on its heels. A review of the National Curriculum in 1995, which released schools from the requirement to teach all nine subjects with the same time allocation, sent a strong message to classrooms that there should be an emphasis on the basics of literacy and numeracy. Coupled with the fact that the first round of OfSTED inspections was under way at this point, it is perhaps easy to see how a prescribed pedagogy for both these subjects was not far off.

In the mid-1990s, OfSTED began to publish its inspection findings as summarised issues for each subject area. It is interesting to see that, according to their overview of English, from inspections in 1994–5, they considered that the teaching of reading was more than satisfactory. It was described as 'effectively taught in most schools, especially in Key Stage 1' (OfSTED, 1996a). The teaching of English was described as satisfactory or better in over four-fifths of schools and teachers' subject knowledge was considered 'generally good'. Although there is more concern over the teaching of writing and over standards of attainments in writing, inspection findings of this period seem to sit at odds with the view expressed in earlier reports and in a second report published in the same year. This gives rise to still further speculation about the weakness in reading and writing standards among UK children being a perceived rather than an actual weakness.

It is this second report that probably paved the way for an aggressively centralised stance on how literacy should be taught in English schools. This report, *The Teaching of Reading in 45 Inner London Primary Schools* (OfSTED, 1996b), drew on observation and reading-test data from pupils in Years 2 and 6 in schools in three inner-London LEAs. The picture was grim. Teaching was described as weak in a third of lessons and as hampering pupil progress. This weakness was observed coming from inadequate phonics teaching, unproductive and routine 'hearing' of reading, which involved very little actual teaching, insufficient resources to fulfil the requirements of the National Curriculum and a general unevenness in the quality of teaching within schools as well as between schools. Where teaching was good it was described as in 'sharp contrast to much that was mediocre or weak' (OfSTED, 1996a, p. 7). Again we see criticism of teaching methods in these weaker lessons: 'At the heart of the problem is a commitment to methods and approaches to the teaching of reading that were self-evidently not working when judged by the outcomes of pupil's progress and attainment' (OfSTED, 1996b, p. 7).

Although not a report on all schools in England and Wales – only on some facing unusually high levels of social disadvantage in their pupil population – it stood as a final indictment of the inconsistency in teaching reading that was seen as 'the problem' at the time. Although, as we can see from the paragraph above, the findings were not necessarily supported by inspection evidence from a wider range of schools, anxiety was fuelled further by the perception that UK pupils lagged behind their European counterparts in reading attainment. We now know that this belief was perhaps misplaced, as evidenced by PISA (2000) and PIRLS (2001) data, which we will discuss later in this chapter.

By 1997, when the NLP was operating in underperforming schools and LEAs in the UK, there seems to have been a widespread assumption that the teaching of English was in crisis and something had to be done about this. There was also no question that this 'doing' had to come from central government. Thus, despite reports that discussed pedagogy as the domain of the teacher and of educationalists, a successful takeover bid for centralised control by politicians and their associated government departments seems to have gone ahead largely unchallenged. Their confidence and the accompanying confidence of the profession in them was perhaps supported by a perception that the NLP had provided the magic recipe through which pupils would improve their reading and writing.

In their review of the NLP (OfSTED, 1998) inspectors spoke in glowing terms of the 'clear improvement in the quality of teaching' and a 10% rise in the number of lessons graded satisfactory or better. Given that the NLP targeted schools where literacy standards were known to be weak, an improvement following additional funding, resources, LEA adviser attention and a programme of in-service training is hardly surprising. Interestingly, there was still a minority of schools for whom standards did not rise and there was recognition that this would only happen in these schools with sustained 'teaching of the highest calibre'. What the review did not address was the fact that it would have been these schools – those most challenged by their intake and with a long history of underachievement – that needed to address school improvement at whole school level before concentrating on only one subject. In this way, the narrowing of inspection evidence to focus only on weak schools using the NLP may have led to two erroneous perceptions. Firstly, that the NLP findings should be generalised to all schools – including those that were already doing well with their chosen pedagogy for literacy; and secondly that the weaker schools were failing with the NLP because of weaknesses in teaching – not because of weaknesses in the Literacy Hour structure or because of wider school improvement issues.

How, by 1998, the country was ready for a national literacy strategy is not straightforward. Whether standards were low seems open for debate and no one seems to have questioned whether a project tried for one year in weak schools should have been generalised to all schools. Regardless of this apparent confusion, a sense of urgency grew to provide the profession with a template based on the better practice observed in schools at the time and to try and address perceived inconsistencies in teaching literacy by imposing a national strategy. Whether the NLP and subsequent NLS were based on anything other than a perception of what constituted good literacy teaching – rather than an informed response to research findings – has been the subject of debate ever since. In order that teachers who have not experienced any other form of literacy teaching do not accept the NLS as 'received wisdom' it is important that we follow this debate with interest.

THE NLS: A REFORM BASED ON EMPIRICAL EVIDENCE?

Turning first to defence of the NLS and of the implementation of a large-scale initiative to radically change the national pedagogy for teaching literacy, much can be found in the writings of Beard (2000a, 2000b, 2003). In a paper arguing against the efficacy of Plowden-influenced individualised teaching (Beard, 2000b, p. 246) he defended the introduction of the NLS on several counts. Firstly he cited weaknesses in classroom practice for literacy prior to 1998, which failed to tackle continuing underachievement in reading and writing (HMI, 1991; OfSTED, 1996b, in Beard, 2000b). Secondly he described the ways in which the model of the Literacy Hour is supported by research.

Beard described a pre-NLS pedagogy for reading, which was largely based on hearing individual pupils read. He depicted a scene of overdependence on brief periods of teacher–pupil interaction, which necessarily characterised teacher time management in teaching reading individually to a class of 30. This one-to-one instruction, he argued, was less efficient in terms of the quality of any teacher–pupil interaction; indeed, teacher–pupil interaction may be simply a *reaction* to errors rather than having a specific teaching focus. 'Such short-burst interactions militate against the kind of scaffolded discourse which can explain and encourage links between reading and writing' (Beard, 2000b, p. 248). Furthermore he cited evidence in school effectiveness research pointing to the advantages of whole, group and class teaching 'over individualised methods in accelerating pupil attainment' (Beard, 2000, p. 247).

One only has to do the sums. With a class of 30 children, and allowing for a maximum of 5 minutes for each child, a teacher would have to spend two-and-a-half hours a day hearing children read on an individual basis. Take off time for assembly, registration and playtime and there could hardly have been any time left for teaching the rest of the curriculum. Or conversely, if the rest of the curriculum was being covered, predicating the teaching of reading on individualised one-to-one sessions would have meant short, snatched unfocused teaching. We should also bear in mind that before the onset of the NLS class sizes were generally greater than 30 and teaching assistants as we know them today were very rare.

In exploring and defending the introduction of shared writing in the Literacy Hour, Beard looked to a number of well regarded studies that have focused on the impact of teacher modelling to improve children's text production. He drew on studies such as those by Derewianka (1990) where children were able to produce high quality text after a long period of research on subject content to aid their writing and a planned input by the teacher to support them in their understanding of structure register and tone for information writing. In other words, children were better able to write when they were familiar with the subject and when they had learned the characteristics of specific writing conventions. This research is further discussed in Chapter 4. It is worth noting at this point that Beard's defence of the NLS, although well argued, came *after* the publication of the *NLS Framework for Teaching*. Others worried by the apparent lack of a foundation in research-based findings related to literacy development have drawn our attention to its virtual omission from the guidance for teachers (Stainthorp, 1999; Bailey, 2002; Earl *et al.*, 2003).

A journal-based debate between Beard and Wyse in the *British Educational Research Journal* in 2003 gives us insight into the continuing tension – 5 years after implementation – between those who argued for the NLS and those who were opposed to its introduction. Attacking Beard's defence of the NLS in 2000, Wyse (2003) set out to unpick Beard's use of empirical evidence and described how the *Framework for Teaching* is not reliably based on either the research related to school effectiveness, inspection evidence or a synthesis of research related to children's literacy development. He challenged Beard's view of pre-NLS teaching as outlined by HMI and asserted that evidence from HMI and OfSTED from 1996 onwards may have reflected the personal views of the current chief inspector and 'resulted in unreliable conclusions about the teaching of reading and writing'. He went on to argue that this perceived change in the emphasis of inspection evidence renders it unreliable as a source of data to support a change in teaching methods.

Turning to the research related to school improvement, Wyse challenged Beard's use of research by Mortimore *et al.* (1988) saying that Beard's (2000b) defence of group and whole-class teaching as a strategy for teaching reading effectively played down their finding that hearing pupils read individually contributed to greater progress in writing. Finally, Wyse explored a range of perceived weaknesses with the *Framework for Teaching*, which he said failed to match empirical evidence related to how children learn to read and write. In conclusion he called for an urgent review of the framework that would include a reduction in the number of objectives and an amalgamation of word and sentence-level objectives; in this way a perceived fragmentation of reading and writing instruction might be minimised. Overall, his call is for a review that ensures a more robust match of the strategy to empirical data related to the teaching of reading and writing.

Defending his earlier work Beard's (2003) riposte acknowledged the 'measured and scholarly' way in which Wyse had found fault with the research he had cited to defend NLS implementation. However, he argued that Wyse in turn had omitted areas from his critical commentary that further support Beard's favourable view of the strategy. This robust debate will doubtless continue. It is interesting for those training as teachers and for those new to the teaching profession to consider that a curriculum document they see perhaps as part of the fabric of primary classroom practice is not necessarily widely accepted as a framework for good practice. Research presented in later chapters will reveal just how effective teachers have drawn on some of those aspects so vigorously defended by Beard, but have modified literacy delivery in response, partly, to questions over its design such as those presented by Wyse and others.

THE TENSIONS SURROUNDING THE INTRODUCTION OF THE NLS, 1998–2004

We look now at the fears related to the implementation of the strategy at a time when many felt that progress in school effectiveness, fostered largely by the increase in OfSTED's role, was not yet firmly embedded in generic school practice. Reynolds (1998) expressed unease over the speed of implementation. In a review of research written after the NLS was piloted in 1996/7 in 13 LEAs across the country, he warned that it was important for the NLS to recognise schools' need to consolidate and ensure long-term development once the teaching materials were assimilated. Reynolds argued that schools need to be effective schools before they can concentrate on effective practice at classroom level. His concern was that a national strategy for the classroom might not address a more pressing local need for school improvement, and thus risked failure in the longer term. The case studies in this book illustrate this very clearly; all those observed had to go through a process of *whole school* improvement before hoping to improve literacy results.

In their paper discussing secondary school improvement in challenging circumstances, Harris and Chapman (2002) quoted OfSTED (2000b) in saying that 'effective leadership is widely accepted as being a key constituent in school improvement.' OfSTED's findings, published in their report *Improving City Schools*, are matched by more recent comments from OfSTED (2002a) and Earl *et al.* (2003). Interestingly their more general findings about leadership and management in schools where the NLS has been implemented successfully match pre-NLS data from Sammons, Hillman and Mortimore (1996) and even older research from Mortimore *et al.* (1988) concerning successful schools. In other words, Reynold's observation that schools need to be first and foremost effective schools before they can be effective using any new classroom strategy is actively borne out by empirical data over several decades.

Stainthorp (1999) described the NLS as 'the big national experiment'. She supported the Literacy Hour's clear reflection of Vygotskian learning theory in its structure but was wary of the rapid and simultaneous introduction of both a new framework and a new pedagogy. This urgency at implementation reduced the NLS to an experiment without a control, she argued; one where we would never know if it was the teaching programme or the pedagogy that most influenced a rise in pupil attainment.

The early warnings from both Reynolds and Stainthorp are reflected in more recent professional commentary. 'Large-scale reform is risky when it is characterised by a reform strategy that requires rapid improvement and significantly increased school accountability' (Earl *et al.*, 2003, p. 25). This report was the third in a series entitled *Watching and Learning*, which was commissioned as part of an independent review of both the NLS and National Numeracy Strategy (NNS) as they became part of the curricular fabric of English primary schools between 1998 and 2002. Although partially superseded by later reports from OfSTED they remain valuable and important commentary that tracked both success and failure in the NLS in its first four years. They provide us with a detailed insight into the strengths and pitfalls of the programme as it rolled out nationally, and analysis as to whether such radical change could be sustained as change for the better. The team from the Ontario Institute for Studies in Education (the OISE team, led by Michael Fullan) comprised independent evaluators who drew on a large sample of schools, teachers, headteachers, LEAs and literacy consultants in a broad-reaching research project that covered every aspect of the NLS's implementation.

Mapping their commentary through the three reports (Earl *et al.*, 2000, 2001, 2003) the team found much to praise, particularly initially. They reported on success with such an ambitious project; they noted particularly strengths in 'leadership (from the centre), policy alignment/coherence, support and pressure, communication, resources and responsiveness and adaptability' (Earl *et al.*, 2000, p. 38). However, even at this early stage in their observations they flagged up concern regarding the need to create sustainable improvements. In particular they highlighted the need to ensure that 'the teaching force has the knowledge and the skills to make the best use of NLNS resources within their unique school settings' (Earl *et al.*, 2000, p. 40).

The flavour of the second report (Earl *et al.*, 2001) was different. The OISE team explained that, although there was still notable success, some weaknesses in teacher subject knowledge and erosion in teacher confidence as they struggled with a new and unfamiliar pedagogy were leading to inconsistencies in implementation. Highlighted successes were that the NLS moved literacy to top priority in primary-school classrooms; that pupil attainment as evidenced by Key Stage 2 results had increased; and that NLS strategy leaders were responsive to problems with implementation by creating new and additional documentation where weaknesses were perceived. Nevertheless, questions remained over the capacity of the NLS to foster deep and sustained changes in teaching that would be supported by increased teacher subject knowledge and understanding of their craft in teaching literacy. Moreover, Earl *et al.* (2001, p. 85) questioned whether the NLS might even create a culture of dependency that 'could reduce the sense of professional autonomy, enterprise spirit and responsibility for continuously seeing ways of improving professional practice.'

In *Watching and Learning 3* (Earl *et al.*, 2003) the team made its final observations and came to a number of conclusions regarding the future of the NLS. Earl *et al.* continued to praise the high quality of central leadership throughout the implementation coupled with substantial funding, an emphasis on accountability, increased focus on leadership and management at school level and the development of literacy assessment in schools. The anxiety surrounding pedagogy continued unabated, however. They remained concerned that the changes were more of an adoption of a system rather than a change that nurtured a better understanding of effective pedagogy for literacy. They accepted that in some schools outstanding practice was driving up standards and that children were being taught a much more focused and engaging curriculum. They argued, nevertheless, that this excellence was not widespread and that many teachers remained deskilled rather than upskilled by the NLS. Their concerns were well expressed in their citation of the work of Dale Willows:

> Training teachers to implement instructional methods when they don't truly understand the underlying rationale is futile. Without understanding teachers do not have the knowledge to adapt an instructional strategy to address various student needs. Without understanding teachers become cogs in a machine, with neither the responsibility nor the rewards of being in control. Without understanding teachers can become inflexible and dogmatic; unable to integrate new research-supported practices into existing approaches.
>
> (Willows, 2002, p. 1)

As the NLS developed, another, highly detailed watching brief grew through the numerous reports from HMI/OfSTED. These reports have ranged from large-scale overview commentary on progress after 2, 3, 4 and more years (OfSTED, 2000c, 2001a, 2002b, 2003, 2005a) to writing with a smaller focus such as the progress of teaching in phonics (OfSTED, 2001b) and the impact of teaching assistants on the effectiveness of NLS (OfSTED, 2002b). Although not strictly research based, and perhaps limited by the brief of an inspectorate, they provide at times an equally insightful and critical view of the NLS as the reports from the OISE team, and have in turn provided schools with useful material on which to base their adaptations of the strategy.

In their first report (OfSTED, 2000b), logging progress after two years of implementation, HMI praised positive effects on the teaching of reading and on subsequent standards in pupil attainment in reading. Conversely they found that progress in writing had been 'limited' and that poor attainment among boys was a cause for concern. Notably, this report drew our attention to those more confident teachers who were better able to teach writing by reversing the introductory parts of the hour and by providing opportunities outside the hour for extended writing. The separation of the shared text work and the independent activities by a word-level slot was, thus, quickly identified as a weakness in the prescribed pedagogy but one that less well informed teachers might struggle with for some time longer. The teaching of phonics came in for criticism as it was insufficient, too slow and lacked a systematic approach, as did the teaching during independent and group work, which many teachers were finding difficult to organise. This report, 2 years in, shows an emerging dichotomy between a rise in test results and some quite marked weaknesses in delivery.

After 3 years the NLS was the subject of a second focused report from OfSTED (OfSTED, 2001a). In this updated commentary, some weaknesses still prevailed. Independent group work was still unsatisfactory in a fifth of lessons – an increase on the previous year; lack of success was linked particularly to poor coherence between the introductory whole-class work and the independent activities and to weaknesses in the quality of the independent activities. Concern over teachers' understanding of the nature of a guided reading session began to emerge and over the loss for schools of the 'broad and balanced curriculum' – so crucial to the success of the National Curriculum as a whole.

Despite some continuing weaknesses there were areas of improvement after 3 years. There was an improvement in the amount of word-level work and phonics teaching – perhaps in response to the NLS publication *Progression in Phonics* (DfES, 2000a). Furthermore, *Grammar for Writing* (DfES, 2000b) was supporting teachers with a more inventive approach to sentence-level work. The OISE team writing in the same year praised this rapid response to weaknesses in pedagogical design with additional guidance. Finally, and of significance to the research findings later in this book, OfSTED identified the crucial role of leadership and management in schools where the strategy was successfully implemented.

In its report after 4 years of implementation OfSTED (2002a) pointed to a yet more mixed review of progress and weaknesses. Standards had not risen sufficiently to reach the government target of 80 % of 11 year olds reaching Level 4 and above in English by 2002 (a target revised to 85 % by 2006). This undershoot was particularly related to writing. The gender gap was closing, although girls still outperformed boys in all aspects of English. There was insufficient focus on speaking and listening – a result of the strategy's writers perhaps intending that this would continue as outlined in the National Curriculum, when in reality teachers had become over-focused on the NLS objectives for reading and writing. Perhaps most critically they called for managers of the strategy at national level to 'undertake a critical review of the NLS, paying particular attention to the clarity and usefulness of the framework as a tool for improving standards in literacy across the whole curriculum' (OfSTED, 2002a, p. 4).

Both the OISE team (Earl *et al.*, 2003) and OfSTED (2002a) warned of the need for consolidation and reflection following initial success for the NLS tempered by a more recent failure to reach targets. Earl *et al.* (2003) perceived that the setting of national targets had distracted schools from effective teaching – particularly during Year 6. OfSTED (2002a) called for schools to be more critical in their own use of the strategy's materials and prescribed pedagogy – 'A great deal has been achieved but further progress will depend on an open, critical approach to the strategy at a national level' (OfSTED, 2002a, p. 36).

Thus OfSTED's own findings reflect those of the concerns of the OISE team. Where the match falls short is in the lack of any reference to the teaching profession and the NLS managers at national level to engage more fully with research. This omission continued in the OfSTED report of late 2003, which looked at progress of both the NLS and NNS. Still critical of teaching in some lessons and of continuing underperformance in SATs by some pupils, the report mentioned the need for teachers to have time to develop subject knowledge. Notably, however, in the main, the recommendations were standards driven. Schools were exhorted to improve their planning and assessment systems in an effort to improve test results rather than to develop their understanding of the ways in which children learn to read and write. Ironically, had they time to develop this understanding teachers might make a better match of lesson content to pupil need and automatically drive up standards. The OISE team's anxieties regarding a SAT-driven curriculum were thus further compounded by inspection recommendations that placed standards over understanding. Further evidence of this concern that teachers were hampered in their efforts to improve their classroom skills when working inside the boundaries of test-driven expectations was presented by Fisher (2004, p. 139): 'it is hard to see how an individual reassessment of pedagogy is possible in a climate where teachers' freedom to explore is limited by a context of inspection and high-stakes assessment.'

Finally, some comment on OfSTED's report on the teaching of reading, published late in 2004, makes an interesting addition to the discussion of the place of inspection commentary in tracking the progress of the NLS. This report, *Reading for Purpose and Pleasure*, was heavily critical of parts of the teaching profession; practice in high performing schools was rightly praised but the practice of underperforming classrooms was likened to that of much earlier, critical reports in 1993 and 1995. It was as if, for these schools, the NLS had not made an impact: 'It is unacceptable that too many children do not learn to read properly because the adults who teach them lack sufficient knowledge to do so effectively. This might have been acceptable a decade ago, but not today' (OfSTED, 2004, p. 5).

The tone was remarkable in the light of OfSTED's own call for NLS review in 2003. Without reference to whether a review of the strategy had taken place, blame for any failure was put firmly at the feet of teachers and headteachers. Yet, if OfSTED considered it pertinent to call for a review of the strategy as a lever for improvement only one year earlier, it is hard to understand why potential weaknesses in the NLS structure were put to one side for this report. If teachers were still unable to teach reading effectively after 6 years of implementation, perhaps the systems, rather than the personnel, were to blame. Guided reading for example – subject of criticism in several earlier reports – was described as unsatisfactory in one third of schools: 'Too many teachers did not understand its principles and struggled to teach it successfully' (OfSTED, 2004, p. 4). The consistent theme is one of criticism for too much variation in standards and for incompetence in teaching across schools. This tone was perhaps born of frustration that the 'one size fits all' approach has not led to greater uniformity either in attainment or for pedagogy. Given the limited empirical evidence to support the pedagogy for the NLS, finding that teachers are 'struggling' with this classroom practice may be more of an indication that the pedagogy itself is in need of review.

Points for action in this most recent report focus again on the need to introduce rigorous action planning and assessment for literacy into schools that are not raising standards. A new point was raised in response to inspection findings for this report, and as a result of data from PISA (2000) and PIRLS (2001). These are international studies of children's academic attainment towards the end of primary schooling. The PIRLS study assessed 150,000 children in 35 countries between the ages of 9 and 10 years. The texts the children had to read were both narrative and informational. The study had sophisticated techniques for equating the texts and the comprehension questions across different languages with different writing systems (orthographies). This was important because, as we will see, English orthography is much more complex than most other languages and therefore more difficult to learn (Seymour, Duncan, Mikko and Baillie, 2005). The average points scored for the tests across the 35 countries was 500. Twenty-three countries were significantly above the average and not surprisingly they were mainly European countries and those with developed economies. The average point score for the English children taking part, who were a representative sample of the population as a whole, was 553. This was third overall behind Sweden and the Netherlands. This was cause for celebration and could make one question what all the fuss about standards had been about because the children had started their literacy education before the onset of the NLS, although they would have been taught under the *Framework* guidelines for their time in KS2. When the PIRLS data are further unpicked an even more interesting picture emerges. The top 25 % of English children were the top of the world. When the top 25 % of all countries taking part are compared, the English children performed better than any other country. However, when the bottom 25 % of each country taking part is compared English children drop to fourteenth overall. This shows that there really is a 'long tail of underachievement', which had been the focus of the NLS as a tool for raising standards. Furthermore, the PIRLS data point to high reading attainment, but much lower motivation to read among English pupils than our European neighbours. Thus, the tone of the OfSTED report had a new focus; this focus was headlined in its title, *Reading for Purpose **and** Pleasure*.

Interesting to any study of the NLS is the fact that commentary from the OISE team, which pointed to the need for all parties to engage with research and so move to a richer understanding of how children learn to read and write, does not seem to sit comfortably with the standards-driven agenda of HMI and OfSTED. OfSTED repeatedly look at failure to reach targets and, now, failure to inspire a love of books in children and yet avoid looking at any possible root causes in either the *Framework for Teaching* or the pedagogy for the hour itself. They do explore the nature of successful schools where literacy practice is stimulating and where pupils make good progress but in calling for action do not seem to see the link between the subject knowledge of teachers and headteachers in good schools and their pupils' engagement; more they see the systems that support delivery and assessment as the key to raising standards. This dichotomy – the need to raise standards on the one hand and the failure to fully address the necessary development of teacher subject knowledge on the other – is a common theme for other researchers watching as the NLS was implemented. Their thoughts bring us back to the fears raised by Reynolds (1998), Earl *et al.* (2003) and Willows (2002) – that schools need to understand the processes that will bring about improvement, broadly and for literacy, before they can properly implement sustainable change.

THE NLS AS SEEN THROUGH THE EYES OF RESEARCHERS

Research carried out by Sylva *et al.* (1999) provided early commentary on the possible benefits and disadvantages of implementing a prescribed literacy programme in schools. They observed teachers using materials similar to those produced for the NLP in reception classes, and compared them with teachers teaching as they had always done. Their research in 1996–7 was specific to a certain context – it was carried out in Westminster schools where teachers were engaged in a precursor to the NLS called the LIFT (Literacy Initiative for Teachers) project. This was a project whereby teachers received a considerable amount of in-service training prior to using the materials. Importantly, their training emphasised not only the organisational aspects of literacy teaching – using whole-class, groups and individual input as appropriate – but it also gave them knowledge of the *theories* related to early reading development.

The advantages of using a structured literacy programme appeared striking. The authors described effects such as the programme having changed the way that teachers teach literacy and the way in which children learn; in both cases there was improvement in terms of pupil outcomes. They also observed children engaged in far more peer tutoring, choosing to carry on reading and writing in their unstructured lesson time and playing less. The loss of play, however, was not necessarily seen as an advantage for such young children when play is such an important part of wider personal and social learning. Teachers were seen using more higher order questioning techniques; questions were likely to be instructional. Overall they noted that it seemed likely that the organisation and structure of the literacy lesson was more important than time spent on teaching reading.

The advantages seemed to far outweigh any problems. By the time of publication in 1999, this research would have been read against a backdrop of the nation's primary schools having adopted the NLS fully. It could have been read as a resounding endorsement of a focused literacy-teaching programme such as NLS. However, Sylva *et al.* were keen to point out that generalising from their study would be dangerous. They explained that, for the LIFT project, teachers were given substantially more in-service training and had the opportunity to coteach with a demonstration teacher. Further to this, they criticised the NLS 'light touch' training that did not look at theories associated with how children learn to read. In summary, it is likely that the LIFT project was successful because of the high levels of time and funding devoted to training teachers using the materials, the recognition of the need for modelling of the practice by effective practitioners and, crucially, because teachers were encouraged to understand the theory behind the practice. As we turn to later commentary, we will see that, in the findings of researchers, this link of theory to practice is perceived as missing in the NLS. Willows' (2002) warning of the problems inherent in adopting a pedagogy without understanding the principles underlying it, is played out time and again.

Fisher, Lewis and Davis (2000) and Fisher (2002, 2004) presented findings from a project that looked at a sample of teachers teaching in small, rural schools as the NLS rolled out between 1998 and 2000. Their research (Fisher, Lewis and Davis 2000) focused on a number of aspects of NLS including whether children were making progress in reading and writing with the new framework and how teachers were adapting their chosen pedagogy for teaching literacy. They found a wide variation in practice and that only six out of 20 teachers had actually fully adopted the prescribed hour as set out in the *Framework for Teaching*. This variability has been a recurrent theme in the commentary discussed already in this chapter.

Notwithstanding this variation in practice – which they cite as a cause for concern – they found several aspects of the new pedagogy for literacy, which were cause for celebration. Children were making progress in reading – although many teachers were not using guided reading to teach this – and, in classes where teachers had made full use of the framework, they found progress in writing. In particular, they note, writing progressed most effectively where children were given specific instruction according to NLS objectives during shared and guided writing sessions. Teachers who had fully understood the model were planning their modelling of the conventions of writing in a more focused way than previously.

In a follow up study, interviews and observations of the case-study teachers revealed the same mix in practices adopted or discarded as these practitioners had developed their use of the *Framework for Teaching* (Fisher, 2004). Fisher described the teachers as having mostly adapted the Literacy Hour by marrying changes to their practice made as a result of using the NLS with those practices they used pre-NLS. The team was concerned, however, that there was a mismatch between how far teachers felt that they had come with the NLS in terms of developing their practice and what was observed in their classrooms. Echoing the words of warning from the OISE team (Earl *et al.*, 2001, 2003), which had questioned how deep the changes wrought by the NLS could be in light of its speedy and wholesale introduction, Fisher concluded that teachers' pedagogical development may have slowed down after the first flush of radical change in 1998. She warned that teachers need to 'take stock and reconsider pedagogy' as this research uncovered that teachers' underlying pedagogy for literacy may be more 'resistant to change' than has previously been thought.

Consideration of the ways in which teachers have changed their practice since the advent of the Literacy Hour has been the focus of several studies, including those mentioned above. Research has concentrated on individual features of the prescribed Literacy Hour in an attempt to analyse how far teachers are using each part successfully, or whether they are using it in the ways intended by the authors of the *Framework for Teaching*. Changes to pedagogy introduced by the Literacy Hour were the use of whole-class teaching in the introduction and the use of shared texts, the use of guided groups to teach reading and writing, planning for independent groups to work on tasks related to the introductory activities while the teacher worked with these guided groups and the use of a plenary to consolidate learning and check understanding against the lesson's intended outcomes. Huxford (2002) explained the expectations and intentions of the NLS *Framework for Teaching* in a description of its structure and impact. Teaching required for successful delivery of the Literacy Hour should be discursive, interactive, well paced, confident and ambitious. Matched to this high expectation of teaching practice is a framework for the hour that involves a mixture of whole-class and group teaching, of focus on learning objectives, careful scaffolding of those objectives to allow for independent work and the use of guided reading and writing to foster literacy development.

We have already discussed the progress of the different parts of the hour in terms of inspection evidence from OfSTED between 2000 and 2004. Empirical research has included the grouping of children during the Literacy Hour (Hallam, Ireson and Davies, 2004), teachers' understanding of 'interactive whole-class teaching' (Dombey, 2003; Hardman, Smith and Wall, 2003; Hargreaves *et al.*, 2003) and the success of teacher–pupil dialogue during guided reading sessions (Skidmore, Perez-Parent and Arnfield, 2003).

Hallam, Ireson and Davies (2004) reported on a large-scale study of schools' grouping practices during 1999. Their focus was on how schools had changed their grouping practices during the 1990s in order to raise educational standards. Interestingly, one of the key influences on changes in classroom groupings had been the introduction of the NLS in 1998; a third of the 2000 schools questioned cited this as a primary influence on change in practice. In some cases the NLS had fostered changes to classroom practice not just in literacy lessons but in other subjects as well. Schools identified that modifications to groupings were made in order to facilitate ease of teaching with the new framework, to facilitate planning and delivery and to promote more effective differentiation within their teaching. Interestingly, there was some disparity in schools either adopting or rejecting setting for pupils. Some had abandoned setting as it was specifically discouraged by the NLS guidance, whereas others had adopted it as a means of facilitating delivery. In an interesting coda to this discussion, Hallam, Ireson and Davies (2004) cite evidence to suggest that setting does not improve pupil performance; indeed it may even inhibit it (Sainsbury *et al.*, 1998; Whitburn, 2001). Perhaps schools, caught up in the standards-driven commentary of inspection findings, felt that setting might best achieve improved pupil performance even though it might not be best practice for literacy teaching.

Interactive whole-class teaching, a pedagogical tool encouraged overtly by the NLS *Framework for Teaching* and referred to by Beard (2000a) in his match of the NLS to research, has been the subject of several large-scale studies. Hardman, Smith and Wall (2003) carried out a detailed investigation into teacher–pupil interactions with a view to analysing whether these constituted effective, interactive whole-class teaching. In essence, at its best, this approach should encourage higher order dialogue with children where teachers' high expectations of children's responses to open questions should foster deep learning. This team was concerned that the NLS had called for use of interactive whole class teaching in its guidance, but that there was 'no clear definition and little practical advice on what interactive whole class teaching is, and how teachers should use it in the classroom' (Hardman, Smith and Wall, 2003, p. 197). Their conclusions, following systematically analysed observations of 70 teachers, were that teachers using the NLS were more likely to use a very teacher-led form of directive teaching than to engage children in effective dialogue. They raised concerns that the NLS is leading to a form of teaching that goes against the social-constructivist theory of learning where children must engage fully and actively with their learning in order for it to be effective.

Their findings are further supported by a second large-scale study carried out by Hargreaves *et al.* (2003). This team took a different approach, using video analysis by teachers of their teaching to encourage reflection regarding their practice of teaching whole-class sessions. Disappointingly they found that teachers made very few adjustments to their practice when they had analysed its effectiveness. The teachers showed an understanding of inter-active teaching at a 'surface level' but seemed to have little understanding of the principles underlying this approach. Both studies concluded that Key Stage 1 teachers in particular were more likely to ask closed questions and to inhibit pupil responses during whole-class sessions. Even more worrying was the fact that the Hargreaves *et al.* (2003) study found pupil responses in Key Stage 1 lessons *other* than literacy to be of a much higher order.

A third much smaller study by Dombey (2003) sheds further light on this important set of findings. She looked at three teachers as case studies and examined their interactions with pupils during shared text activities. Again she found that the tight focus on planning and covering of objectives for the NLS may lead some teachers to dominate conversation in whole-class sessions almost to the preclusion of pupil interaction. Where teachers were more inclined to teach reading for meaning this was less likely to happen in prac-tice, and questioning was more effective in encouraging genuine dialogue about the text. She concluded that we need to further explore what we mean by interactive teaching. She went on to suggest 'that the guardians of the NLS need to take a more analytical look at the nature of children's participation in classroom dialogue' (Dombey, 2003, p. 57).

It is useful at this point to return to the areas for criticism raised by OfSTED (2003, 2004) and see where they match trends in the findings of academic research around the same time. In 2003, OfSTED talked of 'a stubborn core of around one in three lessons where the teaching remains satisfactory rather than good' (OfSTED, 2003, p. 3). They criticised the fact that 'The literacy hour provides opportunities for pupils to discuss tasks with partners or in groups, but these are not taken up frequently enough' (OfSTED, 2003, p. 19). Furthermore they alluded to just those shortcomings in teacher–pupil interaction highlighted in the research:

> Teachers may delude themselves that clearly structured lessons, with planning derived from the frameworks . . . exemplification materials in literacy or com-mercially published materials, lead to good teaching. However, this superficial sense of order can at times belie the quality of the teaching.
>
> (OfSTED, 2003, p. 21)

Thus, inspection findings echoed those of researchers watching the NLS as teachers grappled with its prescribed pedagogy with varying degrees of success.

To conclude this section, a number of issues have been raised and discussed that give us a detailed picture of the NLS as it emerged and dominated class-room practice between 1998 and 2004. Firstly, it undoubtedly introduced change on a massive scale and in some instances that change was for the better. The framework gave teachers a set of objectives that perhaps promoted a greater focus in their teaching of reading and writing than previously.

Across all the research and inspection evidence considered there was broad recognition of this positive effect. However, a number of concerns emerged that remain the subject of commentary. Weakness in teacher subject knowledge was highlighted repeatedly by both OfSTED and OISE and was described as potentially damaging by Fisher, Lewis and Davis (2000). You will remember that this was identified as an issue in the Kingman Report some 12 years earlier. A lack of understanding about the nature of some parts of the hour – particularly those of guided reading and of interactive whole-class teaching – has been examined across a number of studies. We also see an insistence on raised standards of pupil attainment resulting in a narrower curriculum and inhibiting teacher creativity. Nevertheless, the NLS is with us and seems likely to stay (Fisher, 2004; Moss, 2004). So what is it that teachers should be doing with the strategy in order to use it as the tool for raising pupil attainment that it purports to be, while ensuring that pupils remain motivated and that their learning is sustained?

EFFECTIVE SCHOOLS, EFFECTIVE TEACHERS: WHAT DO THEY LOOK LIKE?

Following such a lengthy account of successes and weaknesses in the NLS during its first 5 years of implementation it is useful to pause and examine wider definitions of what makes effective teaching – both for literacy and more generally. Moreover, it is important to consider not only the classroom context but also the wider school setting and the ways in which strong leadership and shared ethos foster pupil attainment. We focus in particular on leadership in inner-city schools as this reflects the nature of those schools studied for inclusion later in the book. That said, the features identified are common to school settings in the full range of social contexts.

We have referred earlier in this chapter to the work of Mortimore *et al.* (1988), Sammons, Hillman and Mortimore (1996) and Reynolds (1998) in identifying the need for schools to be effective schools before they can manage change successfully. In their report *Improving City Schools*, OfSTED (2000a) defined those characteristics of schools that make progress despite having what might be commonly regarded as a challenging pupil intake. They noted that these schools made progress 'against the odds' and that they were improving at a greater rate than schools overall. In the most effective schools studied, positive leadership was demonstrated by all senior staff and not just by the headteacher. Governors played an active and supporting role and management systems were kept simple. In observing the ethos in these schools they found that they provided safe and supportive learning environments where poor behaviour was tackled by providing clear boundaries and by motivating pupils through high expectations and a stimulating learning environment.

These findings are matched by further comments from OfSTED (2002a) and Earl *et al.* (2003), which refer to a wider range of schools. These reports describe the effective leadership in schools where the NLS has been implemented successfully as sharing the following qualities: a clear structure to the management system, supported by the headteacher so that coordinators can fulfil their roles effectively, efficient use of assessment data to improve teaching and learning, systematic monitoring of teaching and the effects of change, the confidence to adapt the framework to suit the needs of the pupils. The recognition that schools and teachers are effective where they are 'assessment literate' – that is, where they actively use assessment to inform planning – is common to all these reports.

In considering the characteristics of effective teachers, one report – published as the new millennium dawned – stands out as seminal. A large-scale study by Hay McBer (2000) presented a wide-ranging set of features that effective teachers hold in common. These relate specifically to the classroom and more generally to their professionalism. In their research into teacher effectiveness, Hay McBer (2000) used 35 micro-behaviours identified by Reynolds and others to focus their questions about what the teaching skills of effective teachers looked like. Among their detailed findings they observed that effective teachers set high expectations for pupils, are good at planning, employ a variety of teaching strategies, have a clear structure for pupils' behaviour management, manage time and resources wisely and are assessment-literate. Overall they found that effective teachers had well over 90 % of their pupils on task through a lesson, and that their lessons flowed naturally with an appropriate balance of whole-class, group and individually targeted teaching techniques. In addition to their teaching skills, effective teachers demonstrated professional attributes such as confidence, analytical thinking, initiative, flexibility and a passion for learning.

Without straying too far from the context of this book, we should pause briefly to further define this often-used phrase 'assessment literate'. At the time of our observations and of much of the research featured in this section of this chapter there was a growing body of evidence relating to the power of using formative assessment in effective teacher delivery. Publication started in 1998 with Black and Wiliam's *Inside the Black Box*. This was followed up by more commentary from the same team and others in later years. Writing by Clarke (2000, 2003) offered straightforward guidance into how primary school teachers might incorporate the strategies identified by Black and Wiliam in their research amongst assessment literate teachers. By 2005 the concept of 'assessment for learning' had become widely used in schools and it became a method of working that LEAs would exhort schools to adopt in their drive for continuing school improvement.

Where teachers employ 'assessment for learning' they use their knowledge of pupils' needs actively to influence their planning and delivery. Furthermore they are more likely to use open-ended questions, to give formative feedback as children work and to encourage children to evaluate their own learning through self and peer assessment. In their delivery they are likely to refer explicitly to the learning objectives – in child-friendly terms – to explain the purpose of the day's activities and to make clear what they expect to see as possible learning outcomes by the end of the lesson. They may also incorporate success criteria into their lessons; through this they articulate for children the small steps necessary to succeed with their tasks and to move forward in their learning. The identification of this particular range of teaching strategies as beneficial both to pupil performance and understanding came at a time when teachers were being encouraged to use the prescribed pedagogy of the NLS and NNS. What was exciting about Black and Wiliam's research was that it identified characteristics that were to do with innate or learned skills – not with the use of a package or published programme.

In their pamphlet *Inside the Black Box* (Black and Wiliam, 1998), the authors set out the evidence from research that showed the power of using formative assessment as an integral part of classroom delivery. However, they were keen to investigate how this theory might work in practice. In much the same way as we wanted to analyse the detailed features of effective literacy teaching, Black and Wiliam, along with a team of other researchers, set up a two-year project looking at good practice using formative assessment in schools in two LEAs in order that they could provide practical examples for busy teachers. As a result of their project they identified that the key areas of practice relating to effective use of assessment for learning were questioning, giving feedback, sharing success criteria and the use of self-assessment among pupils (Black *et al.*, 2003). The teachers involved in the project reported positive pupil outcomes beyond simple text scores. They were more to do with children understanding more about their own learning, raised expectations of themselves and taking responsibility for their learning. This dual positive effect – of teachers understanding more about their pupils and the pupils understanding more about themselves – was clearly a part of the success of the literacy lessons we observed.

There were, however, other features common to our expert practitioners. Evidence from Black *et al.*'s research could well describe nearly all of them, but there are skills specific to the effective teaching of literacy that need discussion. Over the next few paragraphs, we chart some research relating to effective teachers of literacy and their differences from and similarities to effective teachers generally. Hay McBer's general review of teacher effectiveness is amplified by the findings of Wray, Medwell, Poulson and Fox (2002) who carried out extensive research specifically into the nature of effective teachers of literacy. Observing a group of 26 teachers, identified as effective literacy teachers using a range of measures including pupil performance and LEA recommendation, they sought information regarding these teachers' classroom practice but also their knowledge of and beliefs about literacy teaching. Their research included a validation group of 10 less effective teachers in order to provide a meaningful benchmark for comparison.

Interestingly, some of their initial questioning of both groups of teachers showed that there was little significant difference in what teachers might identify as effective literacy activities for the children. Thus, their key findings relate to the pedagogy as well as the subject knowledge and attitudes of the effective teachers. Overall they found that effective teachers of literacy were more likely to link the teaching of word- and sentence-level objectives into meaningful text-based experiences for their pupils. In shared text work – either reading or writing – they were anxious to make connections between text, sentence and word functions explicit in order that children assimilated the purposes for reading and writing across genres. Lessons were conducted at a brisk pace using extensive modelling and careful differentiation. Matching the findings of Hay McBer (2000), these teachers were 'assessment literate' and they demonstrated comparative depth and confidence in their subject knowledge. Furthermore they believed that the creating of meaning in literacy was fundamental to success in teaching reading and writing; they also shared a background in and a passion for their subject.

An important study from 2003 summarised the findings of 12 studies looking at the key features of effective teachers of literacy. In their review of the nature of effective literacy teaching for children aged 4 to 14 years, Hall and Harding (2003) attempted to synthesise the findings of these 12 studies – many of which were from the US – in order to identify what the professional characteristics, beliefs and classroom approaches of effective literacy teachers might be. They drew our attention to the fact that in all the studies – and indeed in selecting the teachers for the research in this book – effective teachers were chosen by a process of nomination by others. In this way the sort of robust evidence we might want from a sample for research does not support their selection. However, in the absence of other studies using 'stronger' selection criteria, the findings and recommendations from this meta-analysis remain important.

Hall and Harding found that the features of effective literacy teachers were similar to those observed by Wray, Medwell, Poulson and Fox (2002). Their in-depth review showed that effective teachers of literacy 'have a wide and varied repertoire of teaching practices and approaches', they skilfully integrate the skills needed for reading and writing and they are careful to match their planning to pupils' needs. Such detailed differentiation was acquired through their use of continuous assessment of children's understanding and progress. The following observation has particular resonance for this book, as it describes in essence the confident quality demonstrated by our three case-study teachers:

The 'effective' teacher of literacy uses an unashamedly eclectic collection of methods, which represents a balance between the direct teaching of skills and more holistic approaches. This means that they balance direct skills teaching with more authentic, contextually grounded literacy activities. They avoid the partisan adherence to any one sure-fire approach or method.

(Hall and Harding, 2003)

In a much more recent study, Topping and Ferguson (2005) built on the findings of both Wray *et al.* and Hall and Harding, in an effort to further define what might characterise effective literacy teachers. Choosing five teachers who were recognised as effective by a combination of children's high literacy attainment and expert nomination they explored the teaching behaviours common to the group. In contrast to the earlier research by Wray *et al.*, they wanted to analyse the pedagogy of their group independent of any programme. The teachers, all in one district of Scotland, were teaching using methods similar to the English Literacy Hour but with some differences. Topping and Ferguson focused particularly on their teaching of reading. They were interested in following up the assertion by Hall and Harding (2003) that curricular approaches may work or fail, but that the teacher's skills are crucial in developing children's skills in literacy. In the context of this book, their findings are very interesting.

Using previous research-based findings relating to effective teaching, and effective teaching of literacy, Topping and Ferguson found that their five teachers exhibited a number of the qualities correlating expert teaching with high pupil attainment. They noted that their teachers attained a skilful balance of different types of instruction and of motivating and consolidating pupil performance. There were high levels of interaction and demonstration during shared and guided reading and questioning was more open than closed. However, such glowing findings were tempered by some criticism. For example, these teachers did not often make the purpose of activities explicit to their children, they used praise rarely and were not observed regularly summarising learning. As you read later chapters of this book you will notice that the teachers we observed demonstrated the characteristics of effective teachers found across all the studies outlined here but that they also used those strategies identified as missing in Topping and Ferguson's teachers.

One further point is important here. Topping and Ferguson identified that their teachers undoubtedly employed high-order teaching skills and were rightly nominated as experts at teaching literacy. However, they also found that these teachers were not always aware of when they were employing these skills. They were not consciously responding to pupils during open-ended questions for example and were not necessarily engaged in explicit strategy instruction. Moreover, they were unaware of their own effective behaviours – 'the teachers were actually using more complex behaviours than they reported perceiving' (Topping and Ferguson, 2005, p. 141). In our study we did not interview the teachers with a view to gathering their perceptions of their own teaching. However, had we done so it is likely that they too might have found it difficult to define their excellence in any detail. This is not to detract from their skill but upholds Topping and Ferguson's final point that there should perhaps be more opportunities for all teachers to reflect fully on their own practice in order to improve; to observe what they do and to enhance their own metacognition. This book goes some way to supporting that move.

This discussion of the features of effective schools and leadership in schools, of teachers generally and of teachers of primary literacy has given us a template from which to judge our own practice and that of others. In observing the schools and teachers studied for this book, these characteristics emerged repeatedly and will be further explored in later chapters. Perhaps the key to understanding how schools and teachers become 'effective' is to notice that there is no mention of an adherence to one specific method of teaching; on the contrary, Hall and Harding (2003) describe professionals who do just the opposite. Research cited throughout this chapter supports the notion that effective teaching of literacy, and perhaps of all subjects, is about understanding how children learn; to understand what motivates them, how to make connections across learning and to pitch lesson content carefully to their developmental needs. The NLS has provided us with a useful framework that can give necessary rigour to our teaching. However, it is perhaps time to move away from the straightjacket of the 'clockface' and to adopt a pedagogy that grows from a deeper understanding of how reading and writing might develop in a meaningful context.

To this end, *Excellence and Enjoyment* (DfES, 2003) gave a green light to schools to move away from prescription and develop 'creativity' in their teaching approaches. At the time this looked like a tacit recognition that the NLS had been overprescriptive and had led to some very dull teaching and a corresponding lack of motivation among pupils. More worryingly, from a politician's point of view, standards were still failing to meet government targets for literacy. Frustratingly, observations from OfSTED (2005b) in the year following publication of this guidance showed little evidence of schools taking up the challenge to regain control of their own pedagogy:

> So far, schools have made only limited progress in plotting a coherent creative dimension across the whole curriculum. In some schools with strong leadership and high standards, there has been a more innovative response, involving a more substantial reorganisation of the curriculum, such as allocating a day a week to teaching by subject specialists, or implementing subject or theme weeks, which broaden the curriculum and enhance the opportunities for pupils' learning. However, the depth and richness of some subjects, such as geography, design and technology, and RE, often remain unexploited because teachers have neither sufficient enthusiasm nor the robust subject knowledge to develop these areas. Rightly, many schools are concerned not to lose their focus on raising standards in English and mathematics and they need support to be innovative within that context.
>
> (OfSTED, 2005b, para. 62)

Perhaps, after years of tightly observed practice and exhortation to follow a particular style of teaching, the profession felt risk averse and confused as to what the expectations of inspection might hold? Or, could it be that *Excellence and Enjoyment* itself replaced one set of curriculum guidance with another? Far from freeing teachers to teach according to their objectives and their pupils, it may have been read – wrongly or otherwise – as another attempt to control classroom practice.

As a coda to this discussion we cannot ignore one more article, published by Robin Alexander in 2004. Thirteen years earlier Alexander had been one of the 'three wise men' whose report called for review of teaching practice in the early 1990s. In his commentary *Still No Pedagogy?* he attacked the newly formed Primary National Strategy – of which *Excellence and Enjoyment* was a published doctrine – in openly hostile terms, finding it to be 'ambiguous and possibly dishonest, stylistically demeaning, conceptually weak, evidentially inadequate and culpably ignorant of recent educational history' (Alexander, 2004, p. 7).

Central to his criticism he drew on earlier work by Simon (1981) whose article 'Why no pedagogy in England?' identified a problem with English classroom practice: that it was inferior ideologically to the practice of our European counterparts and was neither 'coherent nor systematic'. While not necessarily accepting Simon's criticisms as justifiable, Alexander was dismissive of successive government attempts to control classroom practice since 1997 as they have not been rooted in the thinking intended by Alexander, Rose and Woodhead (1992). Their report had stipulated that it is not for governments to tell teachers *how* to teach. Further to this, Charles Clarke, the Education Secretary introducing *Excellence and Enjoyment* (DfES, 2003), is recorded as saying that through this document 'teachers have the power to decide how they teach'. Alexander was sceptical of this apparent release from central control and wary of a document that reduced the concept of pedagogy to 'what works' and 'best practice'. His reservation was based on his belief that education must be viewed as profoundly affected by the context in which it is delivered. For this reason, he asserted, a prescribed pedagogy is inappropriate. It automatically negates the child from the centre of the learning process. He attacked the relationship of political perception and pedagogy thus: 'Under our now highly centralised and interventive education system, those who have the greatest power to prescribe pedagogy seem to display the poorest understanding of it, and discourse becomes mired in the habitual bombast, mendacity and spin of policy speak' (Alexander, 2004, p. 29).

Such bile-filled criticism is perhaps hard to comprehend for those teachers new to the profession. You need support in seeing how you might best teach at a time when our understanding of appropriate pedagogy for literacy is developing fast but when literacy teaching is also such a political football that the experienced teachers you work with may be anxious to toe a government line for fear of being lambasted by inspectors. Arguments between politicians and academics are important – and often entertaining – but they don't help you find answers for your own practice.

The case studies presented in this book show schools and teachers that maintained a strong sense of who they were and what they were about through the years when the NLS was first implemented and through the subsequent developments arising from the establishment of a Primary National Strategy in 2003. They retained a pedagogical approach that they knew suited the needs of their children while actively embracing the rigour of the NLS and its termly objectives. Furthermore, because they all had high numbers of bilingual learners, they addressed and internalised the processes involved in teaching children to read and write in a way that transcended the detail of the printed guidance in the Literacy Strategy. As such they provide clear models for schools and teachers regarding how they might combine the best of the NLS with the necessary understanding of research that underpins successful and creative teaching for literacy. Indeed, they represent the type of pedagogues that the Kingman Report might well have recognised as effective: they have a rich understanding of the nature of language and linguistic development coupled with a detailed knowledge of how they might best transfer this subject knowledge to their pupils.

3 Writing Systems and the Development of Reading

This chapter gives the reader a detailed understanding of how children learn to read. It includes reference to the English spelling system and to research-based models of the psychological processes involved in developing early reading.

The context for this book is the educational system in England. The teachers whose work is celebrated were teaching children to read English although many of the children did not have English as their first language. These Key Stage 1 children were at the start of a journey that we hope will end in the vast majority of them being able to achieve fluent literacy skills. This will mean that as adults they will have the freedom to read with understanding anything they might choose or be required to engage with and to be able to communicate their ideas in writing successfully. There will always be individual differences in terms of ability and motivation but it is the responsibility of the education system to ensure that children are given the chance to achieve as highly as possible.

This chapter and the next one present some of the research evidence about reading and writing that has been published in recent years. When we present the evidence about the activities of the three exceptional teachers discussed in Part Two of this book it will be possible to draw connections between the theory and the three teachers' very effective practices, which were drawing out the best in their pupils. Before we present the models and evidence about how people learn to read we will consider the characteristics of writing systems.

ORTHOGRAPHY – THE WRITING SYSTEM

All writing systems have in common the fact that they have been created in order to provide a visual representation of language (with the obvious exception of Braille). They allow writers to translate ideas into words on the page, which have a degree of permanence. This means that writers can communicate their ideas to others. Of course, there is the requirement that the writers and readers share the same orthographic system just as in oral language the speaker and listener have to share the same spoken language.

Writing systems have a degree of commonality but they are also very diverse. They may represent the language at the level of the word, the syllable or the phoneme.

One of the oldest known systems was the Egyptian system of hieroglyphics where each character stood for an object or concept. These characters were in the main pictograms. They were stylised but figural representations of the objects they symbolized. Hieroglyphs could be written sequentially to create sentences. This system therefore represented language at the level of the word and generally speaking if one did not know the hieroglyph–word correspondences one could not read or write. However, even at this early stage of the development of writing systems the sounds of the language were represented, although not systematically. A hieroglyph could represent either the concept, and thus be employed as a pictogram, or could be a phonetic hint to the sound of the word. The hieroglyphs of an owl and a reed could represent the objects or when written together they could stand for the word THERE because when spoken together the words OWL and REED sounded like the word THERE (Sacks, 2003). It would be rather like using a rebus so that the word BEFORE could be written as:

The Chinese system of writing is an example of an ideographic system that is still in use today. The characters vary in visual complexity depending on the number of strokes that constitute them. Most of the characters are composed of two parts: a semantic radical on the left-hand side and a phonetic on the right. The written language is an enduring aspect of Chinese culture. The characters have been modified over the centuries but they have retained their characteristics. Each character represents the same word regardless of the language that the social group uses. Thus written Putonghua (the main language of mainland China) is the same as written Cantonese (the main language of Hong Kong). A Cantonese speaker may not be able to speak Putonghua or understand a Putonghua speaker but if they are both literate they will be able to communicate through the written medium.

Written Japanese is composed of two different orthographies. There is a form, which is based on the Chinese system, called Kanji where there is a character for each concept. However, in addition there are kana syllabri scripts called Hiragana and Katakana. These are sound-based systems. They represent language at the level of the syllable. Children generally learn the Hiragana characters before they go to school. There are 48 syllables in the language and therefore 48 kana characters. The system is completely regular so that each character always stands for its own unique syllable. In order to learn the correspondences it is only necessary to be aware of the syllables of the language. There is no necessity to be explicitly aware of any units of sound smaller than the syllable.

However, many languages have orthographies based on sound units that are smaller than syllables. Their units are the phonemes, which are the smallest units of sound in a language that change meaning. For example CAT is a word with three phonemes: /k/ /a/ /t/. If the /k/ phoneme is changed to a /m/ then the word meaning changes from a four legged furry animal to a flat piece of cloth that is placed on a floor. Systems based on these smaller units are generally characterised as being alphabetic systems. Modern scripts based on the alphabet can be traced back to the Phoenician alphabet, which dates from before 1000 BCE. The Phoenicians developed an alphabet where each consonant sound was represented by a unique letter. The vowel sounds were not represented. A modified form of this system, with different letters, is still in use today. Hebrew represents only the consonant sounds with diacritic marks for the vowels augmenting the letters when children are first learning to read. Vowel letters were developed by the Romans when they created the alphabet that we still use in English.

Some systems are highly transparent. For example, in modern Turkish each letter represents a unique phoneme and each phoneme is always represented by that same unique letter. The Roman alphabet is used with some letters being augmented by diacritic marks to cover the full set of Turkish phonemes. This means that Turkish children simply need to learn stable letter–sound correspondences and then they have a system in place to enable them to decode written words.

This is not the case for English. It is not a myth that English has a difficult orthography. Children learning to read English have to cope with a system that is highly opaque and fairly irregular. Let us consider this further.

ENGLISH ORTHOGRAPHY

We can assume that the majority of readers of this book are highly competent readers with adult reading skills in English. In order to understand the journey that children have to undertake it makes sense to start with the literate adult reader who can cope with the complexity of the writing system.

As we have said English orthography – the spelling system – is alphabetic. This means that 26 alphabetic letters are used to represent the sounds of the spoken language. Each word has its own spelling, which is written from left to right with a space before and after it on the page. However, unlike Turkish, Greek or Spanish, where the sound–letter relationships are transparent and largely consistent, English has one of the most complex alphabetic systems in use. The English spelling system is said to be *morphophonemic*. This means it is based on phonemes and morphemes: sounds and meanings.

To characterise it as being *phonemic* means that it is sound based, such that the individual letters represent the sounds of the language. Thus the word BED is composed of three phonemes. There are approximately 44 phonemes in English depending on one's specific accent. Table 3.1 lists the English phonemes and the characters of the International Phonetic Alphabet that are used to represent them. It becomes immediately clear that because there are 44 sounds to be represented but only 26 letters, the orthographic system will not be a simple one.

The phonemes of BED are /b/ /e/ /d/. BED is said to be a regular word. Each phoneme is represented by a single letter: the /b/ phoneme is represented by the letter B; the /e/ phoneme is represented by the letter E; and the /d/ phoneme is represented by the letter D. This is a simple transparent example and no alternative pronunciation is likely.

To characterise the system as being *morphemic* means spelling also has elements of meaning represented beyond the sounds. The word ROBED is composed of four phonemes. These are /r/ /əʊ / /b/ /d/. It is also composed of two *morphemes*. A morpheme is the smallest unit of meaning. One analysis of robed is that the two morphemes are /r əʊ b/ meaning among other things 'to be dressed in' and /d/ meaning 'in the past'. The past-tense morpheme is often represented in writing by the letters ED. In the word BED the letters ED represent two sounds but in ROBED they only represent one. Adult readers can use their implicit knowledge of the system to read and write these words successfully. They do not have to think about the fact that the same letters represent different sounds and meaning. Indeed many adults are surprised when this is pointed out to them. They appear to read automatically going directly from print to meaning effortlessly and without analysis. Depending on the phonemic structure of the verb, the letters ED may be pronounced /d/ as in our example of ROBED; /t/ as in the word DRESSED or /Id/ as in the RATED.

Let us take the letters R O B E D and add another B in the middle. This gives us ROBBED /r ɒbd/. Another word that is easy to read. You will have moved effortlessly from pronouncing the letter O as /əʊ /: a long vowel sound, to pronouncing it as /ɒ /: a short vowel sound with the resulting word having a completely different meaning, though again syntactically it is a past tense of the verb.

This illustrates another characteristic of English spelling. It is morphophonemic but it also includes what are called *orthographic rules*. One such rule is: when the medial vowel sound in a verb is a short one and the final consonant sound is represented by a single consonant letter, the final

Table 3.1 International Phonetic Alphabet symbols for English consonant and vowel phonemes for received pronunciation

IPA symbol	Example word containing the consonant phoneme	IPA symbol	Example word containing the vowel phoneme
p	**p**at	i	tree
b	**b**at	ɪ	sit
t	**t**at	e	wet
d	**d**og	æ	cat
k	**c**at	ɑ	father
g	**g**oat	ɒ	plot
f	**f**at	ɔ	saw
v	**v**ote	ʊ	put
θ	**th**umb	u	shoe
ð	**th**ey	ʌ	duck
s	**s**at	ɜ	girl
z	**z**oo	ə	banana
ʃ	**sh**op	eɪ	play
ʒ	trea**s**ure	əʊ	go
tʃ	**ch**ip	ai	sigh
ʤ	**j**ug	aʊ	now
m	**m**at	ɔɪ	boy
n	**n**ot	ɪə	here
ŋ	si**ng**	ɛə	there
l	**l**og	ʊə	pure
r	**r**at		
j	**y**ellow		
w	**w**atch		
h	**h**ello		

consonant is doubled when the past-tense morpheme is added. Thus we have RAT-RATTED, NET-NETTED, DIP-DIPPED, DOT-DOTTED, TUG-TUGGED.

There is a very frequent orthographic structure where a long medial vowel is represented by the vowel letter plus the letter E placed after the final consonant letter: GATE, KITE, BONE. This marker E is not sounded. We can see its influence in the words ROBE, RATE and DOTE where the letter E signals the change in the vowel length from the words ROB, RAT and DOT. Adult readers are able to read these words with no difficulty. They have implicit knowledge of orthographic patterns.

Because spoken English has 20 vowel sounds, but written English only has five vowel letters plus Y, the spelling of vowel phonemes is inevitably complicated. This means that letter combinations are used. Letters may have to be parsed together to stand for the vowel. For example the letters AI generally stand for the phoneme /eɪ/ as in MAID and PAID; and the letters OA generally stand for the phoneme /əʊ/ as in COAT and ROAD. Vowel letters are not always used in vowel phoneme digraphs. For example the letter R may be used as in FAR, FIR, FOR, FUR; L as in WALK, FOLK or W as in PAW, NEW, COW. Caveats always have to be added when presenting accounts of English orthography. In standard English pronunciation and many English regional accents the letter R is part of the digraph for the single long vowels being represented. However, in Scottish English and some regional accents words such as car and fur do not have two phonemes but three with a final /r/ sound at the end.

The spelling of long vowels also shows how inconsistent English orthography is. Though the digraph AI generally represents the phoneme /eɪ /, there is an exception: SAID; the digraph EW generally represents /u/ as in FEW NEW STEW; but SEW rhymes with GLOW. The degree of inconsistency found in English varies for reading and spelling. The letters OW are not consistent in the sound they represent as we can see in the words FOWL and BOWL. Conversely, the sound /əʊ/ can be spelled with the letters OW or with OA as in COAL. The sound / eɪ / can be spelled in many ways: WAY, MAID, SAVE, GREAT, REIN, REIGN, EIGHT, FETE, STRAIGHT, CHAMPAGNE, GREY.

This complex orthography presents challenges to children when they are learning to read and write with the result that it takes longer for children to learn to read words efficiently than in other languages. Seymour, Duncan, Mikko and Baillie (2005) have found that it takes two years longer to learn to read English than Finnish. This complex orthography also presents challenges for teachers. They need to find ways to ensure that children are able to master word reading and spelling but it is also useful for them to have an understanding of the system in order to make sense of the errors that children often make when they are learning.

WORD READING

The words we have presented so far to illustrate aspects of the English orthographic system are all high frequency words that adults are likely to have encountered many times throughout their reading history. It is likely that they are read seemingly automatically because they are instantly recognised as whole units without having to be analysed. Under such circumstances it may be that a process of direct visual recognition is used to identify the words. They can be said to be read via a *lexical route* (Ellis, 1993; Coltheart *et al.*, 2001). To be able to read a word in this way there is an assumption that we have stored a complete description of the word, what is called its *orthographic identity*, in memory. This identity comes to be stored as the result of repeated exposure to the word. It could be that all that is required for recognising any word is repeated exposure plus information that the particular sequence of letters stands for a particular word, for example that CAT stands for /k æ t/.

However, even as adults we occasionally come across words that we have never seen in print before. Under such circumstances we cannot 'recognise' them. We therefore cannot initially read them by the lexical route so we must have another process that enables us to read newly encountered words. The process by which we do this is thought to be one of decoding whereby we translate each letter into the sound for which it stands and then construct a blended sequence of phonemes. The letter sequence CRASK can be sounded out by adult readers successfully showing that they are able to use a decoding process. They are said to be able to use a *sublexical* route to word reading. Pseudowords such as 'crask' are used to illustrate this skill because, as they have no meaning and are very unlikely to have been met before, they have to be decoded.

Many readers will be familiar with the following lines from *Jabberwocky*:

> 'Twas brillig, and the slithy toves
> Did gyre and gimble in the wabe:
> All mimsy were the borogoves,
> And the mome raths outgrabe.
> (Lewis Carroll, *Through the Looking-glass*)

The ease with which people read this poem shows their skill at decoding. However, it also illustrates how we use our implicit knowledge of the orthographic patterns beyond simple one-to-one mapping of the letters and their sounds. The usual reading of 'toves' and 'borogoves' is /t əʊ v s/ and /bɒ r əʊ g əʊ v s/ to rhyme with COVES. However, because English orthography is so inconsistent, these nonsense words of Lewis Carroll could also be read as /t u v s/ to rhyme with MOVES; or /t ʌ vs/ to rhyme with DOVES.

Anyone who read 'toves' to rhyme with 'doves' would be said to have been using analogy. When reading a word by analogy we are making use of our knowledge of the pronunciation and spelling of words that we usually read by the lexical route because we have memorised them and stored them in what is called the orthographic or visual lexicon. We are also using our ability to decode.

THE DUAL-ROUTE MODEL OF WORD READING

The model of word reading that tries to capture the behaviour of adults when they read words and pseudowords is called the dual-route model. It proposes that there are two routes to word reading. When we encounter a word we either read it by the sublexical or the direct lexical route. When we read a word by the sublexical route we map the letters onto their phonemes, construct the phonological identity of the word and use this to identify its meaning (if it is a real word whose meaning we know). When we read a word by the lexical route we access the visual/orthographic identity because multiple encounters with it have led to a permanent trace of it in the orthographic lexicon. The meaning is accessed directly before the phonology. In reality literate adults probably have an extensive orthographic lexicon so they will access the majority of the words by the direct route. However, the sublexical route is there as a backup. The original model conceived of this as a horse race. Both routes would be activated and once the word had been identified the 'loser' process would be terminated.

Regular, consistent words can be successfully read by either route. DOG, CAT, PIG, SHEEP are all such regular consistent words. However, there are many irregular, inconsistent and unique words that would be pronounced incorrectly if they were read by the sublexical route. Words such as WEDNESDAY, COLONEL and YACHT are classical exemplars of such words.

English has many examples of words that are called *homographic-heterophones* – words that have the same spelling but sound different from each other. The meaning of these words can only be disambiguated by identifying the correct meaning in context. BOW meaning a pretty hair adornment or neckwear and BOW meaning to bend forward from the waist to acknowledge another person can only be disambiguated through being identified accurately in context. Likewise TEAR meaning the drop of water coming from the eyes when crying and TEAR meaning to rip paper or cloth.

Much of the evidence used to develop the dual-route model came from adults who had been fluent readers but who had suffered brain damage leading to them developing a condition known as acquired dyslexia. Some of these people were found to be able to read regular words such as DOG and pseudowords such as TRANT successfully but they would regularise irregular and exception words. Thus HAVE would be read to rhyme with WAVE and ISLAND would be read as /I z l æ n d/. However, other people were found to be able to read both regular and irregular inconsistent words correctly but they would be unable to read pseudowords at all even though they could successfully identify each letter.

The dual-route model was developed to account for the patterns of performance observed in normal adult readers of English and the breakdown found in adult acquired dyslexics. However, it has been found to be a useful theoretical framework for considering the processes that children need to develop in order to become skilled word readers (Jackson and Coltheart, 2000).

There are alternative accounts of how people read words. One that is informing much contemporary research is the connectionist account. Connectionist models of word reading (see, for example, Seidenberg, 2002) have been developed from computer simulations. They have in common the view that there is only one process by which words are read. The suggestion is that though people appear to be behaving as though they are using a letter–sound rule they are simply responding to environmental frequencies. In the simulations, the computers learn to 'read' simple letter strings by 'guessing' at their sound and then amending the guess as a result of getting feedback from overall performance. The computer 'learns' to read the input but at no time is it 'taught' the letter–sound connections. At the present time these connectionist models are in their infancy. They also do not seem to be very helpful as a framework for considering the way children may learn to read. As we shall see, learning the letter–sound correspondences and applying them seem to be very important for enabling children to develop their word-reading skills.

THE SIMPLE DEFINITION OF READING

So far we have been considering word reading only. This is the basis of literacy. Unless we can read the words accurately we cannot access the meaning. Accessing meaning is the rationale for reading. The simple view of reading proposed by Hoover and Gough (1990) is that reading is the product of decoding and comprehension:

$$reading = decoding \times comprehension$$

This means that reading results from an ability to decode the print and to comprehend the language that is thus unlocked. Reading is not an activity carried out for its own sake. We read because we want access to the information that is encoded in the squiggles on the page. The simple definition clearly situates reading as a behaviour that is language based. However, it is more than that because it involves the application of skills that are not language based. Decoding is a separate cognitive process because it involves the extra process of translating the visual stimuli into language. In order to understand what the writer intended one has to be able to do this translation accurately. Of course, accurate translation is not enough. It is possible for many adults to read every word of the instruction manual for programming a video machine to prerecord a TV broadcast but not to be able to understand what they have read. Given that such instructions are complicated, they would be made even more incomprehensible if word reading was not accurate and fluent.

At a more simple level, if you are left a note that reads 'please buy flour, milk and eggs' and your word reading was so inaccurate that you read it as 'please buy fish fingers and Marmite' the writer would be unable to create the intended pancakes. Readers cannot play fast and loose with the text. This means that children have to develop efficient accurate word-reading skills in order to access the meaning and comprehend writers' intentions. If they cannot read the words accurately, they do not have a window into the writer's intentions.

THE DEVELOPMENT OF WORD READING SKILLS

Ehri (1995) has proposed a model of the development of word reading skills. This is not the only model of reading development (see Marsh, Friedman, Welch and Desberg, 1981; Frith, 1985) but it is useful, empirically based and connects well with effective teaching programmes. This model accounts for the development of word reading skills in English specifically. Ehri considers that on their journey to acquiring fast, accurate word reading children pass through four phases. The phases are:

1. Prealphabetic
2. Partial alphabetic
3. Full alphabetic
4. Consolidated alphabetic

This procession through the phases does not happen in an unconstrained way. The development of literacy is not like cognitive development where the pattern of performance seems to be roughly similar across all cultures, at least until children are around 7 or 8 years old. The vast majority of children need to be taught to read. The phases they pass through are influenced both by the teaching they receive and by the level of cognitive development they have achieved. Learning to read does not have its own timetable quite like the development of language. Reading is parasitic on language but it is not acquired in the same way. Language is a biologically determined behaviour that has its own timetable and is almost a defining characteristic of being human. Literacy is a behaviour that is culturally determined. Writing systems are manufactured.

THE PREALPHABETIC PHASE

Children may be characterised as being in this phase before they have really developed any efficient word reading skills. They are not starting in a totally naïve state. In the UK children begin compulsory schooling with formal reading instruction at a younger age than most of the rest of the world but, even so, by the time they arrive in school they have made considerable progress in their cognitive development. They may also have had many cultural experiences that will mean that they do not begin to internalise their literacy instruction without any knowledge of reading. They will already have developed strategies for dealing with the world, which they can apply to trying to learn to read. They will have had many visual experiences and used their memory systems to form internal images of these. Ehri suggests that at the start of literacy instruction children will apply simple memorisation strategies to try to remember the names of written words. They may well have already learned to 'read' abstract visual symbols. They may be able to name many logos of shops, foodstuffs and toys. This is evidence of learning through multiple exposures to these abstract symbols. It results from informal opportunities to learn rather than from formal explicit instruction.

During this phase the children strive to remember the words by forming connections between the visual attributes of the individual words and their pronunciations. This can be a useful starting strategy for remembering the words that any particular sequence of squiggles represents. However, in this early phase the internal 'descriptions' of these symbols seem to be fairly crude. Ehri points out that the attributes that children use for identifying any particular word are arbitrary and unsystematic. Connections do not relate to all the letters in the correct sequence. In a classic study by Seymour and Elder (1986) a child read the word 'ball' as 'yellow'. The reason she gave for this was '. . . it's yellow because it's got two sticks.' She had remembered the word yellow presumably by forming a connection between the 'll' element and the pronunciation. On seeing the word ball she identified the 'll' and so concluded it was yellow. Clearly it is possible to develop a small visual vocabulary during this phase but there are too many words that look very similar for this to be an efficient strategy. Individual differences may determine the size of this early vocabulary. A child who has a good visual memory may well appear to be able to 'read' many words. However, this 'reading' is nongenerative because in the end there are too many words with 'll' in them. The children are also dependent on others to tell them all the words they do not know.

THE PARTIAL ALPHABETIC PHASE

The second phase comes about when children are able to read words by forming limited, partial connections between a few of the letters in a word and the sounds they can identify in the pronunciation. This is the beginning of a decoding strategy. When they try to read a word that they do not recognise they are able to use their knowledge of the letter–sound correspondences to make an informed guess at what the word is likely to be. Stuart and Coltheart (1988) showed that being able to use the first and last letters to hazard a guess at the word was indicative of the child who was about to take off in reading. However, although the attempts at working out the word are not arbitrary they are unlikely to yield fast, accurate word reading. For example, in English there are 14 four-letter words that begin with the letter F and end with an L: FAIL, FALL, FARL, FEEL, FELL, FILL, FOAL, FOIL, FOOL, FOUL, FOWL, FUEL, FULL and FURL.

THE FULL ALPHABETIC PHASE

In the full alphabetic phase children are able to use a complete decoding strategy for analysing new words. The letters are mapped sequentially onto sounds, resulting in a sequence of sounds that can be blended into a word. When a new word that they are attempting has a regular orthography such as BED they successfully come up with the correct pronunciation. During this time they can generally take account of the marker E rule so they generally do not sound out the final E. However, they will tend to regularise words. This means that if they do not know SWAN they are likely to regularise it to rhyme with RAN.

During this phase they become much more skilful at mapping the letter-sounds to work out what the words are. Though Ehri does not directly map her model onto the dual-route model, it is possible to suggest that during these second and third phases children are establishing the sublexical route to reading. Repeated rereading of words enables them to set up fully analysed descriptions in a lexicon, which can then be directly accessed.

THE CONSOLIDATED ALPHABETIC PHASE

The more children read the greater exposure to print they get so they become more skilful in using their decoding strategy to form the links between the letters and the pronunciations. In the consolidated phase they are able to decode unknown words on the basis of multiletter units. This reduces the demand on the system and means that when they encounter unknown words their decoding is faster and more accurate.

When children have reached this point they have become successful word readers and just need to continue to read as much as possible so that their word reading becomes both accurate and fast. The more they read the larger their visual lexicon becomes, so word reading *per se* is no longer a limiting factor. Comprehension then drives the system.

NECESSARY KNOWLEDGE FOR BEGINNING TO READ

We now have to consider the knowledge that children need to gain in order to begin to bootstrap their way into literacy. There is now evidence that the amount of exposure to print that children have had prior to beginning literacy instruction, the degree of phonological awareness and the number of letters of the alphabet known are highly predictive of later success in reading. The more the better.

EXPOSURE TO PRINT

Children in the industrial world live in a print-saturated environment. They see texts everywhere: in the street, in the shops, on the television; on almost every object. Cipielewski and Stanovich (1992) have shown that there is a strong correlation between exposure to print and ability to read. However, living in a print-saturated environment and reading ability do not seem to have the same correlation. If this were so then children in the UK today should have significantly higher levels of literacy than children living in the UK 50 years ago. Exposure to print therefore does not imply simply being in an environment where there is text. It means being actively engaged with texts. The phrase 'exposure to print' might be better reworded as 'interaction with print'. Before a child can read it means observing other people who are important to one, like parents, carers and siblings, enjoying reading and using their literacy skills for everyday activities. It means having people read lots of stories to you and seeing how they handle books and other types of texts. The Sheffield University group under Peter Hannon (1995) has been involved in projects designed to support parents in providing their children with opportunities to interact with print in the environment and with books.

Through sitting listening to a story being read from a book in a cosy intimate setting children learn implicitly about the structure of a book and how print operates. They learn about the linearity of print and that the text is fixed, that the reader is not making the story up but that the writer chose the words that are on the page. Children also value such interactions and so develop a positive attitude to reading and writing in general.

Increasingly children in industrial societies and in the UK in particular are attending nursery schools and preschool childcare groups. One of the aims of these institutions is to support children's language development and to enable them to have the type of experiences that will ensure they do not begin school with no skills in relation to literacy.

Effective exposure to print ensures that children understand how print works. They will have experienced the form and the language of stories. They will have engaged in play activities where they have taken on the roles of readers and writers. There is the apocryphal tale of the thousand-book child who may have listened to a thousand stories being read before beginning school and may also have listened to one of those stories a thousand times. Such a child has a head start because the topdown aspects of literacy have been cracked. All that remains to be learned is actually how to read the words. Robbins and Ehri (1994) have shown that rereading is a very powerful aid to learning to read.

Even when children come from families where English is not the first language spoken in the home, children may still be exposed to print and have active interactions with literate others. The language through which these experiences take place may be less important than the activities themselves. However, where children start school from situations where the home literacy system is different from English it is important that the teachers are aware of this. As we said above, English script works from left to right in rows. Arabic and Hebrew work from right to left and Japanese is in top-to-bottom columns that go from right to left. Children from homes where these languages are read may start turning the pages of a book from the back, if considered from an English-language perspective.

Exposure to print gives the head start but it does not in itself give the reading skills. Interactions with books with a sensitive adult ensure that opportunities for learning how to read and write can be taken. These may include the two other important prereading determinants of phonological awareness and letter knowledge.

PHONOLOGICAL AWARENESS

Phonological awareness relates to being aware of the sound structure of words and being able to manipulate those sounds effectively. When we were discussing decoding above we pointed out that this involved the mapping of phonemes onto letters. It is not possible to do this mapping without having some idea about the two systems that have to be mapped. There is now an overwhelming body of evidence that supports the view that phonological awareness is the key to learning to read words. However, being aware of the sounds in language does not necessarily require knowledge of the letters. Work by Lundberg, Frost and Petersen (1988) showed that a simple programme of games and activities designed to enable children to be explicitly aware of sounds before school was very effective. Nevertheless, integrating teaching about sounds and letters may actually be more efficient.

Early work in the UK by Bradley and Bryant (1983) showed that children who were aware of sounds at preschool age went on to be better readers and spellers by the time they were 7 years old. They were also able to show that a programme of teaching children about the sounds through playful activities in association with letters had a significant effect on later reading success.

A programme called *Sound Foundations* developed in Australia by Byrne and Fielding-Barnsley (1991b) has shown that the positive effects of teaching children to be able to identify the initial and final sounds in a word in conjunction with teaching them about letters was detectable 3 years later.

There has been a considerable debate in the psychological literature about what is called the size of the unit in phonological awareness. Byrne's programme, which has been subjected to a number of longitudinal reviews (Byrne and Fielding-Barnsley, 1991a, 1993, 1995; Byrne, Fielding-Barnsley and Ashley, 2000), is based specifically on the phoneme. However, an important feature of the programme is that children begin by working with a small set of consonant and vowel sounds and their respective letters and they work on the phonemes as elements of words both at the beginning and the end. This helps them to become attuned to the phonemes themselves as elements of words that can occur anywhere in a word and not just as initial sounds. The view was that working on just alliteration, as many previous 'phonics' programmes had done, did not help children to become aware of the phonemes as entities in themselves.

This focus on the 'discrete' aspect of the phoneme is what characterises much of the contemporary approach to early literacy education. Teaching about the phoneme in conjunction with letters is the basis of what is called synthetic phonics (Lloyd and Wernham, 1992; Watson and Johnston, 1998). The term itself is perhaps unfortunate because in everyday parlance 'synthetic' has come to mean artifical. Some people have been misled into thinking that synthetic phonics is about working on artificial sounds. This is not the case. 'Synthetic' in this context relates to the original meaning of the word from *synthesise* meaning to blend, fuse or combine. Synthetic phonics therefore relates to teaching children about the units of sound – the phonemes – and how to blend them together to form words. This is done in conjunction with learning about letter–sound correspondences so that children learn how to translate the words on the page into a sequence of sounds that they can then synthesise into words.

The controversy about the size of the unit to be used in teaching children about sounds in words may have stemmed from the work of Treiman (1992) and Walley (1993) who suggested that the developmental sequence of phonology seemed to go from large (syllabic) to small (phonemic) units. Therefore, in developing language, children initially use words that they store as complete unanalysed units and then they begin to focus on syllables followed by the subsyllabic units of onset and rime. Certainly, in English people seem to be sensitive to the syllable and the rime but find it more difficult to be sensitive to phonemes unless they have been trained. A famous study in Portugal of illiterate and newly literate adults found that phoneme awareness – awareness of the smallest unit – seemed to be related to literacy status (Morais, Cary, Alegria and Bertelson, 1979). However, it appears that even highly literate people lose explicit awareness of the phonemic character of words. Stainthorp (2004) showed that highly educated graduate teacher training students had no difficulty in counting the number of syllables in words or finding rhyming pairs but they were very unsure about the number of sounds in words like 'rust' and found it difficult to specify the second sound in 'bride' or the last sound in 'trough'. (Incidentally the correct answers are: four sounds in rust, /r/ /ʌ/ /s/ /t/; /r/ is the second sound in bride and /f/ is the last sound in trough.) Answers to 'how many sounds in rust' varied from 1 to 4; and the second sound in bride was given as /r/ or /ai/ or /ai d/ or /rai d/.

The argument has been that because the rime is such a salient unit in English, this should form the basis of early phonological awareness teaching (Goswami and Bryant, 1990). This has influenced the NLS. Certainly, learning nursery rhymes and playing rhyming games (Goswami and East, 2000; Maclean, Bryant and Bradley, 1987) are very important preliteracy language experiences for children, and teachers believe that children find such activities enjoyable. However, the latest research suggests that once children begin to learn to read they need to map the letter–sound correspondences quickly in order to bootstrap their way into literacy (Share, 1995; Stuart, 2004). This means learning grapheme–phoneme correspondences.

The report called *Teaching Children to Read* from the American committee, the National Reading Panel, set up to investigate learning and teaching reading, analysed all the quality research papers published on teaching phonological awareness and concluded that a short sharp programme of teaching *phonemic* knowledge was very beneficial.

KNOWLEDGE OF THE ALPHABET

It cannot have escaped your notice that it has been almost impossible to write about phonological awareness without mentioning the alphabet. Because of the nature of English orthography, the letter–sound correspondences in English are tricky. However, it is impossible to read if one does not have accurate knowledge of the letters and their usual corresponding sounds. The letters are the basis of reading and spelling. Children need to have complete knowledge of them. By 'complete' we mean knowledge that the shape 'b' is called 'bee' and stands for the phoneme /b/; that the phoneme /b/ is represented by the letter that is called 'bee' and looks like 'b'. They also need to be able to write the letter and to know that the letter they are writing is called 'bee' and makes the sound /b/. Stuart (1995) suggests that knowledge of about 50 % of the letters is needed to really begin to 'take off' in reading. The more letters a child knows at the start of literacy education the more likely that child is to make progress in reading. However, we need to be careful in interpreting this information because it may not be knowledge of the letters *per se* but the experiences that a child had whilst becoming aware of the letters (Adams, 1990). Nevertheless, there is no doubt that knowledge of the alphabet combined with awareness of the phonemes enables children to map the letter–sound correspondences and so begin to learn how to decode.

Teaching phonemic and alphabetic knowledge gives children a means of decoding words and so enables them to begin to have an independent and generative system for tackling any words. They will be setting up the sublexical route of the dual-route model. Certainly, in the early stages they will need to have plenty of feedback about their attempts because so many of the words will be irregular or exception words.

As we have said, it appears that exposure to print, phonological awareness and knowledge of the alphabet seem to be the best predictors of later success in reading when given formal reading instruction. Children who have much of this knowledge in place when they begin school have an advantage. Reception class teachers need to assess individual children's level of knowledge when they start school so that they can bring all children up to speed.

WORD RECOGNITION

Exposure to print can be considered at different levels. One element can be the words themselves. Many of the high-frequency structural words in English that provide the architecture of sentences are short and irregular. A useful strategy for learning them might be to learn them as sight words rather than through decoding them. By learning such a sight vocabulary children can begin to set up the direct lexical route to word reading. The NLS suggests that children need to learn a sight vocabulary at the same time as they are being taught phonics. There is no evidence that children find this confusing. Some people advocate that children should be given a strict diet of phonics with no whole-word teaching or book reading until they have mastered their decoding skills. This extreme view does not have empirical evidence to support it and seems to fly in the face of both the argument about the importance of exposure to print and the importance of motivation. We want children to enjoy reading books right from the start. Many of the high-frequency function words that provide the basic architecture of the English sentences are irregular or exception words. Ensuring that children can recognise these as sight words while building up their decoding skills gives them a strong basis for tackling books. However, although the NLS recommends this strategy, the word lists provided are somewhat idiosyncratic and do not relate to the frequency of occurrence of words in the books that children will be encountering in school (Stuart, Dixon, Masterson and Gray, 2003).

COMPREHENSION

The simple model of reading we cited above includes two elements: decoding and comprehension. In much educational literature the term 'reading comprehension' is often used to depict the understanding of texts to differentiate this activity from comprehension of language when listening. This is slightly misleading because the comprehension processes are the same whether the language comes by ear or by eye (Joshi, Williams and Wood, 1998). There is nothing special about reading comprehension. The difference is that when the language is coming by eye there is the additional effort required to decode the words, which takes up processing capacity leaving less available for working out the meaning. This difference is not trivial. We have concentrated so far on word reading because unless one can work out what the words on the page are, it is not possible to access meaning. The meaning of the print comes through the results of deciphering the squiggles on the page.

This is clearly demonstrated in the passage below printed in Wingdings font:

> ♀✂◆♒✂■ ◆♒♍ ●♋■♈◆♋♍, ♐□□ ♍⌘♋□□●♍,
> ♋ ●□■♈◆♋◆♋■♍● □♍●♋◆✂□■ ♌♍◆♍♍■ ◆♒♍ ♍⌘◆♍■◆ □♐
> □□♋● ●♋■♈◆♋♍ ♋■♋ ●♋◆♍□ □♍♋♈✂■♈ □□□♐♓✂♍■♍♓
> ♒♋♍ ♌♍♍■ ♈♍□□■◆♋□♋♍ ◆✂◆♒ ◆♒□♍♍ ♌□□♋♈●♓ ♈♍♐
> ✂■♍♈ ◆♓□♍ □♐ ♍♒✂●♈□♍■, ◆♓□✂♍♋●●♓ ♍♍✂♍●□□✂■♈,
> □♍♋♈✂■♈♋♍●♋♍♍♈□♋♍, ♋■♋ ●♋■♈◆♋♈♍♍♍♋♍♍♋♍.

Even when we tell you that the sentence is about language and reading, if you do not know the code it will take a long time to work out. The task is possible because you understand about the alphabetic principle. The letter E is the most frequent in English and in this text it occurs 33 times followed by A, which occurs 23 times. Armed with this information you could probably spend happy hours gradually getting closer and closer to the original. However, just in case you cannot spare the time to do this we have printed the original below:

> Within the language domain, for example, a longitudinal relation between the extent of oral language and later reading proficiency has been demonstrated with three broadly defined types of children, typically developing, reading-delayed, and language-delayed.
>
> (Whitehurst and Fischel, 2000, p. 55)

This statement by Whitehurst and Fischel is important in our consideration of comprehension in reading. If decoding is held equal, differences in children's ability to understand the texts they read relate to differences in their language skills. However, this relation is much stronger for older readers than for beginners (Vellutino, Scanlon and Tanzman, 1994; Whitehurst & Lonigan,

1998). We would suggest that this is because, in the early years, those children who are able to read the words have direct access to meanings whereas those children who cannot read the words have to try to work out the meanings from the context (West and Stanovich, 1978). This process of working out meaning via context requires guessing, which is effortful and slow and may actually be misleading. Increasing word-reading efficiency means that children do not have to concentrate on the words but can focus their attention on the meaning of the text itself (Perfetti, 1985; Ehri, 1995).

Understanding language requires grammatical competence and semantic competence. Much of this is mediated through vocabulary. Children who have larger spoken vocabularies have fewer problems in learning to read and are able to understand what they are reading with greater ease. Growth in vocabulary in the early years comes about through listening and talking. Some of this listening will be through listening to stories and there is evidence that the more experience with story books children have before school the greater their vocabularies are likely to be (Sulzby and Teale, 1991). Eventually, of course, much of children's later vocabulary development beyond Key Stage 1 is augmented by independent reading (Nagy, Herman and Anderson, 1985; Stainthorp and Hughes, 2004). In the early years they need spoken language support for vocabulary and syntactic development. This is true for all children but even more crucial for children whose first language is not English. Recent work by Dockrell and Stuart (personal communication) has shown that many children whose first language is not English as well as those who are native English speakers from impoverished backgrounds start school with unacceptably low levels of language skills including vocabulary and grammar even after a minimum of a year in a preschool setting. They argue that children need very focused supportive language to give them the grammar and vocabulary that will enable them to understand the simple texts that they will be learning to read in Key Stage 1. This is important because reading comprehension and vocabulary are highly correlated (Stanovich, 1986; Baumann and Kameenui, 1991) and because reading comprehension and listening comprehension involve the same processes, by increasing children's vocabularies one can boost their general language and their reading skills.

We have said there is nothing unique about reading comprehension as opposed to language comprehension but there are differences between written and spoken language particularly at the text level. Many of the early texts that children read tend to be chronological narratives – they read stories and although this genre is found to be the easiest to follow, there is a schematic structure that authors use that is not necessarily immediately obvious to children. This is where exposure to print again plays a role. Children who have listened to many stories being read to them at home come with an advantage. They recognise the genre (though they would not put it like that) and are comfortable with the structure (Van Kleeck, 1990). Repeated reading activities of the same stories and exposure to a wide variety of stories enable children to develop story knowledge, which then facilitates comprehension (Mason and Allen, 1986; Van Kleeck, 1990). Where children come to school with limited experiences they need to have more direct instruction in this through dialogue and questioning.

Work by Oakhill (Oakhill, Yuill and Parkin, 1986) has shown that there are children who develop normal word-reading skills but who have difficulty in comprehending texts. However, their difficulties are subtle. They understand texts at the literal level but they have difficulty in inferring meanings not explicitly stated in the texts. We have already stated that reading comprehension processes are the same as listening comprehension processes but through a different medium, so it will not be surprising that Oakhill has found that these 'poor comprehenders' have subtle difficulties with language comprehension in general. The problem with reading comprehension is that as children's word reading skills become fluent they gradually read longer, diverse genres, which often have more complex, demanding grammatical forms that require far more inferencing than spoken language. The strategies that were found to help older poor comprehenders included requiring them to ask themselves questions such as who, what, where, when, and why as they were reading the texts. In the early stages of learning to read, this type of questioning technique can help develop comprehension, knowledge of schematics structures and vocabulary. However, in the early stages it seems that children are helped in their comprehension by having teachers ask them the questions. The questioning techniques we observed in this study show how effective this can be in developing and reinforcing children's comprehension of the texts they read.

It is clear that Hoover and Gough's definition of reading as the product of decoding is far from simple. It is rather like the elegant swan smoothly gliding over the water but paddling furiously below the surface. Learning to read words in English is a complex task that needs sophisticated instruction from highly educated professionals. However, word reading is not enough; it is essential that children have the language skills necessary to utilise the products of their decoding so that they do not just read accurately but with comprehension and enthusiasm.

In presenting some of the evidence about the development of reading in this chapter it has been impossible to avoid reference to writing – the other side of the literacy coin. A characteristic of the successful teachers in this study was their ability to integrate reading and writing successfully but writing is not just the flip side of reading. It is much more complex than that so in the next chapter we focus specifically on this important aspect of children's journey to literacy.

4 The Development of Writing

This chapter outlines the processes involved in the production of text. It explores the complexities of the writing process and the psychological processes involved in the development of writing. Reference is made to research-based models of writing and to the role of long-term and short-term memory.

It is a truth universally acknowledged that writing is more difficult than reading. This means that learning to write is much more difficult than learning to read. The three successful teachers in Literacy Hours that we observed spent much of their time teaching writing. They were able to integrate the two related activities, ensuring that writing was supported by the children's growing competence in reading. In order to explain why writing is the more demanding task we need to make a short diversion into an aspect of psychology called human information processing. We have alluded to this approach in the previous chapter by saying that when word reading is not efficient it takes up processing capacity that might otherwise be dedicated to comprehension.

HUMAN INFORMATION PROCESSING

Writing is an example of human information processing in action. It is a highly complex task that requires the orchestration of a number of different activities simultaneously and thereby places great demands on the cognitive system. There are some widely different views and approaches within cognitive psychology but there are a few basic principles on which most agree (Kellogg, 1997). Two of these seem central to an understanding of the demands of writing. The first is the assumption of a limited capacity and the second is an assumption that a control mechanism is required.

LIMITED CAPACITY

This assumption states that the amount of information that the brain can process at any one time (and therefore from moment to moment) is constrained. This means that there is a finite and limited amount of processing capacity, which may vary from individual to individual and therefore correlate with overall individual differences. Any aspect of a task that is difficult for the individual will require greater amounts of the finite capacity to be devoted to it for successful completion. The consequence of this is that there will be less capacity available overall for the other aspects of the task. This is particularly so if it is a highly complex task like writing. It is generally not possible to write a three-volume novel whilst cooking the dinner. This is true for the adult who may be relatively skilled. It is therefore even more the case for the child who is still developing cognitively and who is learning new tasks for the first time. A child who is just learning to write and who may have some exciting ideas to communicate may, for example, have difficulty producing the text because of a lack of sufficient skill to generate the motor movements necessary to form the letters. The physical act of writing may take up so much processing capacity that there is little left over for generating an extended text. Ideas may become opaque to the reader in the struggle to produce sentences that conform to the syntax of written discourse.

Writing has a communicative function. We write to communicate to others or to communicate to ourselves. In the early stages of writing, when skills are fairly rudimentary, this communicative function may be considerably reduced.

The example below illustrates a problem for the reader when the spelling aspect of writing has not become sufficiently skilled. In this instance the little boy aged 5 years 6 months who had written the piece was asked to 'read' it back immediately to an adult (Hughes, 1997). The translation we give in the grid underneath the sample of writing below is therefore a faithful recording of the child's intentions. However, the next day it would not be possible for the writer to discern his own intent.

T w a s a b a h e g L the m L F e s L e the v the p r a a 2 p p w e

T	w	a	s	a	b	a	h	e	g	L	the
There	was	a	storm	a	big	egg	hatched	it	got	lost	the
m	L	F	e	s	L	e	the	v	the	p	r
mummy	look[ed]	for	it	she	look[ed]	in	the	village	the	people	ran
a	a	2	p	p	w	e
away	only	2	people	play	with	it

The strategy the child appeared to be using was to give an initial letter for each word apart from the three instances when the highly frequent word 'the' was written correctly. As the grid shows, there is evidence that the child was phonemically aware with accurate knowledge of the letter–sound correspondences for consonant sounds. This knowledge was slightly shaky for vowels with only the vowel letters A and E being used. However, they were always used for words beginning with a vowel.

The context for this piece of writing was a series of line drawings. The child was asked to write an unaided piece in response to the pictures. This meant that the task demands were reduced in that the child did not have to create the events but simply had to tell the story in his own words. The translation shows that the child was able to produce a coherent narrative that faithfully represented the pictures. However, in order to do this the strategy was to abandon any attempt at spelling beyond the initial letter. The child was clearly working at the limit of his capacity.

CONTROL MECHANISM

The second principle is that a control mechanism is required to process information and carry out tasks. This mechanism has an executive function, which is conceptualised as overseeing the processing, storage, retrieval and utilisation of information. This means there always has to be a proportion of the available capacity taken up by the executive function. When one is learning a new task more processing power is required by the central executive than when one is doing something that is routine and overlearned. The adult writer who writes a lot will have highly practised motor movements, spelling skills, and command of the syntax of written discourse styles. This means that the act of writing *per se* will take up very little capacity. Under such circumstances the central executive can devote more power to the compositional aspects. The person who has a fluent extended vocabulary will have to spend less power searching for the exact words to translate the concepts into the language necessary for communicating concepts to a reader. This reminds us how important it is that children develop a wide vocabulary through listening and reading to support their communication skills in both speaking and writing.

WORKING MEMORY

Having introduced the concept of limited processing capacity we now want to turn to the concept of working memory to develop the argument about why writing is challenging and more difficult than reading. The working memory system makes use of knowledge and experiences stored in long-term memory to enable activities to be performed from moment to moment. The working memory system is conceptualised as having three components – a central executive and two slave systems: the phonological loop and the visuo-spatial sketchpad (Baddeley, 1985).

The central executive is the control system. It is responsible for planning, selecting the appropriate strategy and monitoring the task performance.

The phonological loop is responsible for manipulating and maintaining speech-based information within working memory. It has two components: 1

a phonological store, which holds information for about 2 seconds, and 2) a process of articulatory subvocal rehearsal. This rehearsal capability can extend the time material can be maintained in the phonological store. There is considerable evidence about the development of the phonological aspect of working memory. We have known for many years that immediate memory span, the number of unrelated items that can be recalled in order immediately after presentation, increases from about two or three items at the age of 4 years to seven items in adulthood (Miller, 1956). Measures of immediate phonological memory are routinely used in most IQ tests (see, for example, the Wechsler Intelligence Scale for Children (WISC) and the British Ability Scales (BAS)). In addition we know that children do not tend to use spontaneous rehearsal for deliberately remembering things until about the age of 7 years (Keeney, Cannizzo and Flavell, 1967). An efficient slave system may be important when attempting complex tasks because it frees up capacity for the central executive. This means that there are additional constraints imposed on children in KS1 when they are writing because their working memory capacity is still developing. Working memory is also involved in the spelling component of writing and we will return to this later.

The visuo-spatial sketchpad is responsible for the generation, manipulation and retention of visual images. There has been far less research undertaken into the functioning of this slave system and its role in writing is as yet undetermined. This may be a fruitful area for future research.

Kellogg (1996) has provided us with a helpful model of working memory in writing adapted from Brown *et al.* (1988) (see Figure 4.1).

The systems of writing are designated as *formulation, execution* and *monitoring*. Each of these systems involves two further basic-level processes. Formulation consists of *planning* the content and *translating* this into sentences: from concepts to language. The output from this system is then the input for the execution system. There a *programme* has to be generated for outputting the language via writing, which then has to be realised in text. In other words, it has to be *executed*. This, once produced, will be *read* and available for *editing*. As can be seen from the model, the arrows indicating the flow of information show that the systems are all interconnected. Kellogg makes clear that this is not a simple feed-forward, one-way system from formulation through execution to monitoring. All the processes may have simultaneous activation. The skilled writer may be formulating the next ideas at the same time as writing down the current phrase or sentence, which may be undergoing online editing even as it is being executed. However, this level of sophisticated orchestration is only possible when the execution processes are highly overlearned to the point of proceeding virtually automatically. As we all know to our cost, formulation in particular will remain in many respects controlled and effortful. You will read how the teachers whom we studied for this book clearly engaged in activities that supported all these six writing processes.

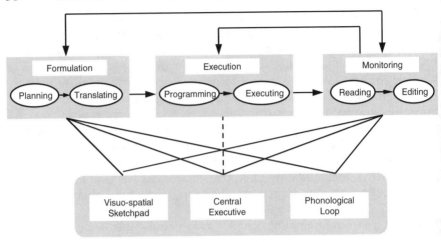

Figure 4.1 The resources of working memory used by the formulation, execution and monitoring system.
Source: Kellogg (1996).

The connections from the working memory system to the processes indicate how they are controlled. The dotted line to the execution processes indicates that these processes are the ones that may become more or less automated. When they do become automated they take up less processing capacity and therefore free up capacity for generating (formulating) and editing (monitoring) the text. In the early stages of learning to write the execution processes may take up so much processing capacity that there is very little available particularly for editing.

A MODEL FOR BEGINNING AND DEVELOPING WRITING

The principles of human information processing have been incorporated into the models of the processes in writing developed since the early 1980s. The first, most influential model of skilled writing was proposed by Hayes and Flower (1980). This was subsequently amended by Hayes (1996). However these models are based on the processes thought to underlie adult skilled writing. For our purposes the most useful model of writing is the one proposed by Berninger and Swanson (1994) (Figure 4.2) in their adaptation of the original Hayes and Flower model. The adaptations and additions made by Berninger and Swanson are printed in bold italics in the figure.

Here we see that the major writing processes are conceptualised as *planning*, *translating* and *reviewing*. In the original Hayes and Flower model reading was directly named as an essential writing process. In the model

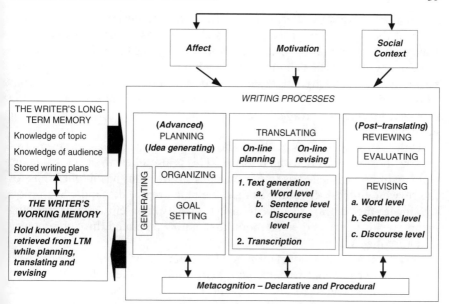

Figure 4.2 Modification of the Hayes-Flower model for beginning and developing writing.
Source: Berninger and Swanson (1994). Reprinted from Berninger, V.W. & Swanson, H.L. (1994) Children's writing. Towards a process theory of the development of skilled writing. Vol. 2.

above you will note that reading is still conceived as being essential to writing but it is labelled 'evaluating'. It is not possible to review a text without reading it. Reading also influences writing indirectly through the information about the topic stored in long-term memory. The model also recognises that working memory plays a central role in writing.

Affect, motivation and the social context are seen as influencing the writing processes. Positive orientation to writing and beliefs that one can write are important in enabling children to produce texts. The reverse is of course also true. Children who believe that they cannot write will find it very difficult to produce texts. A supportive social context with feedback on positive aspects of texts and strategies to help improve texts will enable children to have a positive motivation towards writing. The praise given by the teachers in this study was very important in supporting positive motivation of the children. The social context of writing will also be influenced by the long-term memory in terms of the child's awareness of audience. Recognising the needs of the theoretical audience when reading what one has written is a sophisticated cognitive act, which requires the child to have developed a good theory of mind.

A major innovation of Berninger and Swanson's model is the greater elaboration of the translation processes. This element was underdeveloped in the Hayes and Flower model because they were considering the processes involved in skilled writing. When children are developing their writing skills the transcription processes have still to be learned and automated. They will be controlled and effortful and therefore take up a considerable amount of processing capacity, leaving less available for planning – and probably very little for reviewing.

At the word level, when spelling is not automated the choice and transcription of words is controlled and effortful. This is also likely to mean that many words will be misspelled as in our example above. This has implications for the revising process. It results in there being a greater demand when proofreading for the central executive to divert capacity in order to identify spelling errors. If this happens then attention to meaning mediated through sentence structure may suffer.

This developmental model stemmed from Berninger's empirical work with developing writers and students with learning disabilities (Berninger *et al.*, 1992, 1995). She adapted the Hayes and Flower model because she felt that there are developmental constraints on children's writing as well as limited processing capacity constraints. These developmental constraints operate at three levels.

At the first level there are neurodevelopmental constraints, which include motor activities. Until children have perfected their skills for automated letter formation and gained a degree of control over spelling, there will be considerable extra constraint on their written output. We have noted that in the UK children begin to receive literacy instruction at an earlier age than much of the rest of the world. Their neuromotor development at the start of literacy instruction is therefore less mature than the child beginning to write in Switzerland, for example.

Handwriting was one area of literacy teaching that was not seen during the Literacy Hours that we observed. It has been a much-neglected aspect since the Bullock Report (Bullock, 1975) rather downplayed its importance. From an information-processing perspective it can be argued that if children have to devote much of their limited capacity to remembering how to form the letters they will have less available for the content. The NLS recognised that this was a problem and included specific information about the teaching of handwriting in the guidelines. However, teaching a motor skill, albeit one that is literacy driven, does not lend itself to inclusion in the Literacy Hour and these teachers wisely taught it in other parts of the timetable.

At the second level there are higher level linguistic constraints. Throughout the primary years, children are still developing their linguistic skills. In particular, they are developing control over the more sophisticated aspects of syntax. This involves the spoken domain but is much more evident in the written domain. In her seminal work, *Children's Writing and Reading*, Peren

(1984) documented the development of the production of late-acquired syntactic forms such as used of extended subjects, acquisition of phase verbs and control over subordination.

In addition, during this time, children are continuing to extend their lexicons through reading as we detailed in Chapter 3.

At the third level, ability and experience in planning, translating and revising continue to constrain output. These processes are not achieved automatically by many children and should therefore be explicitly taught and practised. This model reminds us that children need to have many opportunities to write. As with all learned skills, if writing skills are not practised then performance deteriorates. When an activity is still very much in the acquisition phase practice is even more essential because without it every time one returns to a task one has to catch up with the level one had previously achieved, which for a young child can be very demotivating.

Writing is such a complex activity that it makes considerable demands upon our limited processing capacity. For some children the task demands may be so great that they literally cannot start and certainly may not be able to write well formed sentences that form logical, meaningful texts that others can read. In the early years of literacy instruction in the UK – in Key Stage 1 – children are still developing their memory functioning so their capacity is going to be constrained and considerably limited. Even in the later primary years, writing skills are still developing so there is only limited automation of many processes, particularly editing.

Kroll (1981) identified four phases in the acquisition of writing ability. These are: *preparation, consolidation, differentiation* and *systematic integration*.

In the preparation phase, children need to acquire the technical skills that enable them to represent language in written form. This means, as Berninger and Swanson suggest, that children need to learn the transcription skills of letter formation, spelling and punctuation. Kroll argues that by gaining control over these children are able to draw 'more freely' on their language competences. If the physical act of writing and the spelling of the words takes up too much processing capacity then there is less available for accessing the language needed to express the ideas. Within Berninger and Swanson's model, the text generation may be constrained to be at the word-by-word level rather than at the sentence and discourse level. The only way to overcome this hurdle is through experience in composing and through opportunities to develop language by making the planning processes of idea generation, organising and goal setting overt through talking. Just as exposure to print is essential for reading, so it is for writing. Children who have a wide experience of story form find it easier to reproduce coherent narratives.

Kroll's second phase is one of consolidation when children have begun to gain control over the technicalities so that processing capacity is freed up for generating texts. However, at this point he noted that writing and speaking are relatively integrated. Children use the syntactic structures of spoken language in their writing. This means that their texts will tend to be chronological narratives with simple verb forms. They may well produce strings of very long sentences, which are actually many short sentences all joined by the conjunctions 'and' or 'and then'. Writing at this stage may be characterised as being in the form of 'knowledge-telling' as detailed by Bereiter and Scardamalia (1987). When children write like this they tend to produce unstructured texts, which simply detail everything they know about a particular topic, particularly when writing informative texts.

Through direct teaching and experience in writing children begin to be able to differentiate between the discourse styles of spoken and written language. In this differentiation, phase writing and speech diverge. This does not come about automatically and is best taught explicitly. At this point, the writing may take on the characteristic of 'knowledge-transforming' as identified by Bereiter and Scardamalia. The meanings of the ideas that the child wishes to express are mediated through the syntax and the overarching structure. The child is beginning to gain control over the translating processes so that more investment can go into the planning and reviewing processes. The NLS has incorporated the view that children should be taught the different structural forms of written genres although Kress (1996) cautions against taking too rigid an approach to genres. However, it is during this phase that the use of extended subjects and objects with complex sentences and embedded clauses begins to emerge in children's writing as they gain control over written syntax. They will have been exposed to these forms in their reading for a number of years before they emerge in writing.

The final phase of consolidation is when control of both written and spoken forms enables integration. Writers develop flexibility in both modes and can select appropriately from both to serve the purposes of communication. Many adults feel that they do not gain complete competence in this phase!

A small-scale intervention discussed by Derewianka (1990) makes a useful illustration of Kroll's description of the transition from preparation to systematic integration, although in her example the project enabled the children to use appropriate written tenor at a younger age that Kroll appears to envisage. The 7-year-old Australian children in Derewianka's study were engaged in a geological project on rocks. The project lasted over an extended period of 3 weeks and involved the children in physical as well book-based research to support their investigations, which were eventually recorded in sophisticated texts using appropriate written language. Throughout the time of the project the children had the opportunities to use oral language to support their growing understanding of the field and acquisition of topic-specific vocabulary. The activities, discussions, draft writing and feedback enabled the children to learn about the field and to consolidate this knowledge in written form. Derewianka calls this a 'distancing' process whereby the children move from involvement in the present immediate detail and become able to step back and take a more integrated objective perspective. She argues that it is important to give children opportunities to engage in activities that enable them to discuss, record, revisit and reflect in order that they can gradually move towards successfully making the connections between the 'action' spoken end of the language continuum and the more reflective, crafted, 'frozen' end, which is written language. The lessons we observed for this study showed that the teachers were very good at providing these sorts of opportunities for their pupils.

In the early years of learning to write, when children are in Kroll's preparation phase, it is arguably important to ensure that the processes that place additional constraints on writing are supported by direct instruction and opportunities to practise. From the perspective of the psychology of skill acquisition, we know that skilled performance comes about from supported practice with feedback. There should also be planned, short, focused, frequent opportunities to practise so that performance gradually becomes more automated rather than controlled. This should be the case for writing instruction. Derewianka's study showed how important opportunities to revisit and work on a sustained topic are.

The content aspect of writing probably never becomes automated. We always have to think about what we write so it necessarily involves higher level processes. However, if we ensure that the transcription processes are highly practised then there will be more capacity available to generate and control ideas. This means that time needs to be set aside for explicit instruction in the transcription skills of letter formation and spelling.

Children need to become skilled, fast, fluent writers so that their writing keeps up with their generation of ideas without losing too much legibility. In a recent survey of handwriting policy and practice in primary schools (Stainthorp, Henderson, Barnett and Scheib, 2006) we found that schools had clear policies about letter formation and writing style but they did not include strategies for developing fast, fluent, legible skills. Berninger (1999) found that the transcription skills of writing speed (and thereby fluency) and spelling contributed significantly to individual differences in the overall quality of writing in the elementary years (approximately 40 % to 60 % of the variance). However, Connelly and Hurst (2002) found that in the UK they are still making a significant contribution to writing quality in Years 7 and 9. The effects of slow, laboured handwriting are now known to be very long lasting, so they can affect performance at degree level. In a study of undergraduates, Connelly, Dockrell and Barnett (2005) found that, although handwriting fluency did not contribute to the variance of writing under unpressurised conditions, it did when writing final examination papers under pressurised conditions.

Both Berninger's and Kroll's models can act as a positive framework for pedagogy. A knowledge of these models can help teachers to keep track of the demands being made on children by the writing tasks with which they are presented. Teachers need to be able to articulate to themselves which aspects of writing they are focusing on at any one time in order to ensure that all processes are addressed. It may well be necessary to teach some skills with a degree of isolation.

A particular feature of writing may be embedded in a specified text that children are studying. It may be necessary to highlight that feature and isolate it for some direct, focused teaching. During the primary years, children may not have the cognitive capacity to focus on word, sentence and textual features all at the same time without explicit teaching at each level. In addition, once a particular element has been considered, children will need to have opportunities to try out their control of the particular feature and then have opportunities for extended practice to ensure that they consolidate their learning to achieve sufficient automaticity.

Berninger's model makes clear that developing writing is not just a scaled-down version of skilled writing. There are overt linguistic constraints resulting from the development of syntax during the primary years. Perera identified the syntactic changes, with writing as the pacemaker, which occur in the later primary years. We now know that these need to be taught explicitly so that control is not left to chance. The NLS goes some way to actualising this.

SPELLING

As will be clear from what we have said about the writing processes, word spelling can be a major constraint on writing. Just as it is essential to focus on word reading in the early years it is also essential to focus on word spelling.

In parallel with the dual-route model of reading, so there is a dual-route model of spelling. The two routes are the addressed and the assembled routes. The addressed route maps onto the lexical reading route and the assembled route maps onto the sublexical route (Barry, 1994). In addition to her model of reading, Ehri has detailed a parallel model of the development of word spelling (Ehri, 1997). She suggests that there are four levels of spelling: *pre-alphabetic, partial alphabetic, full alphabetic* and *consolidated alphabetic*. The levels are characterised by the approach to spelling that *predominates* (our italics) at that level. Development at the final two levels is contingent on development at the earlier levels, but development at level 2 is not considered to be contingent on level 1. This means that once children have begun to learn the letter–sound correspondences they have a rudimentary system in place for spelling. They may have experimented with spelling at a prealphabetic level by producing protowriting that superficially resembles cursive script but this will not be derived from letters, sounds or their relationship to each other. Children who have engaged in this protowriting will understand that this is a valued activity that adults undertake and be positively motivated to do the same. However, it is only when they move to a level of using the alphabet to represent sounds that their writing begins to be at least partially accessible to others. We saw this in the example of the dragon story that we presented above.

At the partial alphabetic level, children will begin to represent the sounds of words with letters and often select only the most salient sounds. Thus, they may often only use consonants. In this early stage, their capacity to map the phonemes may be limited by their letter–sound knowledge and their level of phonemic awareness when attempting to segment a word into its constituents. It is often the case that children will miss out the letters 'n' and 'm' which stand for the nasal phonemes /n/ and /m/ when they occur in word final consonant clusters like sand and stamp. They may also be good at representing the initial phoneme but have difficulty in sequencing the rest of the letters.

At the full alphabetic level they are able to segment words successfully and map the resulting phonemes onto letters so their spelling is readable but, because of the nature of English, it is not always accurate. Accuracy occurs at the consolidated level when they have learned about the morphophonemic character of English orthography and the multiplicity of letter patterns.

It is important to stress that these levels are characterised by the dominant strategy that a child uses. Right from the start there will be some words that children can spell accurately because they have memorised them. In today's educational climate there is a hope that children will arrive in school able to spell their own names and those of some of their family members. This is word-specific knowledge and is therefore not systematised. Words that are spelled in this way are spelled by an addressed route. Teachers can capitalise on this to develop the assembled route where the words are generated using alphabetic and phonemic knowledge. Treiman, Kessler and Bourassa (2001) have shown that knowledge of 'own name' letters is very important in children's early spelling attempts and teachers may well use this when beginning to teach children how to use the alphabetic principle to spell words.

Words generated by the assembled root are in a sense 'invented'. Any word spelled in this way is not stored in memory so it has to be generated. Sounding out is a good strategy but in the early stages, this sounding out may be based on incomplete knowledge. When segmenting a word, children may 'hear' letter names and so use a single letter to stand for the CV or VC of the letter. The word TEA could be spelled T and the word EAT could be spelled as ET.

Eventually, when children have expanded their knowledge of words, they may use analogy. If they can spell LIGHT correctly they may use analogy to spell RIGHT and FIGHT. Of course, analogy can lead to the wrong spelling being chosen. Some IGHT words are heterographic homophones, such as MIGHT – MITE; RIGHT – RITE; SIGHT – SITE.

The learning of word spelling is highly dependent on the working memory system (Service and Turpeinen, 2001). A new word needs to be processed and practised if it is to be 'written' into the orthographic (visual) lexicon. If the words one wishes to use when writing do not have complete, accurate representations in the orthographic lexicon, the letter sequences will have to be generated in a controlled way rather than automatically as we have discussed above. This will require more processing capacity and leave less available for the generation of ideas. In languages with a transparent regular orthography such as Turkish and Spanish, memorising the simple grapheme–phoneme and symmetrical phoneme–grapheme correspondences will take little cognitive energy and accurate spelling can be achieved quite efficiently. In a language with a morphophonemic, irregular, opaque orthography, such as English, the task becomes much more complex. The grapheme–phoneme and phoneme–grapheme correspondences are not symmetrical. Many words have irregular spelling patterns. Admittedly it is always possible to map the sound–letter relationships but these may be unusual, as in SHOULD (/ʃ/ /ʊ/ /d/ = SH OUL D), or even unique, as in WEDNESDAY (/w/ /e/ /n/ /z/ /d/ /eɪ/ = W E(D) N(E) S D AY).

This means that becoming a fluent, accurate speller in English requires considerably more time and effort than in many other orthographies. We might note that the list of words required to be learned by heart at Key Stage 1 tends to be composed of irregular exception words. These have to be learned when children have not yet developed an ability to use rehearsal as an effective mnemonic. This means that teachers have to give children many opportunities to learn the spelling of these words accurately by scaffolding their rehearsal for them.

Evidence from SAT performance suggests that at the end of primary school many children are not achieving the level of writing that is expected of children as they enter secondary school. This is particularly the case with boys. As we said at the beginning of this chapter, writing is hard and much harder than reading. It may be that the levels expected of 11 year olds are unrealistic given the other demands of the curriculum. However, the data from the schools that took part in this study show that it is possible for schools in challenging situations to enable their children to achieve highly. The writing performance of all the schools at KS1 was very high. The three teachers whose work we celebrate were able to bring out the best in their pupils.

5 Children for whom English is an Additional Language

This chapter explores the issues for children learning English as an additional language (EAL). It identifies the difficulties that learning to read and write in English might present but also the advantages for pupils who are bilingual or multilingual. In particular this chapter explores the linguistic metacognition that EAL learners often demonstrate. Reference is made to research-based findings related to children learning in another language and also to the practices of the three case-study schools examined in the later chapters of this book.

A significant characteristic of the schools that we focus on in this book is not just that they were good and improving but that they all had a high proportion of pupils for whom English was an additional language. In order to set the accounts of the Literacy Hours in context, a discussion of the issues surrounding the teaching of primary-aged pupils for whom English is an additional language is essential.

Let us start by clarifying the expression 'English as an additional language', more commonly referred to by the acronym EAL. There are a number of terms used to describe pupils who come to school in England with a home language that is not English. Among these are *bilingual, second language learners, pupils learning English as a second language* and so on. It is generally acknowledged now that many pupils may well be operating in a third or fourth language. Take for example a Tamil-speaking child who has spent some time living in France before the family successfully claims asylum in the UK. Such a child may have varying degrees of proficiency in at least three languages. For this reason, we adopt the term EAL in this book in order to give a more accurate description of many of the children in the schools studied. Nevertheless, the alternative names listed above are likely to appear in this discussion because they will have been the preferred terms of writers and researchers cited as part of the commentary. The important thing for teachers is to know enough about their pupils to understand where their spoken English may lie in relation to other languages they use outside school.

Increasingly teachers in the UK, regardless of their schools' locations, are likely to have one or more pupils in their class whose mother tongue is not English. Edwards (1998, p. 2) explains that this is not a new phenomenon and that there have been references to the teaching of pupils for whom English is an additional language since the nineteenth century. For some schools the teaching of pupils with EAL will be the mainstream. An example of this would be a school in an East London LEA where 90 % or more speak Sylhetti/Bengali. In other schools the percentage of EAL pupils may be high but the pupil population may come from very diverse geographical locations with some 40 or more languages being spoken. A further percentage of schools will have individuals who may be the only EAL pupil among their peers. These are the children who Statham (1993) terms 'isolated bilingual learners'. Each scenario presents challenges for the children, their families and their teachers. However, there are consistent findings in research and some clearly identified features of schools that manage to support their EAL pupils well, which are significant for all settings and a useful reference point for teaching.

THE BENEFITS OF BILINGUALISM: METALINGUISTIC AWARENESS

We may be familiar with the idea that children with EAL have a greater knowledge, albeit implicit knowledge, about the nature of language; that somehow children who are learning in more than one language are actually at an advantage compared to their monolingual peers because of enhanced metacognitive skills. This *linguistic metacognition* can be described as the knowledge these children have about languages because they have to think in two or more languages. They are perhaps more keenly aware of how language operates because they have to address the differences between their languages all the time. But what exactly are these advantages and how do they present themselves in ways that teachers can recognise and exploit to the pupils' advantage?

Bialystock (1997) studied monolingual and bilingual 4 to 5 year olds in order to gauge their print awareness. She found that bilingual children had a more advanced understanding of the representational nature of print than monolinguals: 'they knew that the written form carried meaning and that the picture was irrelevant. Moreover, they understood this equally for both languages' (Bialystock, 1997, p. 437). Interestingly Bialystock found that French/English bilingual 4 year olds outperformed Chinese/English bilinguals in developing concepts about print. However, by 5 years old Chinese pupils were leading both the bilingual French group and their monolingual peers. From this she surmised that there might be initial confusion for children learning in two languages, particularly for Chinese children who are used to an ideographic rather than a sound-based writing system. However, 'when the confusion is resolved, the benefit of the richer experience enables children to apply their new knowledge to both languages' (Bialystock, 1997, p. 438).

Further evidence of this 'richer experience' can be found in the writing of Helavaara-Robertson (2002). In her case study of Ikram – a 7-year-old bilingual of Pakistani background – she observed simultaneous development of reading in three languages. Ikram was taught English as part of the standard Literacy Hour in his primary school, read Urdu during a lunchtime club and attended Qur'anic classes at the mosque in order to learn Arabic. In addition to this his home language was Pahari – an unwritten dialect of Panjabi. The writer was critical of what she saw as the failure of Ikram's primary school to acknowledge his varying literacy experiences. Instead, this child's weakness in spoken English led to his being taught always with the least able children in class and given simple exercises that did not take account of his highly developed literacy skills such as his ability to read for meaning in different contexts and give personal responses to texts. She summed up this tension by defining the different values attributed to different types of literacy, which affect the pupils themselves and the ways in which their teachers perceive them:

> Appropriate participation in different literacy classes is characterised by different sets of values. In the Qur'anic class literacy is rooted in religion. Whilst Urdu literacy is linked to learning to belong to Pakistan, English literacy is directly linked with general educational success.
>
> (Helavaara-Robertson, 2002, p. 122)

There is a body of evidence showing that the advantages of children's bilingualism and biliteracy can be negated by cultural and political attitudes to bilingualism and to the perceived status of the children's home language. Cummins (2000) described US policy related to bilingualism, particularly to the teaching of the very many Spanish-speaking children in some states, as rooted in xenophobic and misinformed prejudice. He cited opponents of teaching pupils in their home language during the early years at school and explored media responses to the issues in relation to social class. Where bilingual teaching programmes such as French immersion for Canadian children are reported, the view is favourable because – Cummins asserted – 'these programmes serve the interests of dominant middle-class majority language children'. However, when focusing on those programmes that seek to support the more marginalised sections of society through bilingual teaching, the media take a far less positive view.

Perhaps something similar happens in the UK. When children arrive in English classrooms they are assessed only by their proficiency in English, which may automatically devalue their home language. Our language is, however, very closely matched to our sense of self. Thus, if children are given a sense that their home language is not important they may suffer poor self-esteem. Siraj-Blatchford and Clarke (2000) explained that children will learn their new language best when they are in a state of emotional wellbeing, secure and have a positive self-identity. Cummins (2000) and others cited already in this chapter would argue that this starts with a recognition of what the child brings to the classroom and an understanding of the benefits of maintaining the home language in school. The following sections define the more specific issues for EAL pupils in developing spoken and written English.

ACQUIRING SPOKEN ENGLISH: CHILDREN IN THE EARLY YEARS

It is important to understand the differences between the acquisition of a first language (L1) – a 'mother tongue' – and the development of a second or subsequent language. First language development occurs from birth and largely in the home setting, whereas second-language acquisition may happen at any time and probably in what is an unfamiliar setting. In a home or family setting children are exposed to language used in a context that is familiar. For example, as a parent dresses a child he may name the items of clothing as they are put on and will also be using a range of positional and functional language related to getting dressed. Also, this action will be repeated daily and the repetition will support understanding. As the young child starts to use words for himself he will receive lavish praise from adults and siblings in the home, thus fostering a sense of pride and excitement at correctly using the words he had heard at first hand at home.

Consider then, the young child starting school for whom English is not a first language. New names will have to be learned for objects first learned in the home setting in meaningful contexts. These may be learned in abstract contexts without the support of visual cues and everyday actions. There is unlikely to be the close one-to-one attention of a parent or relative to support the language. Depending on the culture a child comes from, objects in the home corner, which are so familiar to children in the UK, may have no cultural reference so that the name and use have to be learned together for the first time. This suggests that meaning may have to be worked out in confusing and unfamiliar contexts. Added to this learning may be taking place in an environment where the first language is not regarded as important, adding pressure onto the need to acquire English when the first language does not have the vocabulary for the contexts.

The above presents us with a basic picture of the challenges for the child. Siraj-Blatchford and Clarke (2000) also warn of the danger in generalising the needs of young EAL pupils and failing to take account of individual difference. Because of their fundamental linguistic difference it may be that teachers are not sensitive to character differences that will affect children's capacity to acquire their new language. Expectations may be uniform rather than differentiated. Some children will be natural risk takers who are motivated to learn a new language whereas others may lack confidence and risk rapid isolation as English-speaking children tire of trying to communicate with them through their initial silent period (Siraj-Blatchford and Clarke, 2001, p. 47). Evidence of this important issue is referred to by Parke and Drury (2001) who included in their research among nursery children the words of a bilingual interpreter working for families to support transition from home to school:

> The reception of bilingual children when they first enter nursery decides the direction in which they will proceed during their school life. The outgoing, confident children will find their way through, while others will stay inside their shells and not come out for the time they are in school.
>
> (Parke and Drury, 2001, p. 124)

Parke and Drury (2001) followed the progress of three Pahari-speaking nursery-aged girls, as they entered nurseries in Watford. In three case studies they observed quite clear differences in the ways in which the process of language acquisition affected the children. One, Nazma, found the transition very difficult and maintained her home language while at school. Relationships with English-speaking children were limited and she was described as 'coming alive' only when working with the bilingual support assistant. The other two girls made the transition more quickly, were confident, were considered able by their teachers and started the process of operating in English and Pahari as soon as they arrived. One of these, Samia, elected for some periods of silence – a recognised necessary feature for developing bilinguals as they assimilate their new language. The most able child, Maria, benefited from targeted language support from her teacher who recognised her as 'brighter than the other bilinguals'.

In the context of the need to acknowledge individual difference among bilinguals, it is interesting to note that three children with very similar backgrounds and entering very similar schools should have such different experiences of acquiring their new language. It is also worrying to observe that perhaps those children who find the transition least troublesome and make the most obvious progress may be rewarded with additional support. While it is inappropriate to generalise from just this one case study, it does illustrate an example of how there may be potential 'Matthew effects' (Stanovich, 1986) in children's second language development. The child who is most quickly able to engage with her teacher is rewarded with additional attention and, therefore, increased opportunity to learn more vocabulary. She feels pleased with her progress, her teacher is pleased, and her self-esteem is high. Conversely, the child for whom the whole process is traumatic is, perhaps for the best intentions, left alone by her teachers and probably her peers and is dependent on the limited time available to her from a teaching assistant.

It is widely recognised that children who come to school with no spoken English are likely to move through a range of stages as they become familiar with their own language. It is important for teachers to recognise what these stages may look like, in order that they can respond appropriately. This is crucial for the children who do not make the transition easily, as outlined above. Table 5.1 shows Clarke's analysis of these stages.

ACQUIRING SPOKEN ENGLISH: CHILDREN IN KEY STAGES 1 AND 2

The difficulties experienced by older children arriving for the first time in school with a home language other than English will mirror those of the younger bilingual but they are potentially subject to a greater range of obstacles. Changes in curricular expectations as children mature may lead to a change in teacher expectation. In an early years setting it may be the case that children are able to develop their spoken English gradually in a supportive environment where the pressure to read and write in English is absent. However, as children enter formal education, the parameters change. In Key Stages 1 and 2 children of all backgrounds are subject to the same testing and levelling culture that has characterised English primary schools for over a decade. Thus, those children for whom English is an additional language may be part of a less fluid classroom protocol where talk cannot flourish in order to support their acquisition of a new language. Indeed, they may be asked to start reading and writing in this new language before they have mastered it orally.

The overwhelming importance of allowing children with EAL – regardless of age – to develop fluency in their new language first is highlighted by a

Table 5.1 Stages of development in second language acquisition

1. Continued use of the home language in the new context
2. Use of nonverbal communication
3. A period of silence
4. Use of repetition and language play
5. Use of single words, formulae and routines
6. Development of more complex English

Source: Siraj-Blatchford and Clarke, 2000.

number of authors. In a study looking at Turkish children learning to read in Dutch schools, Verhoeven (1994) argued not only for bilingual literacy instruction but also for a greater emphasis on oral development in the second language before children are asked to read and write in it. In particular he noted that the Turkish children's word recognition and reading comprehension were most strongly influenced by their oral proficiency – or lack of it – in Dutch. Thus, more time spent in developing children's spoken English will reap rewards when they come to read and write in it.

Furthermore, there is shared concern that teachers should recognise that pupils who are apparently fluent in 'playground' English still have gaps in their technical understanding of standard English. Failure to address the need for support in developing sophisticated use of spoken English is cited as a possible cause for comparative underachievement in children with EAL. In a study observing adult 'talking partners' supporting bilingual 5 to 8 year olds, Kotler, Wegerif and Le Voi (2001) observed the lack of opportunity for EAL pupils to acquire the oral competence that would support higher order skills of reflection and reasoning in the current curriculum for English. They noted, importantly, that this may also cause the educational underperformance not just of bilingual children but of some groups of pupils for whom English is a first language (Kotler, Wegerif and Le Voi, 2001, p. 403).

One final case study is valuable to this discussion about the ways in which children acquire a new language, particularly those who arrive later than normal school starting age. Long (2002) tracked the second language of her own 8-year-old daughter as the family moved from the USA to Iceland. Using a range of data such as observations of her daughter and interviews with her schoolteacher and new Icelandic friends Long distilled a range of classroom features that were most effective for her daughter in supporting language development. The least useful setting was where her daughter was expected to listen to 'streams of unsupported teacher talk' (Long, 2002, p. 114). More favourable conditions included the use of visual aids and physical demonstrations that were consistent with the verbal message. Routine and the gradual build up of a range of familiar words that were then used in teaching a new concept were important, as was a change in tone that matched the meaning of an explanation. Added to this, the child responded more actively when her prior knowledge about a topic was activated before moving forward with the introduction of new language. Opportunities for the child to observe and follow others were helpful, as was the need for meaningful learning in a 'risk-free setting'. This sequence of suggestions points to an essentially Vygotskian model for supporting language acquisition.

So, schools must recognise individual difference and provide support for pupils even after they have an apparent fluency. Principles identified across research and the writings of those with an interest in the development of EAL pupils' language acquisition point to the following:

- the need to embed learning of the new language in a meaningful context
- the importance of maintaining the home language and allowing the child to operate in two languages in school
- the recognition of and respect for a necessary period of silence while children assimilate new terms and language customs
- opportunities to listen
- opportunities to work with trained bilingual assistants
- use of visual props and cues to support meaning and understanding
- the need for support in understanding and using subject-based language, after 'everyday' fluency has been achieved (it takes 5 to 7 years to become fully competent in a second language)
- the need to develop the understanding of the different registers of language between home and school.

Later chapters of this book will explore how our focus schools tackled the crucial need for their pupils to develop spoken fluency in English and to use oral language at all times to support writing.

LEARNING TO READ WHEN ENGLISH IS AN ADDITIONAL LANGUAGE

> Fluency in spoken English is usually achieved within two years (five to seven years to become fully competent), but the ability to read and understand more complex texts containing unfamiliar cultural references and write the academic English needed for success in examinations takes much longer.
>
> (Footnote in OfSTED, 2000a, p. 27)

Having explored the main issues for children acquiring their new spoken language, we turn our attention to the development of reading in a language that is not a home language. Table 5.2 shows the factors affecting proficiency in reading for all pupils but draws our attention to the additional difficulties that children operating in a new language might experience.

We have already alluded to the fact that, in developing reading, pupils with EAL need to develop their proficiency in spoken English first. Many of the points raised in this table serve to underline that. However, there are a range of taught reading strategies that pupils with EAL may benefit from in particular if they are to develop comprehension skills that match those of their English-speaking peers.

Much has been printed in recent years referring to the need to increase the teaching of phonics to children in Key Stage 1. It is considered that there is sound research-based evidence to support this and the NLS has championed phonics teaching through its own package *Progression in Phonics* (DfES,

Table 5.2 Factors affecting reading proficiency

Factors affecting proficiency in all readers	Potential differences for children with EAL
Language knowledge	May have to unlearn some pre-existing language knowledge
Decoding skills – grapheme-phoneme correspondence	May have contrasting phonological knowledge or knowledge of a symbolic writing system
Reading strategies – e.g. comprehension, monitoring	Syntax differences – use of plurals, English has no gender, verb tenses vary across languages
Prior knowledge of text type, organisation and structure (e.g. the difference between a novel and a brochure)	An unknown lexicon – children will be having to read words for which they don't have a meaning
Experience of the purposes of reading	These may differ considerably – e.g. case study of Ikram The child's own proficiency in spoken English Cultural references in the text with which the child is unfamiliar

2001) and other related support materials. Research by Stuart (1999, 2004) shows that the use of a structured phonics programme as a basis specifically for teaching children with EAL, prior to teaching reading, can prove highly beneficial.

In her first study (Stuart, 1999) and subsequent followup study (Stuart, 2004) young beginner bilinguals in inner-city primaries were given one of two forms of teaching. The first group were taught using a commercial phonics teaching programme, *Jolly Phonics* (Lloyd and Wernham, 1992), while the second were taught introductory reading strategies using an approach named 'Big Books' in which the emphasis was on word-level work using whole texts. The results from the initial study showed 'strong, specific and significant positive effects of the Jolly Phonics intervention on the development of reading and writing' (Stuart, 1999, p. 603). Furthermore, the followup study showed that the children given phonics training as their first introduction to reading tuition in reception sustained this lead over peers taught with the Big Books method through to the end of Key Stage 1.

However, teachers of reading are well aware that phonics is just one part of the jigsaw that children need access to in order to comprehend fully the text they are reading. Extracting meaning from text can be particularly problematic for children with EAL. In fact, Stuart's finding was that the EAL children in her study performed less well at the SATs than their monolingual peers, possibly because of their underdeveloped oral language. This, she hypothesised, was because a delay in oral language development led to a subsequent delay in their ability to read and understand continuous prose and to respond to open-ended questions. Yet again we find evidence supporting development of oral language proficiency alongside instruction for reading and writing.

Hutchinson, Whiteley, Smith and Connors (2003) picked up on this concern in their study following the developmental progression in comprehension skills of both bilingual and monolingual children from Years 2 to 4 in the transition from Key Stage 1 to 2. They cite a wide range of research that described the negative impact of poor vocabulary knowledge on the development of reading for children learning either in their home language or in another language. Furthermore, they discussed the fact that while developing the phonological awareness of pupils with EAL may not be problematic, the development of reading comprehension is much more complex and challenging. The following sums up this dilemma succinctly:

> As children learning EAL start school they have to simultaneously learn to speak and read a new language in a learning environment that is not directly structured for language learning to occur. The development of early English-language skills is facilitated by verbal interactions with teachers and monolingual peers . . . However, in later school years, as the language of text becomes more advanced and requires the understanding of more complex ideas, language learning may not keep pace with the requirements of the text.
>
> (Hutchinson, Whiteley, Smith and Connors, 2003, p. 21)

In analysing where the challenges for pupils with EAL lie, this study identified a number of specific features of reading that pose difficulties, while others may mask lack of knowledge. In common with Stuart's study, reading *accuracy* among children with EAL was not found to be a problem. In fact, by Year 4, there was also very little difference in terms of reading comprehension when the children were tested with monolingual peers. However, the writers were keen to point out that difficulties with reading *comprehension* can be masked where pupils are able to copy chunks of text to respond to questions and where questions give clear clues about the sentences to which they might be referring. This allows pupils to guess accurately and produce a 'correct' answer without necessarily understanding what they are writing.

The real difficulty for these pupils lay in their comprehension when listening to stories. At this point their lack of expressive vocabulary – that with which they could give an answer – hindered their capacity to respond to questions. Without the visual cue of the text they had to memorise paragraphs and were less able to answer successfully. In conclusion, the authors suggested a programme of direct language teaching for pupils with EAL in order to close their 'vocabulary knowledge gap'. We need to support pupils with EAL after they have acquired a working fluency in order that they can be supported with specific subject-based comprehension for their reading.

LEARNING TO WRITE WHEN ENGLISH IS AN ADDITIONAL LANGUAGE

In Chapter 4 we presented a range of research related to writing. This identified that, basically, writing is really hard! Remember that, in order to write successfully, the child must have spoken vocabulary, an understanding of context, genre and appropriate tone, phonic knowledge for accurate spelling and have mastered the mechanics of pencil control and letter formation. Writing is all the more difficult when an individual is thinking in an additional language.

Consider the difficulties for the second language reader identified in Table 5.2 and add to those the complexities of the writing process. The fact that young children can learn to write successfully in English – in the case of our focus schools very successfully – is quite extraordinary. It also worth noting at this point that the process of writing successfully in English can be as challenging for some indigenous English speakers as it is for our pupils not operating in their home language. This is because children need to understand the different registers of language used in written as opposed to spoken English, and this can have as much to do with social class as with linguistic background.

The figures for writing performance in SATs at Key Stage 2 show that children are continuing to find it difficult to achieve the age-appropriate level as laid down by the QCA. In 2000, 63% of girls and 48% of boys achieved Level 4. These figures rose to 69% and 52% respectively by 2002 and then remained static.

The range of research related to how children with EAL acquire literacy in English is limited. That related to how children with EAL learn to write in English is even harder to find. However, a report for the DfES (Cameron and Besser, 2004) gives us the view of professionals working within a research-based framework, and identifies a range of features in the writing of fluent and able EAL pupils as demonstrated by their performance in the Key Stage 2 writing test of 2003. This research sought to fine tune our understanding of how EAL pupils might have both a richer and poorer understanding of written English by segmenting the myriad tasks required of the fluent writer and analysing the performance of monolingual and bilingual pupils in each. The overall aim of the study was to identify those key features of language that pupils with EAL appear to handle less confidently than pupils who speak English as a mother tongue (referred to in the report as EMT speakers).

Their key findings related to a multiplicity of areas involved in the production of text and, interestingly, did not all demonstrate a reduced understanding on the part of pupils with EAL. It is important to understand that they analysed the texts of pupils performing at Levels 3, 4 and 5 of the National Curriculum for English Attainment Target 3; thus their findings differed quite radically according to the attainment levels of the pupils studied. The tasks for the test in that particular year were interesting because they had changed quite significantly from previous years in an effort by the QCA to stop the formulaic and prelearned responses to the written task that had started to emerge as a result of teachers feeling under pressure to 'teach to the test'. Thus children were asked to produce a longer written task, a story, and a radio advertisement as a shorter written task.

Key findings related to each of the areas of written output studied are illustrated in Table 5.3.

Several of these points deserve further explanation. Starting with the most able children, it is interesting to note that there were fewer differences between the two groups. Thus, we could surmise, that once writing at Level 5, EAL pupils have perhaps bridged a developmental gap and moved towards a fuller assimilation of English for writing purposes. However, as always with research, it is dangerous to generalise and we must remember the findings of research related to reading, which demonstrated the continuing need for direct vocabulary teaching for EAL pupils long after an apparent fluency had been reached. Furthermore, the second point in Table 5.3 highlights the fact that the culturally specific nature of some tests may disadvantage the most able EAL pupils

Table 5.3 Key findings from Cameron and Besser (2004) relating to the differences between pupils with EAL and EMT when writing in Key Stage 2 SAT of 2003

- The best writers at this age, using either EAL or EMT, were found to employ all the resources of written English with flexibility and to create strong story characters and plots, and effective persuasive writing.

- However, many EAL learners, even high-achieving pupils, handle adaptation to a variety of genres less confidently than monolingual English peers.

- EAL pupils writing at levels 3 and 4 were more likely to have errors in using prepositions and in the composition of formulaic phrases (see below). By level 5 these differences were less significant.

- EAL pupils writing at levels 4 and 5 tended to use more figurative language – similes and metaphors – than EMT writers.

- Lower achieving EAL writers handled certain features of language less confidently; for example adverbs, verb tenses and endings and the subordinators used to link clauses.

- In many ways EAL writing at Key Stage 2 was more fluent and accurate than writing seen at Key Stage 4.

writing with EAL. Pupils of all attainment levels with EAL, when compared to EMT peers, wrote the radio advertisement task less effectively. The language use was less confident and the openings and slogans less 'catchy'. Cameron and Besser draw our attention to this built-in disadvantage: 'Writing tasks that offer advantage to pupils who are familiar with specific genres should be used with caution in assessment' (Cameron and Besser, 2004, p. 84).

The high number of missing prepositions among pupils with EAL writing at Levels 3 and 4 is possibly not surprising. Prepositions, of all the parts of speech, are perhaps the most variable between languages and the most difficult to apply accurately. In French for example the word 'attendre' means 'to wait'. In English the word 'wait', in order to express its object, also needs the preposition 'for'. Thus, the French-English speaker must know the translation for the verb and understand that its meaning is carried effectively only when united with an appropriate preposition. In Asian languages there are no definite or indefinite articles before the noun. Thus the sentence 'he was bad boy' lacks its necessary 'a' and the sentence's meaning is less transparent. Overall, the small words, such as those among prepositions and articles in English, pose particular problems for EAL learners and considerably reduce their capacity to write fluent texts.

A discussion of the misuse of formulaic phrases by pupils with EAL is particularly constructive when it comes to identifying common errors in their written English. Cameron and Besser provide a series of examples of this error related to phrases made of word strings, or word orders, that always go together in conventional written English. For instance:

Word order errors:

Can I go with you shopping?	go shopping with you
He thought they should go or stay	stay or go
His best of all friend	his best friend of all

Word choice errors:

He quickly wore (put on) *his shoes*
It costs (is) *expensive*
A bundle (bunch) *of people*

(Cameron and Besser, 2004, p. 75)

In identifying where problems persist at Level 5 writing among EAL pupils, they noted that children have learned some formulaic words and phrases, and used them in the right context but have not understood emphasis. One example of this is a pupil who wrote 'I barged everyone out of the way'. He had understood the meaning of *barge*, but not that it can't be used as a straight replacement for *push* (Cameron and Besser, 2004, p. 75). The authors call for explicit teaching related to common formulaic words and phrases in spoken English in order that pupils can transfer them successfully to their writing.

The greater use of figurative language, related most commonly to animals, by the EAL pupils is an interesting one. Cameron and Besser did not put forward any particular hypothesis for why EAL pupil writing at Levels 4 and 5 should have this tendency to use more simile and metaphor in story composition. It could be the case that these pupils have, for whatever reason, better assimilated the process of creating similes as a result of direct literacy teaching. This could be that, because they are thinking in two languages, they have drawn on their linguistic metacognition and have a more detailed understanding of how figurative language works in storytelling.

An anecdote from the headteacher of Ballard Primary – one of our case study schools – may provide further support in the quest for an answer. She described those pupils with EAL who were in the gifted and talented group in her school as 'by far the best story writers'. Her understanding of their superior talent was that they were exposed to a rich storytelling culture at home and at the mosque, and thus had a greater awareness of the conventions of successful narrative. Whatever we might hypothesise as to the reasons, it is clear that EAL pupils learning to write in English may learn differently from their monolingual peers and that they bring with them a source of language knowledge that may provide certain advantages.

Verb tenses were a difficulty, in the Cameron and Besser study, for less able pupils. So too was the use of modal verbs (can, could, would, will, must etc.), which are always used in English before a verb in the infinitive without 'to': *He can swim, I may leave early, etc.* Japanese and Chinese lack the range of verb tenses that we use in English. In Bengali the verb component of a sentence can consist of one, two or three parts. The first part of the verb is in root form with inflection to indicate tense. Thus the need for a specific verb ending, found in many European languages, does not exist. Perhaps most confusing for these children is the positioning of verbs, as in Bengali (the majority language spoken in two of our focus schools) the verb comes at the end of the sentence rather than before the object as in an English sentence. This demonstrates that a basic understanding of the differences between a child's home language and written English will greatly enhance the skills of a class teacher in supporting her pupils effectively as they develop literacy for writing. Increasingly local education authority Web sites contain helpful information for teachers needing to research this.

In the final point covered in Table 5.3, Cameron and Besser referred to an earlier report (Cameron and Besser, 2004) in which the author analysed the writing of pupils at Key Stage 4. Cameron and Besser noticed a difference between the two cohorts of pupils and commented that Key Stage 2 EAL pupils writing in 2003 showed more accuracy and fluency generally than their older counterparts at Key Stage 4. They explained, 'These differences would seem to be linked to the teaching that the younger children have received through the National Literacy Strategy' (Cameron and Besser, 2004). In other words they felt that the two sets of analyses provided evidence that pupils who did not receive the kind of direct language teaching that characterises the NLS framework for teaching were less well equipped to write in their additional language. They don't support this assertion with other evidence but it is likely that their hypothesis bears some weight; interviews with EAL coordinators at our focus schools included comments in favour of the NLS as a tool for direct teaching about the conventions of English, which in turn serves to support pupils learning English as an additional language.

The Cameron and Besser study provides a very useful reference for teachers wanting to understand the detail of just how writing in English as an additional language is even more complex than the writing process for English-speaking children. It is particularly supportive in the absence of much other research in the field. Nevertheless, some other research, related more to the teaching of pupils in Key Stage 1, is valuable for discussion at this point.

Kenner and Kress (2003) chose to study a quite different aspect of EAL pupils' writing from those covered in Cameron and Besser's report. They observed children who were between 5 and 6 years old both in their primary schools and in the community language schools they attended in addition to mainstream schooling. The home languages spoken by the children were Chinese, Arabic and Spanish. Each was chosen because of salient features of its written form: 'Chinese as a mainly logographic script, Arabic as a non-Roman script with a different directionality, and Spanish as a Roman script with some differences from the English writing system' (Kenner and Kress, 2003, p. 183). Observations took place in the children's language schools but Kenner and Kress, creatively, also elected to watch these children peer tutoring their monolingual friends in writing their home language script. Through this they were able to explore how much the children understood about the written form of their own language because they had to teach its features to another child.

Their findings cross-matched the children's experience in their community schools with their peer tutoring and each setting provided an interesting insight into the advantages of bilingual children's linguistic metacognition. The Chinese pupil showed that she took particular care with line length and formation in her writing, as, in Chinese, the accuracy of the symbols is so crucial to meaning. This attention to detail spilled over into her writing in her primary school and she found the crossing out of errors at first a frustrating process that detracted from the aesthetic appearance of her handwriting. She was, however, quickly able to operate in both the very different Roman script and with a very different set of cultural expectations related to the English classroom. The pupil who had been taught in Arabic was writing his home language from right to left. However, his community language teacher fully supported him in understanding that English script is written in the opposite direction; she continually reinforced this difference in order to support the pupils when they returned to their Literacy Hour. This observation challenges the sometimes racist assumption made by many that the preservation of a home language hinders progress in English and may be a sign of unwillingness to integrate. On the contrary, this child's Arabic teacher was equipping him to operate successfully in either language and clearly understood the importance of his developing biliterate skills.

We now turn our attention to our focus schools and to how their classroom practice integrated research-based findings related to the development of spoken and written English in bilingual pupils.

THE MANAGEMENT OF SUPPORT FOR PUPILS WHO LEARN ENGLISH AS AN ADDITIONAL LANGUAGE: EVIDENCE FROM OUR FOCUS SCHOOLS

Visits made to the schools in January 2005 involved interviews with the headteachers to see how the schools had moved on from when they were first observed in 2003. In addition, two EAL coordinators were also interviewed separately. In one school where the headteacher also took on the role of EAL coordinator, this aspect of her work was treated separately in the interview. This was because we wanted to establish how the systems in the school supporting pupils with a home language other than English might be integral to their work with the NLS. Throughout the observations of the three case-study teachers during the Literacy Hour it had become apparent that support for EAL was essential to the success of the lessons; there was no evidence of the low-level writing exercises or well meaning 'leaving alone' of the teachers observed in some other research with second language learners. Rather, the practice seemed to be a seamless part of delivery – an integral part of practice and not a 'bolt-on'. In order to further understand how this environment flourished we asked the coordinators to describe what they had found most effective in their schools and what they saw as the barriers to EAL pupils' learning.

In all three cases the EAL coordinators had been in post for a sufficient amount of time to develop a strong sense of where their school's overall vision of teaching matched the specific requirements of pupils learning English. In the case of Anderson and Campbell Primaries there were members of staff with a clear role to support EAL; they were both highly informed about the needs of these pupils and neither had a full-time class responsibility. In this way their time and energy was dedicated exclusively to the linguistic development of the pupils who needed it most and to supporting staff in their classroom delivery. In Ballard Primary the EAL coordinator was the headteacher. She saw this as her role because the large number of EAL pupils in the school meant that attention to the acquisition of English was basic to all their consideration of the curriculum. The allocation of staffing for EAL in these three schools is evidence of the high profile it was given and is, perhaps, part of the web of excellence that the three schools each demonstrated.

Both Anderson and Ballard Schools described EAL as being 'the mainstream'; for these schools, where the numbers of pupils were very high, consideration of EAL was not a separate issue from consideration of any other aspect of education. In Campbell Primary the agenda differed because the pupils came in with over 40 different languages and many of them were the children of refugees and asylum seekers. This led to some quite different systems for support; because of this difference and others we will turn our attention to the interviews with the EAL coordinators in each school individually. However, it will become evident that there are common strands to their practice.

ANDERSON PRIMARY

Alan, EAL coordinator for Anderson Primary, explained that EAL was the 'mainstream'; thus good EAL practice, characterised specifically by a focus on developing oracy, was fundamental to all classroom practice. Historically the school had a generous staffing ratio to support its pupils – nearly all of whom had English as an additional language. Following the removal of Section 11 funding – a funding system that targeted pupils with EAL in the 1980s and early 1990s – the school had maintained a high percentage of adults for supporting EAL using its own budget allocation. Alan did not have a class and was used in a tightly timetabled role to support pupils from across the primary age range. He led a team of EAL assistants who were trained in delivering targeted support and for whom training was delivered regularly in issues of inclusion; in particular, staff were trained in identifying differences between language needs and other learning needs that might come under the brief of SEN. Further to this, Alan was an advanced skills teacher with involvement in a DfES-funded research project for EAL.

The status of the children's home language was valued by the school – in keeping with the findings of some of the research outlined earlier in this chapter. Alan felt that it was particularly important for new arrivals to be able to identify and celebrate their culture and language. Once settled in Anderson Primary and operating in English it was important for the school to continue supporting the status of Bengali. This could prove challenging as the pupils tended to use it as a playground language and to speak only in English in the classroom. Swearing, for example, tended to be in Bengali, thus lowering its status. Teachers had to correct and challenge this degrading use of the home language actively. Further support in celebrating language was given through the purchase of many dual-language texts. Widely cited by teachers as an important part of resourcing a school that celebrates diversity, Alan acknowledged that until recently many of these texts had not necessarily been of high quality. This is an important point for new teachers to absorb; the fact that a text is in a child's home language does not necessarily mean that it is an interesting book that will motivate the child to read.

Support for pupils was targeted through the use of detailed assessment systems. Children in the early years were assessed using their home languages; this was possible in a school where nearly all pupils spoke Sylheti/Bengali and there were a number of bilingual assistants who used this home language. Their class teachers then reviewed children as they grew older. They might move in and out of concentrated support as the needs arose. Most recently the school had used a tracking system for speaking and listening. Alan felt that it was obviously pertinent for following children's language acquisition but that it also worked to raise staff awareness about the crucial role of developing oracy in order to support literacy for EAL pupils. He felt that this was particularly important given the low profile that the NLS had given speaking and listening during the years that less experienced members of staff were trained in using the strategy.

There was no specific curriculum for literacy development for the pupils in this school but they had some favourites among their resources. In the nursery, staff were using the Paley technique (Paley, 1990) through which children developed their story composition. Initially they would create a story orally through one-to-one conferencing regardless of their language skills; a 'story' might be just one or a few words. Following this the children would animate each other's stories and perform them. Alan explained that this allowed the children to 'absorb the conventions of narrative over time'. At the time of the interview the school was working on using the technique with reception and Year 1 children as well. A second resource that provided scaffolding for staff's practice was *Learning to Learn in a Second Language* (Gibbons, 1993). This publication explores basic classroom practice that will support literacy development among EAL pupils. It provides a useful tool for staff, particularly in developing their understanding of the importance of oracy.

In developing children's spoken English the school used the resources outlined above. In addition to this Alan felt that staff needed considerable support in providing a talk-rich curriculum. He felt passionately that speaking and listening should not be the 'bolt-on' that the NLS perhaps portrayed it as, and that it should be fully integrated into all parts of the curriculum. He believed, in common with Aidan – the Year 2 teacher chosen for case study – and the rest of the staff, that the children in his school needed topic-based learning that tackled their learning in a more global sense than the compartmentalised National Curriculum. In particular he described the need for a curriculum based on 'functional literacy'; by this he meant that the children needed to see that language was 'a fluid animal' and not something that can be 'put together in bits in the way that the NLS portrays it'.

Despite the school's obvious success in developing spoken English for its pupils, some barriers to learning were still apparent. Alan spoke realistically

about the complexity of ensuring that children were always grouped according to language need, as working with peers who did not match them in
fluency and ability might adversely affect self-perception. He also spoke of
the need for children to take ownership of their learning and to apply their
newly taught skills; it is perhaps the case, for example, that when we provide
highly structured support for pupils they become dependent and deskilled.
This is not to say that this was happening in this school, but that the coordinator was keenly aware that the allocation of support was complex and demanding if the school were to get it right.

A further barrier to children's development of spoken English was identified as the lack of speaking and listening in the NLS. Although this coordinator praised the then newly published speaking and listening materials, he was
critical of an absence of a specific curriculum for EAL pupils. It could be
argued that the materials produced by the NLS to support pupils with EAL
address the issues generally (DfES, 2002) but the detail of support based on
an understanding of the crucial role of oracy is not adequate. Finally, and
interestingly, even in this school where the understanding of how pupils
acquire language was so highly developed, Alan spoke of children who may
be 'culturally isolated'. He was referring to the small number of Somali children in the school. This observation has echoes of Siraj-Blatchford and
Clarke's (2000) reference to the need to recognise individual difference.
Thus, although the Somali children's linguistic development was supported,
they still felt like outsiders in a school where they were effectively the ethnic
minority.

The school's results in reading, particularly at Key Stage 2, showed that
they had tackled the problems associated with learning to read in a new language. They were aware of the comprehension gap identified by Hutchinson,
Whiteley, Smith and Connors (2003) and set out to provide children with
frameworks to support their developing understanding of the innate messages
text might send out. In order to do this, Alan identified a number of ways in
which the school's emphasis on oracy had played a role. Access to language
at the beginning of a unit of work was important; the need to identify and
teach specific vocabulary related to the objectives. Teachers were also asked
to 'link the NLS to an oral curriculum which looks at the functions of language'. Staff were being trained in identifying how to do this. For example,
in teaching children how to move from the first to the third person and to
understand how they create different registers in reading and writing, children might be asked to report an incident during a telephone conversation
where they use third instead of first person. Alan felt that formal objectives
from the NLS could be met using imaginative and oral-based work.

When teaching writing, the school continued in its use of oral language to
produce text. The examples provided by Aidan, which are covered in a later
chapter, were typical of many of the staff's approach to writing. This approach
was characterised by identifying the stepping-stones needed to produce a

meaningful piece of text and to reflect the multiple stages identified by Berninger's (Berninger and Swanson, 1994) model of developing writing. Children's writing was used for modelling and shared writing was used extensively to model correct form and content for a genre. Alan saw this as part of a 'continuous teaching of language strategy'. In other words, although specific skills for writing were developed in the children, the school recognised the need to link oracy, reading and writing for the children in order that skills learned for one might feed the other platforms of expression.

One-to-one conferencing for writing was regarded as highly important for EAL pupils because it allowed them to express what they wanted to write first and to think actively through the structure of their writing. Alan was critical of the lack of time for this in the tightly controlled pedagogy for the NLS. A comment made about children's writing was that the staff found that pupils' use of figurative language was a strength. This is interesting in the light of the findings of Cameron and Besser's (2004) report, which identified greater use of simile and metaphor among EAL pupils.

Overall Alan was critical of the NLS for some quite fundamental changes to classroom pedagogy, which, in his opinion, directly disadvantaged children with EAL. Firstly, he felt that it had 'inadvertently created a problem for schools in squeezing out good foundation subject teaching and producing an overtight framework to support lack of teacher subject knowledge'. Further to this, he welcomed the more creative stance fostered by *Excellence and Enjoyment* (DfES, 2003) but considered that its success would be effectively hampered by the standards-driven agenda through which it had to operate. His comment echoes the fears of Earl *et al.* (2003) and Fisher (2004), that progress away from the overly prescriptive guidance of the NLS will be limited without addressing the testing culture that governs the teaching of English and mathematics in UK schools. Nevertheless, evidence from the interviews and observations in Anderson Primary illustrates that, despite operating in this same target setting culture, the school's success was in no small part due to a commitment to the creativity in teaching recognised as 'the way forward' by *Excellence and Enjoyment* (DfES, 2003).

BALLARD PRIMARY

In Ballard Primary the headteacher – Ms Bradshaw – managed support for EAL. As was the case for Anderson Primary EAL was the mainstream and therefore not subject to separate consideration; it was a part of how the school operated all the time in planning and delivering its curriculum. Interestingly there were differences between the schools. Ballard Primary's pupil population was a little different; 70% as opposed to around 90% EAL and with some white indigenous pupils. However, the majority language and culture in both was Bengali and the schools were only two or three miles apart. A key difference was the fluency of the pupils on entry to the school. In Anderson Primary quite a number arrived with little or no English whereas in Ballard Primary many were from second- and third-generation British-Asian homes and the head at Ballard commented that it was now quite unusual for them to have a child arrive in school with no English at all.

This led, perhaps, to a further difference. In Anderson Primary children were assessed on entry to nursery in their first language and there was a keen awareness of the need to keep their home language active in order to value it. In Ballard Primary there was a general acceptance that English was the medium for education and children were encouraged to use it in school. This was not to say that the school devalued the children's home language but that it had enlisted parents' support in developing school as the arena for English language learning. Ms Bradshaw said that parents were very supportive of this action. This acknowledgement by Asian parents that school is the place for children to learn English is reminiscent of the research by Parke and Drury (2001) where the mother of Samia considered that there should be a clear separation of the roles of home and school in relation to language teaching; school was for English and home was for mother tongue.

This subtle but interesting difference between the two schools highlights the complex journey schools have to make when deciding how they will best support their pupils' linguistic development. It also underlines the fact that there are social and cultural differences within ethnic groups that may play out differently in different settings. The important similarity between the two is that they both valued the children's home languages. Where support was needed for children with limited English in Ballard Primary, it was provided by one of the many bilingual staff. Yet again the school was at an advantage in having only one or two languages spoken and this meant that support could be intensive. Support was always given in class, so that the children were taught their English through immersion in whole-class lessons.

In common with Anderson Primary, Ballard Primary put a great deal of emphasis on developing children's spoken English through drama and role-play. In addition they used a lot of art and music to support language development and to generally enrich the curriculum. Story telling, drama and role-play were key features of the nursery classroom and this was supplemented by intense synthetic phonics using *Jolly Phonics* (Lloyd and Wernham, 1992) while the children were in reception. In this way the children emerged from their Foundation Stage years with a thorough grounding in spoken English and in phonics, which prepared them for reading and writing during Key Stage 1. The use of oracy as a tool to promote successful writing was a key feature of Bridget's practice in this school and is discussed in a later chapter.

Ms Bradshaw was keenly aware of the possible gap in comprehension that EAL pupils might suffer when tackling English text. In order to iron out this potential disadvantage the school had several strategies in place. Children for whom the comprehension of text was problematic were paired with older children, or even with adults, who had higher level comprehension skills. Through this 'buddy' system they were engaged with reading partners who could involve them in the kinds of discussion that they needed to access text more fully. As she said, 'it's about inference, ambiguity and dilemma; picking out what's going on underneath the text.' It was recognised that the children had significant visual literacy skills. Ms Bradshaw cited an example of children being shown a film of *A Christmas Carol* in order to support their understanding of the novel. They were able to pick out inference, predict plot events and hypothesise an ending in ways that they were unable to use when presented with written text.

Ms Bradshaw had an interesting theory relating to why children's text comprehension in an additional language is so much harder than in a first language. She felt that, as first language development takes place in the home, children also develop their skills of enquiry and questioning. They will ask questions and obtain answers and explanation from the family. She saw this as their first exposure to thinking philosophically – to asking questions beyond the literal – and felt that this enhances children's capacity to find inference in the text. Where the text is in a language other than the home language, this sensitivity to inference may be more difficult to nurture. She drew parallels with her monolingual, English-speaking pupils who also had problems with inference. She surmised that white, working-class parents were perhaps less likely to engage their children in thinking about stories and that the ability to comprehend text fully was a class and cultural issue as well as a linguistic one. It is inappropriate to draw conclusions related to class, culture and language from one school's anecdotal experience but the comments are interesting. Teachers should, however, bear in mind key research by Tizard (1984) that found rich literacy experiences for children in white working-class homes.

In teaching writing, Ballard Primary laid the same emphasis as Anderson Primary on developing language through talk first of all. This was so that pupils could 'untangle some of their sentences in their heads and orally before having to write them down.' It is interesting to note that this use of talk for writing is supported both by the research literature related to EAL pupils and the literature concerning how children develop as competent writers. In talking about writing, Ms Bradshaw felt that this was an area where the NLS had actually been responsible for improvements, particularly for the writing of nonfiction by her pupils. She felt that children really knew how to write a letter, a recipe or a set of instructions because the objectives had given them access to the 'formula', which they had been able to internalise. In this way the NLS had perhaps inadvertently supported progress for EAL pupils by overtly teaching the conventions of a wide range of text types.

Anderson Primary had found that its pupils demonstrated evidence of very well developed use of figurative language. In common with this the headteacher of Ballard Primary observed that the truly exceptional story writers in her school – those in the 'gifted and talented group' – were all bilingual. Her comment is illuminating, and gives us more evidence for how children's bi-literate and bilingual skills may enhance their learning:

> I think that some of the great literature in their own language lends itself well to understanding the literature in our language as well. The sort of universals – fables, myths. When you're looking at them in parallel languages they probably reinforce each other. The epic journey, the good over evil, the universal clashes of value that get matched across the two types of story.

Ms Bradshaw was careful to point out, however, that she did not think this advantage was necessarily there for all pupils. She felt that the richer linguistic understanding that bilingual pupils are said to have is related to learning as much as it is to language. Those bilingual pupils who were excellent learners and who could extract and synthesise information were those who showed this greater metacognition. She did not think it was necessarily there for all bilingual pupils as it was perhaps related to higher level processing; the ability to crossreference commonalities in texts for example. Nevertheless, this potential for higher levels of attainment among EAL pupils is borne out further by evidence from the interview with Campbell Primary's EAL coordinator.

CAMPBELL PRIMARY

The interview with Caitlyn, the EAL coordinator from Campbell Primary, provides some interesting contrasts. There were 42 different languages spoken at this school. The most widely spoken language after English was Yoruba, the main language spoken in Nigeria. Bengali, French, and Urdu closely fol-lowed this with Portuguese being the fastest growing language; some of the Portuguese-speaking children were from Africa. More than one in five of the children at the school were from refugee or asylum-seeking families. Thus, we might expect some differences in the way in which this school supported its children with EAL. In management of new arrivals, for example, there were certainly differences, but in the management of curriculum delivery similarities with Anderson and Ballard Primaries were obvious.

Anderson and Ballard Primaries had a mostly stable population of British/Bengali pupils from families that had lived in East London, in some cases, for several generations. Campbell Primary, with much greater mobil-ity among its pupils and a high number specifically of refugees and asylum seekers, had to put considerably more emphasis on its strategies for settling new arrivals'. The systems for supporting EAL, therefore, had a wide remit that covered interpreters to support the multiple languages, support for asylum-seeking families with their claims to the Home Office, finding

ESOL (English for Speakers of Other Languages) classes for parents, advice about GPs and housing. All schools were characterised by supportive relationships with parents but Campbell Primary's relationship had to extend beyond the education of the children and language classes for parents. Caitlyn felt that, for many families, the school was the first and the most supportive point of contact they might have, which could help them with a range of issues relating to their managing some sort of life in their new country.

However, once beyond the initial stages of support and transition, the systems for supporting language acquisition, reading and writing, bear many of the hallmarks of the good practice identified earlier in this chapter. In common with Anderson Primary, home language was celebrated and its use in the classroom encouraged when appropriate. Nevertheless, Caitlyn made the interesting observation that children were reluctant to use their mother tongue, particularly as they grew older. In fact, she spoke also of the sadness of parents whose children were refusing to use their first language at home at all and in some cases were losing fluency in it. Perhaps this underlines the tension for children arriving from war-torn countries to which they know they cannot return. They know that England will be their home in the future and try to identify themselves fiercely with this new culture and its language. This is in contrast to the Bengali children who are perhaps better able to separate home and school and to maintain a more relaxed footing across both cultures. Furthermore, it could be the case that in schools where there are multiple languages English has to be the medium for communication and this passively subverts the use of a home language.

As the school was used to taking in children with a wide range of languages support systems for language acquisition were drawn from the wider community. There were good relationships with community language speakers who came in to work as interpreters when children first arrived in reception and came for an interview with the class teacher. Children, whenever they arrived, were 'buddied up' with a same-language speaker in order to help the process of transition to the new setting. Many staff were bilingual, some sharing the home languages of the children, and classrooms were equipped with a range of resources to help non-English speakers gain access to the curriculum. Children were assessed within 3 weeks of arrival and allocated language support depending on their stage of language acquisition. This assessment was repeated as they progressed through the school and they would move in and out of support as needed. Staffing for support was generous and carefully targeted according to need, operating in much the same way as the team for EAL in Anderson Primary.

Barriers to language acquisition were described in some detail for this school, and were definitely more of an issue than for the other two schools. In particular, learning English was a problem for children arriving in Year 5 and 6. Caitlyn explained that the curriculum for upper Key Stage 2 did no lend itself to children who are new to English, thus access to learning became difficult. It could be the case that this led to frustration among the children, which manifested itself in behavioural difficulties. She explained also that many Albanian children, arriving from Kosovo, had no experience of the school system and needed play and art therapy to help with what was in many cases a quite traumatic transition. Another example of difference was among the Lithuanian children who might arrive at 7 years old, having not yet started school in their own country. They would, therefore, not have the literacy skills of their English peers, but were 'incredibly able' in other ways.

More positively, the school was involved in a project with the Primary National Strategy in using speaking frames with EAL pupils. These frames work using similar principles to a writing frame – in that they provide a framework for thinking and a scaffold for composition – but they start at the level of the language needed for writing, rather than how to structure the writing. Children were introduced to the sort of vocabulary they were going to need to access a text; this would be particularly important in the case of a science lesson, for example, where many new and technical terms might be introduced. Speaking frames would present a piece of text and children were encouraged to note certain tenses, plurals, unknown words and to mark the text where these appeared. In this way they could engage with and familiarise themselves with new language before having to write anything down. This made the pupils aware not only of vocabulary but of the conventions of English language.

Speaking frames are a welcome addition to NLS as their use directly relates to the research-based findings regarding how EAL pupils might best be supported in literacy development. The use of speaking frames supported much of the children's success in reading when they were at higher levels of fluency. Their use helped to eradicate the comprehension problems identified by Hutchinson, Whiteley, Smith and Connors (2003) as detrimental to attainment among EAL pupils. They also help in supporting direct teaching of the subtle complexities of English writing such as use of prepositions and verb tense endings; thus providing a framework that attends to the issues highlighted by Cameron and Besser (2004).

Teaching writing at Campbell Primary had much in common with the study published by Derewianka (1990) where children's writing was shown to be far more developed when they were immersed in their subject. In fact, Caitlyn described their practice as just this – 'immersion in the activity'. An example of this would be a project where staff had wanted children to write about the seaside. They took them on a visit to the sea where they asked them to focus on how things smelled and how they sounded in order to promote a richer, descriptive vocabulary when they came to write about it. They drew comparisons with the seaside in Britain and in their home countries and built up word banks related to the topic in both English and their home languages. Links were made to the geography unit being taught at the time. This practice of making crosscurricular links, in order that children could make sense of their learning, was common to all three schools studied and is a recurring theme in the interviews and observations.

We have described some quite complex problems for the pupils at this school and have perhaps painted a rather bleak picture of the issues for a school where multiple languages are spoken. The school's SAT results for Key Stage 2 said otherwise. When asked if she could quantify how EAL pupils might have a rich metalinguistic awareness Caitlyn drew our attention straight away to the performance of EAL pupils in the Key Stage 2 SAT. She explained that the bilingual pupils do far better then their monolingual peers, with over 90% attaining Level 4 and above. Those who did not reach the all-important sound average grading were those who had not been in the school system long enough to develop their literacy skills to that level. Thus, the school's SAT scores for English at Key Stage 2 were in fact depressed by the poorer performance of white, monolingual pupils – mostly boys. This was due, she felt, in many ways, to the value that the ethnic minority pupils' parents gave to education – 'Their parents see English as key to their future.' In this way, she explained, the children's attainment had as much to do with cultural and social difference as it did with language. Thus, we find a strong correlation in the anecdotal observations of both Ballard Primary and Campbell Primary despite their very different pupil intakes.

We should remind ourselves at this point that only half of the children in Campbell Primary had English as an additional language. Thus, the pedagogy for reading and writing that we have described was used for all the children Caitlyn made the crucial point that 'EMA (ethnic minority attainment) practice is good practice'. In other words, the pedagogy used to support the literacy development of EAL pupils is based on sound principles of how monolingual speakers need to develop their reading and writing. The ways in which this plays out in practice become apparent in the classroom observations described in later chapters.

6 The Schools

In this chapter we contextualise the study that forms the basis of this book. We introduce the three schools from which the three observed teachers were selected for detailed case studies. We show how the schools were comparable because of shared experiences in raising standards and in their pupil intake, but that they had very distinct and individual identities. The discussion grows from inspection and performance data and from interviews with the headteachers conducted in the spring of 2003.

RATIONALE FOR THE RESEARCH

What do teachers do with the NLS in schools where pupil intake is socially disadvantaged but where results are good? This question forms the basis of this book. We decided that three recognised, effective teachers in recently inspected schools, acknowledged to be improving in challenging circumstances, would be researched as case studies. Fifteen schools were contacted and those that responded most positively were selected for the study. This was clearly an opportunity sample. We make no claims that these teachers or these schools are in any way representative. However, as all three schools were acknowledged to be successful through SAT and inspection evidence (Table 6.1) and all three teachers were acknowledged as effective by their headteachers, thus matching the selection criteria of Wray, Medwell, Poulson and Fox's (2002) study, it was felt that each would provide a sound basis for a case study.

The schools and their teachers were suitable for case study because they shared some features in common. For example, they were all inner-city primary schools with a significant percentage – more than 50 % – of pupils eligible for free school meals. Each school had at least 50 % of its pupils learning English as an additional language and all three had a history of school improvement. Thus we feel that the data from each case study are valid for interschool and interteacher comparison. However, it is also our intention to focus on specific and unique features of each school and teacher. The teachers chosen all taught in Year 2 because it was considered that it is during this year that children's fluency in reading and writing makes very significant progress. It is also a year in which children are judged by national testing.

A set of research questions was devised and data collection techniques were chosen. These data collection techniques were *structured observations* and

Table 6.1 Profiles of schools cited for successful teaching of literacy

School	Percentage of pupils receiving free school meals	Percentage of pupils with English as an additional language	1999 Key Stage 2 English results (National average 69.7%)	2000 Key Stage 2 English results (National average 75%)	2001 Key Stage 2 English results (National average 75%)	2002 Key Stage 2 English results (National average 75%)	Inspection history
Anderson Primary	51%	83%	36%	81%	67%	79%	Out of serious weaknesses. 'Very good' report 2000
Ballard Primary	59%	70%	58%	59%	75%	79%	Report shows 'rapid improvement' 1998. HMI (2000) cited as 'improving city school'
Campbell Primary	53%	50%	28%	47%	71%	65%	Out of special measures. 'Good' report 2002

audio recording of three lessons per teacher; *interviews* and *questionnaires* with the teachers and their headteachers; and collection of *performance data* on each school. Following data collection it became clear to us that perhaps the most significant feature of the teachers' practice was not what they *did* with the Literacy Hour – with their planning for example – but what they *said* while teaching. It seemed to us that the nature of teacher–pupil interactions was governing the success of the lesson.

In order to investigate this further we carried out a microanalysis of the nature of 'teacher-talk' during each lesson using the audiotapes. The audiotapes were analysed in order to reveal the categories and subcategories of teachers-talk and a taxonomy was devised for coding these concepts Once identified, the teacher–pupil interaction was coded at 3 second intervals in each lesson and the information converted to pivot tables in order to investigate patterns of interaction. This analysis is commented on in general terms in the chapters focusing on each teacher.

Observations and recordings were made of each teacher teaching three Literacy Hours over a period of one term – the spring term of 2003. Any paperwork relating to the lesson was collected; for example the written plans and any worksheets given to the children. Two sets of interviews were carried out following the collection of all data from the lesson observations. The teachers and their respective headteachers were interviewed using the questions from Wray, Medwell, Poulson and Fox's (2002) study of effective teachers of literacy and from the OISE (Earl *et al.*, 2003) team's broad study of the implementation of the NLS. Additional questions were devised to clarify emerging findings from the observations.

The interviews with the headteachers served several purposes. Firstly they provided information about the school setting that illuminated reasons for the school's comparative success. They also offered detail about the circumstances supporting the effective classroom teachers. The interviews with the teachers set out to question evolving hypotheses formed after the classroom observations. They facilitated exploration of the extent to which the teachers' practice was informed by their own subject knowledge and also enabled the teachers' attitudes towards the NLS and more generally towards the effective teaching of literacy to be established.

Return visits were made to the schools in January 2005 during which the headteachers were interviewed again to see if there had been any changes to their management of literacy since the observations. At this time we also interviewed each school's EAL coordinator as it had become obvious from our overview of all the data from 2003 that their roles were crucial to the successful pupil attainment in these settings.

Performance data were collected from all three schools. The data were used to give background information that supported the choice of the three schools as suitable for comparison. Some comparison of the differences and similarities in the ways in which schools analysed and used performance data was made. However, this proved less useful than the interviews when comparing the schools. As performance data are subject to local fluctuation, such as the number of SEN children in any given year group, the fact that all three schools showed an improvement trend was where the similarity was most meaningful. We also felt that OfSTED inspection commentary provided a fuller picture than the summative score provided by SAT results. The inspection reports from each school supported our choices well.

THE SCHOOLS

As discussed, the three schools shared performance and pupil-intake features. They were all in local education authorities in east London. Two were from one authority, and shared very similar intakes – large numbers of Sylheti-speaking Bangladeshi pupils – and thus had received similar local authority support during the implementation of the NLS. The third was from a neighbouring authority and had a quite different experience of NLS implementation and a more ethnically diverse intake.

It was interesting, however, to discover that similarities and differences were richer and more complex than shared geographical location or the children in the school. Of much greater significance seemed to be the nature of leadership and the confidence with which each school had embraced a new directive. Furthermore, the schools shared a particular well developed sense of what constituted good teaching of literacy. It seemed likely that this was very well served by their having to understand how to teach pupils with EAL. As they had to consider how children's language and literacy developed as part of their everyday practice, they were less inclined to use any guidance without first thinking of the needs of their pupils. Thus their practice could remain truly child centred rather than teacher led. Unlike other schools described in OfSTED and OISE reports at the time, they had not fallen into the rote adoption of the NLS; they had managed to retain what they knew worked well and made it work with the new documentation. This symbiotic relationship between leadership, school improvement and the confidence to hold on to an independent sense of identity emerged as a significant theme throughout this investigation of successful literacy teaching and learning.

ANDERSON PRIMARY

Anderson Primary was a two-form entry primary school where 69 % of the Asian British pupils were of Bangladeshi origin. The remaining intake was made up of small percentages of white British (4.5 %), black British (5.6 %

and other ethnic groups. The total percentage of children in the school with EAL was 83%. There had been a significant improvement in Key Stage 2 SATs results since 1999 (see Table 6.2)

Anderson's results were closer to average than those at Ballard Primary and in some areas improvement had been better than others. For example, reading results in Key Stage 1 were poorer in 2002 than writing results. The staff was aware of this disparity between their reading and writing scores – which continued with the results for 2003. They felt that the amount of time they spent developing speaking and listening had a significant impact on improving the children's writing skills, whereas the use of guided reading groups to teach reading in the Literacy Hour may have left children less confident at performing in the individual reading task and comprehension paper. Mr Abbott, the headteacher, felt that the improvement trend at Key Stage 2 had much to do with the focus on oracy at Key Stage 1. He considered that this gave children a sound basis for accelerated literacy development at Key Stage 2. The drop in results for Key Stage 2 in 2003 is explained by a higher than usual proportion of children having been disapplied for specific learning difficulties. However, despite this disadvantage and its negative impact on the score we can see that this cohort, who would have sat their Key Stage 1 tests in 1999 and are thus included in the table, had maintained their performance overall.

Anderson Primary was inspected in June 2000. A previous inspection in 1998 had found the school to have 'serious weaknesses'. Although this result was successfully contested, reinspection took place only 2 years later when the school was judged as 'very good' across a range of features. Teaching and learning in both Key Stage 1 and 2 was described as 'very good', as was the provision the school made for its pupils' language needs. The senior management team was described as 'excellent' and as contributing significantly to raised attainment of pupils. Although some results at inspection were found to be below national averages, the report points out that pupils' progress, considering their attainment on entry to the school, was 'very good'. Also notable is the fact that pupils were described as having very good relationships with each other and very good attitudes towards school and to their work.

Table 6.2 Anderson Primary performance data

	1999 (%)	2000 (%)	2001 (%)	2002 (%)	2003 (%)
KS1 Reading	65	74	74	63	68
KS1 Writing	69	85	76	83	78
KS2 English	36	81	67	79	67

The headteacher of Anderson Primary considered that the NLS had had some impact on teaching and learning in his school but that he and his staff had never lost sight of their commitment to a broad and balanced curriculum. He was undecided as to whether the NLS itself has raised standards or whether some modification in teachers' pedagogy following the NLS had made the difference. This highlights the dilemma identified by Stainthorp (1999) – that we will never know if it was the curriculum or the changed pedagogy for the NLS that improved children's teaching and learning experience. However, Mr Abbott saw the rigour in the structure of the NLS as something that had 'upskilled' his staff, particularly in relation to word-level work. He also felt that its implementation had facilitated a necessary focus on improving standards in his school and the LEA.

English was led by a coordinator who was supported by two other staff members forming the literacy team. The perception of both Mr Abbot and the Year 2 teacher observed for case study, whom we call Aidan, was that the NLS had been implemented but modified to suit the pupils at the school. This view was common to all three teachers and headteachers used in the research. Mr Abbott described the approach to the strategy when it first arrived in school thus:

> My word to staff when NLS first came in was that we want to get into it quickly so that we can get out of it quickly. This was a way of saying that as soon as we were working from inside the NLS (and NNS) we could start modifying and adapting them ... knowing that we had a strong and experienced staff who wouldn't want to be straightjacketed for any length of time.

Planning for literacy focused on the needs of the children and used minimal paperwork. For example, medium-term planning was taken straight from the NLS documentation; staff highlighted objectives covered across a term. Fine tuning took place at weekly year group meetings where staff put together fortnightly units that grew from the NLS objectives but where work was identified across the curriculum. Thus planning meetings were more about ways to allow children to make connections in their learning than how to put across subject knowledge. This was common to all three schools studied.

The school worked towards targets set by the LEA for its Key Stage 2 pupils, but was largely against forecasting test results for its younger pupils. A range of assessments took place across the year that informed planning and the deployment of support staff. The headteacher saw target setting as an effective way of raising teacher expectation but was firm in his belief that the school's history of providing a broad and balanced curriculum remained the driving force, rather than a desire to reach greater heights with a narrower curriculum.

Mr Abbott considered that recent school improvement gave the school much more freedom to decide on its own curriculum. In common with

Campbell Primary, Anderson Primary felt less able to adapt the NLS in the early years of implementation as it was under the spotlight of inspection and the need to raise standards. However, more recently the school had been able to make adaptations and modifications as required without feeling the need to ask the LEA permission for this. Furthermore, the school had been able to retain a strong sense of stability and identity through the implementation of a national initiative such as the NLS.

Anderson Primary had received very little support from its LEA literacy team and had trained staff in implementation of the Literacy Hour mostly through school-based support among its own staff. Both Mr Abbott and Aidan described demonstration lessons – some from the LEA's Leading Literacy Teacher team – and working alongside other colleagues as their most effective training in using the NLS.

Unusually perhaps for an inner-London school, Anderson Primary had not had a problem with recruitment and retention during recent years. Many staff had been with the school for more than 10 years – including both the head and the deputy head. Mr Abbott believed that this provided a stable source of support for newer teachers. The school had relationships with several local teacher training providers and often recruited NQTs from among the students it had trained. This stability in the staff had affected the school's funds available for literacy development. The headteacher felt that he was able to spend more on school development because he kept supply costs to a minimum; particularly the considerable expense of having to recruit long-term supply from agencies. The school was well resourced and there was a substantial budget for staff training.

Furthermore, the school had been able to retain a strong sense of stability and identity despite the implementation of a national initiative such as the NLS; it had assimilated the NLS rather than been driven by it. The headteacher felt that his stable staff and their strongly held belief that children need access to a rich and diverse curriculum experience in order to develop their learning capacity had made the school less likely to be dominated by external pressures. He was concerned by what he saw as a singular weakness of the NLS and other national initiatives; specifically he felt that in training teachers with what looks like a prescribed curriculum, teacher training courses risk training new teachers who have little understanding about the craft of teaching.

BALLARD PRIMARY

Ballard Primary was a one-and-a-half form entry primary school. This meant that in each year group there was a class made up of a single age group and a second made up of mixed age groups. Therefore, the class observed consisted entirely of Year 2 pupils who had been selected as the higher performing children in the year group, while the remaining Year 2 children were taught in the mixed-age class with a group of higher performing Year 1 children. The school's ethnic profile was made up of 69 % Asian British children of Bangladeshi origin, 24 % white UK children and a very small percentage of other ethnic minorities. The number of pupils with EAL was 70 %.

School improvement had taken place over a longer time and for a sustained period in both Key Stages. Ballard Primary differed from Anderson and Campbell in that it had not had the spotlight of HMI attention following a poor inspection. Prior to observation it had not been inspected since 1998 when inspectors described it as 'a rapidly improving school with an excellent ethos' and as providing 'pupils and staff with an exceptional learning environment'. Looking at Table 6.3 it is clear that results were very good, particularly in relation to national averages and considering the school's social profile. The improvement becomes more obvious when compared with the results from 1995/6. This is why we have included these historical data in the table.

It was interesting that the results in Key Stage 2 had taken longer to rise than those in Key Stage 1. This is perhaps attributable to the fact that the school had to work harder at replacing lost time for its Key Stage 2 pupils. The headteacher, Ms Bradshaw, said that there had been a culture of low expectation when she took over the school eight years previously, where children had very little word-level work and were not given the basic skills necessary to develop as beginner readers and writers. Now the school spends a considerable amount of time in its early years delivering synthetic phonics training using the Jolly Phonics scheme (Lloyd and Wernham, 1992). This was not, the headteacher said, as a result of the NLS but grew from the school's own analysis of its needs in terms of raising children's capacity to read and write. It is noteworthy that Key Stage 2 results for English in 2003 exceeded the national target of 85 % by 2004, despite the changes to the writing test that may have made the SAT more challenging.

Of the three schools observed, this school had probably the least evidence of using the NLS to raise standards. Ms Bradshaw felt that standards had risen to their current impressive levels chiefly because, in common with

Table 6.3 Ballard Primary performance data

	1995 (%)	1999 (%)	2000 (%)	2001 (%)	2002 (%)	2003 (%)
KS1 Reading	34	71	90	82	94	91
KS1 Writing	55	74	90	85	91	86
KS2 English	19 (1996)	58	59	75	79	86

Anderson Primary, she had a stable, highly competent and experienced staff who understood that teaching children how to think and learn took precedence over teaching content. She did, however, concede that the NLS had been helpful in tackling weaknesses in beginner and less able teachers. 'It is a good bottom line for teachers who need more structure' she said, and, 'It acts as a springboard for excellent teachers.' Again, in common with Anderson Primary, she felt that the NLS acted as confirmation for her competent staff that they were teaching an appropriate curriculum but that they had not felt the need to follow it single mindedly.

National Literacy Strategy training from the LEA had been limited. As Ballard Primary was already considered successful in 1998 the LEA chose a model of little or no intervention. This allowed the school the freedom to interpret and use the documentation away from the monitoring eye of local inspectors. In common with Anderson Primary, this school considered inhouse training, particularly in the form of demonstration lessons, to have been most effective in terms of initial consideration of the Literacy Strategy. The experienced staff was more likely to attend literacy training that was not NLS related, using the generous budget for training that was allocated each year. Interestingly, Ms Bradshaw was being trained as one of a team of LEA consultant heads who were due to work with schools to support the implementation of the Primary National Strategy (DfES, 2003). She was keen to take on this role in order that she could 'have an influence on the inside' and because she didn't want to see the emergence of a system that 'further demoralises weak schools.'

In keeping with this view that the NLS had been a useful tool, but not one that the school felt honour-bound to follow with precision, Ballard Primary used a range of literacy curriculum materials. The focus of the materials was to encourage children to engage with full, good-quality texts. Ms Bradshaw decried, in particular, the loss of time to spend on extended writing and in engaging with entire texts – particularly in Key Stage 2, where the need to teach small aspects of fiction such as openings and settings had led to the use of text fragments as examples for the children. The most recent acquisition by the school, to support children's engagement with high quality texts, was a computer program called *Accelerated Reader* (Renaissance Learning, 2002, see School Resources, p. 221). This was considered an appropriate pedagogical tool as it encouraged the children to read with understanding, tested their comprehension skills – both literal and inferential – and simultaneously allowed the school to track individual progress.

In common with Anderson Primary this school was committed to providing its pupils with a broad and balanced curriculum. The headteacher of Ballard Primary had worked at adapting planning procedures in the school so that teachers were relatively free from paperwork and were released to concentrate on their pedagogy. Medium-term planning had become streamlined so that staff worked straight from documentation or school-written schemes of work covering every term. Teachers created fortnightly plans that covered all curriculum areas. This ensured that work was crosscurricular and that these links were made overt to pupils who used skills learned in one subject to foster learning in another subject.

Although teachers did not have to spend time producing written plans for their classes, the headteacher had created a system of extended planning time for teachers and their classroom assistants at the end of each day. Teaching assistants were paid to spend an hour on site after the children had left in order to discuss that day's progress with the class teacher and plan for the following day's activities. This professional dialogue about how the children might learn was considered far more important than written planning.

Regular assessment was a feature of the school's practice. Pupils were tracked using a range of tests twice a year; these included the Suffolk Reading Test, QCA optional SATs, the NLS high frequency word lists and a software package called GOAL (GOAL plc, 2002, see School Resources, p. 221) which gave pupils an end of year National Curriculum level in the subjects it tested. Nevertheless, Ms Bradshaw was not in favour of the target-setting culture abounding in schools at the time. She felt that target-setting alone did not raise results; she considered that 'improvement comes from knowing your pupils' by using a range of data such as that from the tests above but even more so from teaching children how to learn. Although pleased to have results that bring praise for the school, the headteacher felt that 90 % of the success of her school was beyond measurement as it was 'activity that goes on below the water-line'.

CAMPBELL PRIMARY

Campbell Primary was a three-form entry primary school; the largest of the three schools studied. Pupils came from a wider range of ethnic, cultural and language backgrounds than at Anderson and Ballard which is in part explained by the fact that it was in a neighbouring borough with a more diverse ethnic population. There were 38 languages spoken at Campbell Primary with 50 % of pupils having English as an additional language. This EAL percentage was less than for the pupils at Anderson and Ballard but was, perhaps, a more challenging percentage to contend with as so many children spoke in languages not shared with bilingual staff. Nevertheless, an OfSTED inspection in 2002 praised Campbell Primary as 'an inclusive school that provides very good education for all pupils.'

The results in Table 6.4 show a very significant improvement from 1999, when the school was still in special measures. This improvement had been sustained in the years since 1999; a cohort in 2001, with an uncharacteristically low percentage of SEN compared with other years, explains the apparent decline from 2001–2. Results for 2003 showed a continuing upward trend, taking Campbell Primary close to national averages for English at both key stages.

Table 6.4 Campbell Primary performance data

	1999 (%)	2000 (%)	2001 (%)	2002 (%)	2003 (%)
KS1 Reading	43	71	95	79	84
KS1 Writing	68	71	93	81	84
KS2 English	28	47	71	65	70

Campbell Primary's OfSTED inspection commentary from 2002 was unequivocal in its praise for the senior management team: 'It has made rapid improvement under the very strong and effective leadership of the headteacher and her leadership team following a period of instability.' OfSTED's observations provide evidence for their own published finding that 'effective leadership is widely accepted as being a key constituent in school improvement' (OfSTED, 2000a). Moreover, this feature of effective leadership teams, as evidenced by inspection data, was common to the three schools studied.

Ms Chadwick, Campbell's headteacher, in common with staff from Anderson and Ballard, spoke collectively when she described the success of her school in raising standards in literacy. She considered that the strengths and weaknesses of the NLS were as described by Ms Bradshaw; namely that the structure and rigour were invaluable for supporting weak teachers but that the framework had been overprescriptive and had led to the teaching of knowledge rather than skills. In particular she disliked the teaching of snippets of text rather than the enjoyment of a whole book and the lack of reference to speaking and listening. Campbell Primary had adapted its delivery of the Literacy Hour to include guided speaking and listening in order to address this shortfall in the framework.

Ms Chadwick's comments in relation to the schools' changing relationship with the NLS were interesting. Echoing observations of the other two headteachers, she explained that the detail in the NLS while the school was in special measures had been of great value. With the school constantly in the spotlight of HMI it was essential to 'play by the rules'. However, she went on to say:

It is because we've moved beyond the Literacy Hour in the way that we deliver it, that we are a good school. Once you are a 'good school' you can almost do what you like. You'll only ever be satisfactory if you can't be creative and take risks.

Her comments related closely to the need, recognised by both OfSTED (2002a) and OISE (Earl et al., 2003), for schools to adapt the NLS prescription for their own ends; to use its strengths as part of their own wider agenda for school improvement.

Leadership for literacy had evolved since the introduction of the NLS in 1998, although Ms Chadwick did not consider that this was necessarily due to the implementation of the NLS. She described how her own leadership style had changed as a result of her leading the school out of special measures – a task for which she had been specifically appointed. She also felt that studying for an international MBA was instrumental in changing her leadership style as well as being required to implement other initiatives such as the National Numeracy Strategy. Literacy was led by a coordinator (Clare, the Year 2 teacher chosen for case study) but Ms Chadwick believed that the key staff who affected the success of the NLS in her school were her year group leaders. As the school was comparatively large – the roll was 684 including the nursery – she had worked towards a model of devolved leadership in which her year group and phase leaders played a pivotal role. It was the phase and year group leaders who led dialogue with staff related to pedagogy and the provision of an effective learning environment.

The focus on developing teaching and learning, exemplified by the above practice of the phase leaders, was a key characteristic of Campbell Primary. This school had moved away from burdensome paperwork by saving all its planning documentation since the NLS was implemented; in this way planning meeting time was spent in professional dialogue about pedagogy and not content – a practice shared with Ballard Primary. Planning, in common with both Anderson and Ballard, was crosscurricular wherever possible.

The school had worked at teaching the children four crosscurricular skills, described by Ms Chadwick as 'children asking deep questions, making connections, describing their learning at the metacognitive level and evaluating their work'. An example of this practice was observed in the pilot lesson for this school when children, who had been writing in pairs during the independent group work, commented on each other's work during the plenary. Their comments had to include what they liked about their partner's work, how it differed from their own and how they might improve any aspect of it.

Support for implementation of the NLS had evolved as the school's needs had changed. When the NLS first came in to the school, and the school was in special measures, Ms Chadwick described the LEA support from NLS consultants as invaluable. More recently, like Anderson and Ballard, school-based support from the school's own staff, particularly Clare, had promoted their development of the interpretation of NLS. Further support was taken from the professional commentary in reports like those by PISA (2000), OfSTED (2002a) and Earl *et al.* (2003) but not from the NLS materials aimed at headteachers. Moreover, Ms Chadwick, like Ms Bradshaw, was being trained as an LEA consultant head to support the implementation of the Primary National Strategy (DfES, 2003).

Campbell Primary had developed a high level of assessment literacy. In common with Anderson and Ballard there was a range of summative assessments conducted on children across the year. These include termly running records, phonic checklists and NLS high-frequency word lists. These data were analysed in order to check the progress of classes by ethnicity, gender and SEN. In addition to this summative assessment, the school had been influenced by the work of Clarke (2000, 2003) who described the process of helping children to 'close the gap'. This included regularly giving children small targets, sharing the learning objectives for the lesson and discussing the success criteria for that day's objective at the start of the lesson.

Ms Chadwick felt that the success of her school in raising standards in literacy had grown from all of those features described above. In other words, that the success in literacy was part of a bigger picture of success in the school as a whole. This comment is borne out in the wider context of school improvement by Mortimore *et al.* (1988), Sammons, Hillman and Mortimore (1996) and Reynolds (1998). In addition to those areas already mentioned she considered that the school's focus on creativity and engaging children with a range of activities across the arts was crucial to motivation and filling the gaps in children's home experience. Also, she had recruited and retained high quality staff over a period of time, so that the high turnover of staff often associated with schools in special measures had not remained a problem. New teachers were often recruited from among those the school had trained; eight current members of staff had completed their final teaching practice in the school.

Finally, despite the fact that Campbell Primary, of the three schools studied, was perhaps the most closely influenced by the early prescription of the NLS, Ms Chadwick considered that the school had emerged with a strong sense of autonomy. A focus on the generic skills relevant to effective teaching and learning, supported by systematic devolution of leadership to the senior management team, had fostered a culture and ethos that allowed her staff to ask the fundamental question:

'Does this help the children's learning? If not, why are we doing it?'

SUMMARY

The following chapters show a series of lessons observed in the schools we have just described. As you read them consider how the picture of the implementation of the NLS has emerged during this chapter and those preceding it. Consider how, for example, the strengths of the NLS and of improving schools have combined to foster effective learning environments where excellent teaching flourishes. The following checklist covers those aspects of excellence in literacy teaching that we have discussed so far:

- Excellent classroom practice is observed in schools where systems for planning and assessment are rigorous and are based on an understanding of how children learn to read and write.

- Excellent schools raise standards through whole-school approaches to learning that encompass all curriculum areas, not through the piece-meal adoption of a range of different pedagogical styles.
- The NLS is used as a very useful tool to support rigour in teaching reading and writing but it was not embraced as an inflexible dogma by the schools observed.
- Effective teachers have the confidence to teach according to what they know about how children learn to read and write, rather than according to the latest 'received wisdom'.
- Effective teachers of pupils with EAL have to consider language development all the time; it is possible that this may improve their subject knowledge and their confidence generally in planning for their pupils' development in literacy.

You will find reference to the above key messages repeatedly in the following chapters. They are important for the beginner teacher as they explain how some schools and some teachers can perform very differently within the same curriculum framework.

II Three Exceptional Teachers

An Introduction to Part Two

In the following three chapters we report on the detail of the practice of the three Year 2 teachers observed teaching the Literacy Hour. We explain the background to their thinking and planning. In describing their lessons we provide fine-grained analyses of each lesson in order to demonstrate how their practice matched findings related to effective teaching and, more importantly, research related to how children develop as readers and writers. Furthermore we describe how their understanding of pupils' second-language acquisition scaffolded their successful teaching for reading and writing in English.

As we introduce the teachers and their lessons, it will become obvious that the large number of EAL pupils in the classes of Aidan and Bridget had a particular influence on their practice. Those who teach pupils who are all, or almost all, monolingual English speaking pupils may feel that there is little in the material on these two teachers to help them. They may, for example, feel more drawn to the observations of Clare whose class was more mixed and who had had different influences on her practice in terms of school setting. Nevertheless, we urge readers to observe the practice of all three teachers because each has unique qualities and this makes them fascinating to study. The underlying similarities will demonstrate for you the richness of practice that is based on understanding how children develop as readers and writers. There is something that each teacher can show us, regardless of the settings in which we teach ourselves.

When we studied the practice of these teachers in 2003, we observed the very significant role that successful teacher-talk played in scaffolding learning during their lessons. Success in any lesson was due to a combination of careful planning, effective management of pupils and support staff, secure subject knowledge and rich experiences of teaching English; but the way in which these teachers communicated with their pupils during the lesson appeared perhaps most significant. In the original research we coded the types of teacher-talk we observed and produced a range of histograms detailing teacher–pupil interaction for each part of the lesson. Such technical detail is not appropriate for a book of this kind but we do refer to various types of teacher-talk in the descriptions of their practice.

The commentary related to each teacher is divided into observations of each lesson. In order to further illustrate how the lessons were planned and how they matched research-based findings related to literacy development we have included diagrammatic representations at the beginning and end of each lesson section. Each lesson is drawn up as if it were a lesson plan; this is not what the teachers themselves used but it is our interpretation of the practice as related to the NLS framework for teaching. In some cases, notably Bridget's lessons, readers will notice sections of the lesson that don't match the prescribed pedagogy for the NLS. At the end of the commentary for each lesson, there is another figure showing the plan for the lesson and how the teachers' decisions for planning and delivery matched those of research related to psychological processes of reading and writing development, effective literacy teaching and successful teaching for pupils with EAL. We consider that this second representation of the lesson provides a valuable model for how teachers in training might evaluate their own practice.

7 Aidan

BACKGROUND

Aidan had been teaching for 20 years. He had been trained on a PGCE primary course and had a BSc in biology. He was the school's Key Stage 1 coordinator and also had responsibility for mentoring trainees and NQTs. During the 5 years prior to our observations he had taught Years 1, 2 and 3. His training for NLS implementation was covered by days delivered by the LEA literacy team through 1998 and 1999 although he felt his most effective training had been from working alongside colleagues and in having opportunities to try out new ideas in his own classroom.

The class was made up of 29 children: 28 with Bengali heritage and a lone Somali child. Thus the class were 100% EAL, with fluency ranging across all levels from barely conversant in English to confident bilingual speakers.

Aidan had moved beyond the original prescription for the NLS and was at a point where he felt free to adapt it for his class. To some extent this was because the school had been released from the intense scrutiny of inspection, but it was also, as is apparent from the headteacher interview for this school in Chapter 6, because that was how Anderson Primary always planned to use the *Framework for Teaching*. Aidan admitted that, when observed, he was more likely to teach a standard Literacy Hour. Also, because he had a trainee teacher in his class, he felt that it was important to model the intended pedagogy for her in order that she was trained according to the guidance. However, left alone, he might devote entire lessons to drama or to extended writing if that best suited his objectives and the need to keep his children motivated.

He had always been confident with his own understanding of how to teach reading and writing effectively and continued to be most influenced by training from providers other than NLS consultants. Where he did accept that the NLS had improved his practice was in the rigour it had introduced in the teaching of word-level work and phonics. Like many schools in his LEA he used Miskin's *Superphonics* (Miskin, 2000, see School Resources, p. 221) and appreciated the structure that this had given to the school as a whole. He was also of the opinion that all of the staff at Anderson Primary valued the mix of whole-class and group activities that the NLS encourages.

At interview it was noticeable that Aidan spoke collectively in response to many questions. This was because he considered that much of his own pedagogy – in Key Stage 1 at least – would be shared by his colleagues; delivery of literacy grew from agreed understanding of what the NLS should look like in his school. This agreed classroom practice would include a major emphasis on speaking and listening, on talk for writing (perhaps through drama and role-play) and on grouping children for specific word-level work. The school felt strongly that, in order to raise attainment in writing for example, it was necessary to tackle what they perceived to be a weakness of the NLS, namely that it fosters insufficient development of the various stages of written composition.

Aidan's planning for the NLS used an NLS weekly planning format but the detail was limited. Planning was made crosscurricular wherever possible. A good example of this was the Anancy topic, from lesson one, where the fortnight's activities across several curriculum areas supported the literacy objectives of plot development related to character and setting. Choices were made about which objectives the children needed to cover and, in making these, Aidan believed that 'motivation is everything'. He was not keen to promote the amount of technical detail for written English that the NLS appears to support. He felt, rather, that children need to write well – not that they need to understand which parts of speech they might be using. To this end, perhaps, he did not use any of the NLS additional support materials such as *Progression in Phonics* (DfES, 2000a) or *Developing Early Writing* (DfES, 2000b). In fact, the school used no commercial schemes other than their phonics package, preferring instead to rely on 'home-grown' resources.

Other adults played a key role in Aidan's decisions in planning the content and progress of a lesson. For example, in the first lesson observed there were three adults available one of whom was Alan, the EAL coordinator introduced in Chapter 5. This support teacher worked with children who were least fluent in spoken English, and planned a separate set of activities that were matched to this group's needs. A classroom assistant worked with a small group of children who had a specific phonics programme that was used during the word-level part of the introduction while Aidan worked with a third group.

In the second lesson Aidan worked with the least fluent children while Alan worked with the more able group. This decision to change was taken so that both groups of children could benefit from the variation in teaching style of the two teachers; so that Aidan could assess the progress of his lower achievers in collaboration with the EAL coordinator, and in order not to stigmatise the least fluent children by always having their tuition delivered by a practitioner other than the class teacher. This careful deployment of other adults meant that Aidan rarely engaged in whole-class teaching other than in the final lesson where, unusually, he was the sole adult with the class. It also meant that word-level work was carefully differentiated and that, where the class was together, objectives were adapted to suit the wider range of abilities.

Planning for lessons was brief, in terms of overt planning on paper. However, each lesson had clearly been considered in detail as resources were always very attractive, texts well chosen to suit the children's interest and the learning objectives and the teachers and additional adults were very aware of their differing roles and tasks. An impressive feature of this teacher's practice was his attention to planning for a high quality end product. For example, when children were exploring dialogue in text they had large speech bubbles, set against character drawings from the text discussed, in which to record their dialogue. When writing their poetry the children wrote across 3 days so that each section of a poem was carefully constructed. This attention to detail led to highly motivated children who remained on-task throughout independent activities regardless of whether they had an adult with them, and with little reduction in on-task activity when, as in the third lesson, the teacher was the only adult present.

Reading was planned and delivered both during the Literacy Hour and at other times. Aidan felt that the recommended practice of children reading simultaneously while the teacher 'keys in' to individuals was not an effective model for his class. Instead he preferred to have children read silently and to check their comprehension with questions, or to listen to them one at a time in the group. He felt that this latter model in particular was much more effective as an assessment tool as he had the comparative responses of the group to feed his knowledge of their progress. Many children were taught reading outside the Literacy Hour – particularly those with reading difficulties who were listened to regularly by Aidan, the EAL teacher or the teaching assistant. Across a week many of the children would read both individually and in a guided reading session.

Children were grouped by ability and these groups were reviewed regularly. Support was varied according to the needs of the children and in order to share the expertise and differing teaching strengths of Aidan and the supporting EAL teacher. Aidan engaged in a great deal of ongoing assessment in order to change groupings for his class and to allocate additional adults most effectively. This did not necessarily involve formal or summative assessment but was based more on his observations or those of the EAL teacher. However, summative assessment was used for the class. Children were assessed termly according to National Curriculum levels and the school had devised its own gradings within the levels: for example, 'working towards' was divided into W1 and W2, and Level 1 had a 'threshold' or a 'secure' rating.

Target setting, at school level, informed Aidan's practice to the extent that he focused his attention on what the SAT target was and was conscious of it when planning for the various abilities in the class. Nevertheless, he did not set individual targets for the children as he found it unrealistic in the context of planning for units of work. He could see a place for targets but considered that they could tend to narrow down the focus of what he might want to teach the children.

Books for reading were sent home very regularly and parents were encouraged to become involved in the child's choice of book when they came into class in the morning. Children were allowed to choose for themselves and Aidan found that, on the whole, they chose sensibly and from within their current reading ability. Siblings were encouraged to read at home with children in the class whose parents may have had difficulty reading with them because they did not read English. Studies by Gregory (2001), carried out in the same community as Anderson and Ballard Primaries, have uncovered the important role that siblings often play in supporting the literacy development of their younger brothers and sisters. In addition to this encouragement of sibling support, there were four classes run for parents in the school; these included classes in literacy for parents and in mathematics games for home.

Homework was set weekly and tied to the current class work. There was a 50% return rate, approximately, although Aidan was sure that more children than this actually completed the homework. He considered that homework provided another valuable opportunity for parents to become involved in their children's learning and that parents and children appreciated the opportunity to complete it, despite being further committed to additional work for class in Arabic at the mosque school they attended in the evenings.

Aidan considered that the reason his school has been successful in raising and maintaining standards in literacy had much to do with the experience and professionalism of the staff. Many staff in the school had held onto their pre-NLS beliefs about the best ways to teach reading and writing and had assimilated NLS rather than changing their practice to match its requirements. Nevertheless, he felt that this marriage of the two can work well and that, if schools could find a balance between the structure of the NLS and the 'sovereignty' of the teacher the NLS should work effectively to raise standards. How he found this balance is now illustrated as we observe his lessons.

THE LESSONS

The lessons always had a tight focus, with a very limited amount of new information being introduced. This, and the thought he gave to attractive and well-matched resources, was very much key to the success of this teacher's practice. Any new teaching always grew from the children's prior knowledge and was delivered in incremental steps. The majority of children might be working on the same task during the independent activities but with differentiated learning outcomes and targeted support. Guided and independent activities always drew on the text used during shared reading. This match of the text across the lesson was shared in common with Clare, and exemplified the sort of planned coherence noted as a feature of effective literacy teachers by Wray, Medwell, Poulson and Fox (2002) and Hall and Harding (2003).

In general there were no issues with problem behaviour in any lesson observed. Children were aware of the boundaries of appropriate behaviour and their very good attitude to work meant that the issuing of warnings or sanctions was almost non-existent. On the contrary, Aidan took great care to praise children, individually and as a class, on a regular basis. Children were keen to please their teacher and he spent time explaining exactly why some features of their work had pleased him. This increased the available time for teaching because unproductive interruptions were minimal.

We move now to detailed analysis of three Literacy Hour lessons taught by Aidan during the spring of 2003. We will observe that the practice of this teacher was characterised by a very clear focus on his objective, careful modelling, explanation and demonstration and the use of a great deal of one-to-one interaction with the children at whole-class, group and individual level. In this way his practice matched that of the expert teachers observed by Topping and Ferguson (2005). However, he went beyond the excellence described in the Topping and Ferguson study in that the purpose of activities was always very clear and children were aware of how to apply their learning.

LESSON 1 (TABLE 7.1)

We can see from the lesson overview that Aidan had decided to combine several objectives. The children were to focus on character, but could do this through role-play, thus covering two text-level objectives. Further to this, the sentence-level objective grew naturally from the text being used and was combined with text-level input during the introduction and the independent activities. In this way we are given an example of how a teacher may use the *Framework for Teaching* in a coherent way that allows children to experience how different aspects of text are interrelated.

Lesson 1 looked at character in fiction texts, using the traditional tale *Anancy and Mr Drybone* (retold by French, 1998) as a stimulus. In the previous week the children had read the story and this lesson started a followup sequence that was to support them in creating their own Anancy story in a different setting. As a starting point for this, and in order to give them a high quality model of what they might work towards, Aidan had created his own Anancy story – *Anancy and Alligator* – a version of which the children had read in an earlier shared reading session. Straight away we see that learning is supported by the visual aids and physical demonstration that Long (2002) identified as crucial for her daughter's language acquisition; the avoidance of 'streams of unsupported teacher talk'.

Table 7.1 Aidan, Lesson 1

Section focus	Objective	Activity
Word level	*Long vowel phoneme /ow/*	• Say it like a robot • Two letters one sound • Writing words • Phoneme segmentation • Adding endings to root words
Text level	*To identify and describe characters (Y2, term 2, T 6)* *To investigate and recognise a range of other ways of presenting text (Y2, term 2, S 7)*	Shared reading of *Anancy and Alligator* Identification of text features such as 'think bubble'
Guided reading	*To identify and describe characters (Y2, term 2, T 6)* *To reinforce and apply their word level skills through shared and guided reading*	Reading text *Anancy and Alligator* (difficulty level Book Band 6) Answering comprehension questions – literal and inferential
Independent groups	*To prepare and retell stories . . . through role play (T 7)* *To investigate and recognise a range of other ways of presenting text (Y2, term 2, S 7)*	Retelling story using story props Illustrating the text and using speech bubbles
Plenary	*To prepare and retell stories . . . through role play (T 7)* *To identify and describe characters (Y2, term 2, T 6)*	Independent group retells story with props Children dicuss character of Anancy and what he might say to Alligator

Quite apart from having an obvious relationship to the needs of the pupils because their home language was not English, this use of a simplified story model to support understanding of the conventions of writing and the writing process is also consistent with the more general findings of research related to how children develop effectively as writers of English (Berninger and Swanson, 1994, Cameron and Besser, 2004). Furthermore, Aidan had not only considered the use of his own story during the shared reading session but had also planned for its use in the guided reading session. In order that this was done most effectively he had created a text that corresponded to the group's reading level for guided reading for that day. His planning was thus explicitly informed by his assessment of the children's prior knowledge and a careful match of the activity to their stage of reading development (Black *et al.*, 2003). We can see from the lesson overview that Aidan had decided to combine two objectives. The children were to focus on character, but could do this through role-play, thus covering two text-level objectives.

During word-level work the class was divided into three ability groups and supported by one of three adults: Aidan, the EAL teacher or a teaching assistant. Each group had its own programme of word-level objectives that was matched to their need. In this way the children could make maximum progress through a lesson as they were exposed to the next stage in their learning, rather than being asked to work at a level that might either support the least able or be too difficult for them. The class regrouped into two for shared text and sentence-level work on the carpet, and then into independent group work where they were taught either by Aidan or the EAL teacher. This precision in the use of other adults maximised the learning opportunities for the children during the lesson, fostered an environment where assessment for learning was most likely to be used successfully and ensured that pupils were kept motivated and on-task because of the amount of one-to-one attention they were likely to receive.

WORD-LEVEL WORK

Aidan worked with a middle-ability group for this section of the lesson. Their objective was to learn the long /OW/ /əʊ/ sound as pronounced in the words 'know', 'grow' and 'show'. Consider how complex this sound is for all children learning English. How does the child new to this letter string understand that 'cow' and 'show' share a grapheme but not a phoneme? In order to avoid confusion and to enable children to learn the sets of words that shared either pronunciation of the same spelling, Aidan had ensured that he listed only those rhyming with 'grow' for this lesson but was also prepared for errors and misconceptions and made sure that these were corrected with further explanation.

The children had been introduced to the phoneme /OW/ /əʊ/ the previous Friday and had also been taught the alternative spellings for this phoneme. Thus, the dialogue with them during teaching of this session was rich with crossreferences to prior learning. Following a recap and a modelling of how to write the word 'know', Aidan asked the children to use their whiteboards and write down other words for him. As he gave instructions for each word he assisted them with previously learned rhymes, which supported them in sounding out the words for themselves. The dialogue below illustrates this use of a multisensory approach to spelling.

'Can you write down the word "show" for me? And when you've done it show it to me. Show me show.'

'Think, two letters one sound. Two letters one sound – sh – and two letters one sound – ow.' (Models the writing of this word on the board.)

'Can you try this one? Like a robot, can you say "grow"?'

'G-r-o-w' (enunciates this with the children while moving arms like a robot).

'I say g-r-ow' (this time making the final sound from two letters together, and the children repeat after him).

'I say grow' (children repeat).

'Now write it down.'

'Underneath "grow" you could write it again and add another letter to make it "grown", like "grown up".'

Note how the learning sequence is incremental and avoids the simple listing of words that may characterise phonic work in less imaginative literacy lessons. The children were fully involved at all times in creating words and given multiple tools for working out how they might attack unknown spellings; they have to think of the jingle 'two letters one sound' and the game 'say it like a robot'. In addition to this they are taught to think of a root word and to add an ending. His technique would support children of any linguistic background as it engages them fully in their learning and gives them structures for managing their own learning.

As this session progressed, the children started to ask questions relating to other words with the long /OW/ (/əʊ/) sound. Although he had kept the focus on one particular spelling for this phoneme, Aidan took time to explain the differences. Even within this one ability group – only one-third of the class – children were at different stages in their fluency. Thus, with one more able girl, Aidan explored other spellings when she asked 'what about the word "bone"?' He explained that this was the 'o' with magic 'e' spelling and also that there was no easy way of working out which words had any of the three different spellings: 'you just have to know which are which'. His attention to one child's precise level of understanding demonstrates how Aidan could respond to individual need and treat the children's linguistic development at an individual level where needed.

Similarly, within the same teaching slot, a less able child began to write the word 'throw' as 'flow'. Aidan then spent time getting her to put her tongue between her teeth in order to make the sound she needed for the spelling. His teaching was thus characterised by attention to the detailed needs of individuals and a deep understanding of how to react to their misconceptions within any teaching event. A less confident teacher might, for example, miss the problem with pronunciation of 'th' (a common error among many children in London) or might not see the value of allowing some conversation away from the tight focus of the graphemic representation for that day. Thus, potentially rich educational experiences can get lost where teaching is not governed by the confidence that can foster flexibility in response without losing pace and a clear focus on objectives.

SHARED TEXT-LEVEL WORK

Note that word-level work for this lesson bore no relation to the overall object-ives. In a class where children were all or mostly fluent in written English, we might expect to see the same lesson taught with no word-level work at all in order not to demotivate pupils. However, with so many EAL pupils, Aidan needed to invest daily quality time in teaching word-level work so that they could access the interesting text-level work he devised for his lessons (Stuart, 1999, 2004). Flexibility over the positioning of any part of the Literacy Hour characterised the teaching of all three teachers observed.

Aidan, now working with half of the class while the EAL teacher took the remainder for a separate lesson with objectives appropriate to their linguistic development, introduced his home-made book thus:

Now last week, I did the story props for Anancy and Alligator, and as it made you laugh and we enjoyed it, I thought we'd do some more of it for a couple days. I made it into a little book and I got my pictures for it off the computer. But I don't like the pictures very much so I'm going to ask Black group to make their own pictures to go in the book, using the black paper cut out, to go with the story.

His explanation was clear. Children knew what they were working on that day and why. As he read the book – a simplified version of the story read in the previous week – he drew the children into the story with him. Notice how the text (see below) has meaning but draws on a narrow range of words and s written in simple sentences; the vocabulary range was taken from Book Band Level 6 (Hobsbaum, 2003) so that the text could also be used during he guided reading session.

'Anancy did lots of other tricks. He tricked all of the other animals. Alligator did not like the tricks that Anancy did. "I will get rid of Anancy," said Alligator.' (Page turn – 'we need a picture of alligator there, don't we?')
'"My tooth hurts," said Alligator. "Help me Anancy."'
'"I will get my tools," said Anancy.'
(Page turn.)
'He went home. "This is a trick," he said. He got a screwdriver, some sandpa-per, a hammer, a drill and a stick. (We need a set of little pictures to go with that there.)
'He went back to Alligator. "Open wide," said Anancy. (The dentist says that, doesn't he?) Anancy put the stick in Alligator's mouth.' (Has a chat with a child who had something in his mouth at the dentist and wanted to shut his mouth but couldn't.)
'Anancy got in the mouth. He poked with the screwdriver.' ('Can you do a bit of poking?' – to the children.) '"Ahh!" said Alligator. (Do you see how it's written with an "a" and two "h"s and then an exclamation mark?' Children say it for a long time. 'No, it's not that long, it's just a little one.')

'"Ahh!" said Alligator.

'He rubbed with the sandpaper. (Can you do a bit of sandpapering?) He drilled with the drill. "Ahh!" said Alligator.

'"I have to go now," said Anancy. He left the stick in Alligator's mouth. "Ahhhhh!" said Alligator. (I've got a little think bubble that can go here. It says, "you left the stick in my mouth.") But Anancy was gone.'

On ending the reading of this text Aidan spent a very brief time explaining what the children were going to do for their independent activities. Because he had several other adults in the room and the children were very familiar with specific routines for his lessons, explanation and transition were rapid and minimal learning time was lost. One group was to create pictures for the text; another was to listen to the two Anancy stories on tape and play with the story props for each, and a third group was to work with Aidan for guided reading using the story that had just been used in shared reading.

GUIDED READING

The guided reading session was used to practise the type of comprehension questions the children might see in their Key Stage 1 SATs. The children did not know that it was 'SAT practice' but Aidan acknowledged that there had to be some teaching of test technique in order that the children were prepared for the task. Thus, the children were given small versions of the teacher-made booklet read during the shared reading session and a set of questions that required a range of reading skills for accessing the text for answers.

Children read individually to themselves, while Aidan checked for fluency by listening to them one at a time. This system is the traditional guided reading model put forward by the NLS, although not one that all teachers found easy to adopt when the strategy came in. Indeed, as we mentioned in the introductory background, this teacher did not use the group guided reading approach all the time; children were also given one-to-one reading time with adults or might read altogether if that was deemed appropriate for the objective. While listening to each child he gave constructive feedback to support their confidence: 'If you're not sure what that word is then try the other words before and after it. All the words you don't know are ones that you can sound out.'

The text was read fairly briefly – far less than 10 minutes. This was because the key focus for this guided reading session was the comprehension questions and because the children had already spent some time with this text during shared reading. One of the weaknesses in the implementation of guided reading as a strategy is that teachers may not keep a clear focus on their objective, or even understand that there should be a planned objective for that session. Rather than give more time to the skill that matters for that day they may become too bogged down in the mechanics of word recognition for every pupil. Used at its best, guided reading should look more like the practice of this teacher who gives weight to the comprehension of text when he recognises that the word recognition is adequate to support questioning. By giving the children a text that is carefully matched to their ability – the NLS recommends that 90 % of words will already be known by the children – he is able actually to 'teach reading' rather than 'hearing reading'. More examples of excellence in guided reading can be observed in Clare's teaching for her first and third lessons.

Following the reading, Aidan turned the children's attention to their comprehension questions and used his characteristic clarity when talking to them about how they might find their answers and record them. For example, the first question gave the children a series of choices where they had to choose and tick a box next to the word that answered the question correctly. This would be characteristic of one of the types of question that the children would meet in the SAT. Aidan took time to show the children how he would answer the question and took time in ensuring that they answered the first one correctly. By doing this he was ensuring that they had an example from which they could deduce how to answer questions of the same type later in the exercise.

The group were set for ability but, as during word-level work, Aidan demonstrated his knowledge of the subtle differences in their abilities. One question required inference: 'What does Alligator pretend?' Taking one more able child through this he took her to the place in the text where she might consider her answer.

'Here he says, "My tooth hurts." Did his tooth really hurt?' . . . (Pauses and waits for child to respond, then confirms her answer with her.)
   'No, he's just saying that to make Anancy go inside his mouth. But Anancy's clever so he worked out that it was just a trick.'

Here we see evidence of this teacher understanding that the question required the child to see beyond the text in order to reach an answer; she had to think in terms of inference. You will remember from Chapter 3 that Hutchinson, Whiteley, Smith and Connors (2003) identified the problem for EAL pupils in tuning into inference. Giving children a mix of questions and supporting them in finding their answers involved Aidan in the kind of direct teaching of comprehension skills that Hutchinson, Whiteley, Smith and Connors called for. The NLS gives very little guidance about the teaching of inferencing skills.

Another question proved problematic for a child both in terms of her understanding of the text and her understanding of the question. The children had to make a choice and 'name one thing that Anancy did to Alligator's teeth'. She had answered 'screwdriver'.

'You said screwdriver, but the screwdriver is the name of the thing. What did he do with the screwdriver? Do you remember? It says here if you read it. Can you read that word there?'

Child reads, 'he picked . . .'

Teacher responds, 'It's like picked but there's an "o" instead of an "i". It's poked. Do you know what poked means?'

Through this dialogue the teacher is identifying and clarifying a misconception, identifying the correct way to answer the question and exploring the text with the child in order that she is better equipped to answer comprehension questions in future. Thus we see, in one small example of this teacher's practice, evidence of effective teaching as identified by research-based models of how children learn, of how children learn to read and of how children learn to read in a second language.

THE PLENARY

The plenary for this lesson acted both as a vehicle for celebrating the children's work and for checking on the progress of the group that had been working alone. Aidan used the plenary to consolidate learning from the lesson, to check understanding and to extend the objective. OfSTED (2002a) highlighted the plenary as the weakest part of the Literacy Hour. Aidan's practice matches that described as most effective in this same report. It is important to note that OfSTED identified effective closing plenary sessions as occurring

> where the teacher has made the learning objectives precise and has given the pupils tasks that relate to the main theme of the lesson. He or she is then able to focus on and evaluate a specific aspect of learning with the whole class.
>
> (OfSTED, 2002a, p. 14)

In other words, the success of Aidan's plenary session grew directly from the effective practice he used during all parts of the literacy hour. Aidan shows us how the plenary is used to evaluate progress so far and check on understanding, as well as to model the best work for the children in order that the class can learn from the success of a group.

Aidan focused on those groups with whom he had not had contact. Thus the group that illustrated the text (working with a student teacher) presented the book. They had written speech bubbles related to the plot in each drawing and the group who had been working completely independently read these to the class. This same group then retold the story for the class using story props – their task had been to use these during the lessons but they had not been supported with this. It was interesting to note that the story prop group had not only carried out their task but was able to perform it well. High teacher expectations and clear classroom routines meant that these children could work on-task and independently, even though they were used to a quite unusually high staff–pupil ratio in class.

As one of the children retold the story his teacher encouraged his performance and modelled Standard English for him:

> Child telling the story: 'Anancy put the stick in Alligator's mouth and he went in to Alligator's mouth.'
> Teacher: 'Well done, you're telling this story really well.'
> Child: 'He hammered.'
> Teacher: 'And he hammered with the hammer.'
> Child: 'And he got sandpaper.'
> Teacher: 'And he put sandpaper on.'

Overall, this plenary allowed Aidan to refocus on the lesson objectives – character and retelling – so that children remained in a tight learning framework throughout the lesson. This is a clear illustration of Aidan's specific characteristic of keeping a close match to the objective in all activities and developing an incremental progression related to this objective during the lesson. Figure 7.1 shows, in précis, how Aidan's lesson matched research-based findings regarding how children develop literacy.

Aidan, Lesson 1

This sequence of activities is multisensory.
Visual cues consistent with verbal message
Long, 2002

Use of systematic phonics programme, Stuart, 2004

Objectives coherent throughout lesson, Wray et al. 2002

Reading task teaches reference Peakhill et al. 1986, Hutchinson et al. 2003

Plenary consolidates, learning of independent groups is assessed OFSTED, 2002, Black et al. 2003

Section focus	Objective	Activity
Word Level	Long vowel phoneme /ow/	•Say it like a robot •Two letters one sound •Writing words •Phoneme segmentation Adding endings to root words
Text Level	To identify and describe characters (Y2, term 2, T6) To investigate and recognise a range of other ways of presenting text (Y2, term 2, S 7)	Shared reading of Anancy and Alligator Identification of text features such as 'think bubble'
Guided groups	To identify and describe characters (Y2, term 2, T6) To reinforce and apply their word level skills through shared and guided reading	Reading text Anancy and Alligator (difficulty level Book Band 6) Answering comprehension questions – literal and inferential
Independent work	To prepare and retell stories...through role-play (T7) To investigate and recognise a range of other ways of presenting text (Y2, term 2, S 7)	Retelling story using story props Illustrating the text and using speech bubbles
Plenary	To prepare and retell stories...through role-play (T7) To identify and describe characters (Y2, term 2, T6)	Independent group retells story with props Children discuss character of Anancy and what he might say to Alligator

Text work using familiar genre, Kress, 1996

Teaching conventions of written English, Berninger, 1994 Cameron & Besser, 2004

Text matched to children's reading level, Black et al. 2003

Match of introduction and main activity, Wray et al. 2002

Figure 7.1 Aidan, Lesson 1.

LESSON 2 (TABLE 7.2)

In Lesson 1 we saw that Aidan's effectiveness grew from his careful choice of activities and resources so that children were well scaffolded as they worked through their group activities. In Lesson 2 we see evidence of the same but also observe how the use of role-play to foster writing can create an engaging lesson where children make sound progress in their linguistic development. Notice that in Lesson 1 Aidan had covered three objectives as well as the phonic input but for Lesson 2 the delivery is around a sole focus. During this lesson the class was split into two halves and Aidan worked with the least able. The more fluent and able readers worked with the EAL coordinator in a separate room. This is an example of how this school varied the ways in which it worked with its pupils and the groups that worked with the range of adults available.

Lesson 2 focused on developing children's understanding of how to build dialogue into their stories through role-play and on writing dialogue onto

Table 7.2 Aidan, Lesson 2

Section focus	Objective	Activity
Word level	*Final phoneme -ll*	• Do it like a robot • Phoneme counting • Two letters one sound • Writing words using -ll ending
Text and sentence level Shared text *Zomo the Rabbit*	*To prepare and retell stories individually and through role-play in groups, using dialogue and narrative from text (Year 2, term 2, T 7)*	Shared text *Zomo the Rabbit* (part read) Role-play in character Creating spoken sentences in speech bubbles
Independent work and guided writing	*To prepare and retell stories individually and through role-play in groups, using dialogue and narrative from text (Year 2, term 2, T 7).* **Used as a writing objective**	Writing insults from Zomo to Wild Cow on to speech bubbles
Plenary		Performing dialogue between Zomo and Wild Cow Discussion of effective dialogue Introduction to homework, words with -ll ending

speech bubbles for the characters in the shared text. The use of speech bubbles had been introduced in Lesson 1 (a month earlier) and the children were accustomed to using role-play to support their writing development. This demonstrates the importance of repeating and revisiting learning in order that children build up a gradual understanding of how text can be represented. It is also illustrative of Aidan's awareness that the children needed to learn a convention of written English and to implement it in more than one lesson. In other words, he intuitively combined his understanding of how children learn with how children develop as readers and writers.

Teacher–pupil interaction was characterised by one-to-one dialogue across the lesson, by substantial modelling of the activities children were to engage in and detailed explanation of any teaching points related to the objective. Targeted dialogue took place during all parts of the lesson, so that the interaction served as a model for learning and stimulus for discussion for the rest of the class.

WORD-LEVEL WORK

The games and multisensory learning opportunities for word-level work used in Lesson 1 were further demonstrated in Lesson 2. Aidan worked through a range of quick-paced activities to embed the double consonant -*ll* ending and its graphemic representation in the children's visual lexicons:

'Last week as your homework one of our words was "fell" (articulated clearly). One of the things I want to do is to really get that into your heads – how we spell "fell". How – we – spell – "fell" (slowly to draw children's attention to the rhyme).

'Can you say it like a robot? /f-e-l/. Can you do that too now [name])? /f-e-l/.

'OK, how many sounds were in that word "fell"? Hold up your fingers to show me. What do you think [name]? Four? Well three is actually the right answer. Listen to me say it. I say /f-e-l/, I say fell.

'It's a bit of a tricky word. It sounds simple but it's got a bit of a trick to it.' (Draws three lines on board for phoneme segmentation.) 'Who can tell me what the first sound is?' (Child gives him an 'f'.)

'And then the middle letter of the word?' (Child gives 'e'.)

'Now the last sound is /l/, but how do we write that /l/? Double ll, well done. It's one of those two letters one sound. Shall we sing that?' (Sings their 'two letters one sound' jingle with the children.)

'Today, the two letters one sound is a double "ll". When we get the /l/ sound at the end of the word, usually it's a double "ll".

'To get it into our heads and to make sure we all know it, let's look at some other words that are spelt the same way.

'Put up your hand and tell me what you think that's a picture of? That's right, it's a bell. Can you say that like a robot? /b-e-l/. Hold up your fingers and tell me how many sounds?' (Repeats phoneme segmentation exercise.)

'Sometimes now we get our water from the tap but sometimes people have to go deep down into the ground with a bucket and they pull the bucket up. Do you know what that's called? A well – well done! Can you all say that?' (Children chant 'well'.) 'No, not whale – it's "well".' (Repeats it with an exaggerated short 'e' sound for the medial vowel.)

'Say "well" like a robot. /w-e-l/. How many sounds? I say /w-e-l/, I say "well".' (Then phoneme segmentation is repeated.)

'Well done – and when I say that, it's written the same way.'

Note how in this session, the progress is incremental, as in Lesson 1, but also that children are engaged in having to switch quite rapidly between different ways of thinking about the same spelling throughout the lesson. Furthermore Aidan produced pictures of the well as it was likely that many of the children would not have experience of seeing one. He was aware that the children needed visual cues to support their understanding of new words (Long, 2002). Throughout this teaching sequence Aidan checked in particular on accurate pronunciation of the words introduced – an example of which is his correction for 'well' above. The need to model pronunciation in standard English is very important when teaching pupils with EAL in order that spelling in our opaque language is not made even more difficult than it already is for their monolingual peers.

SHARED READING

The shared reading activity was very closely matched to the independent activity – even more so than in Lesson 1. The NLS objective for this lesson was 'to prepare and re-tell stories individually and through role-play in groups using dialogue and narrative from text' (Year 2, term 2, reading objective 7). This is interesting in itself in the context of this lesson. The objective is a reading objective but Aidan had chosen to use it as one that would also support writing. In this way the children were being taught to make connections in their learning and to combine their knowledge of the conventions of story writing in oral retelling, reading and writing. This plan to provide coherence for the children in their literacy development is reminiscent of the practice of the effective teachers of literacy studied by Wray, Medwell, Poulson and Fox (2002).

In this lesson the teacher read the shared text *Zomo the Rabbit* (a traditional tale retold by McDermot, 1996). In the story Zomo – a trickster who is set the challenge of retrieving certain things from other characters – set out to fool Wild Cow into giving him some of her milk. He succeeds in making her so angry that she runs at him and gets her horns stuck in the soft trunk of a tree. Having listened to a repeat reading of this part of the story the children were invited to pair up and to practise throwing insults at each other while acting in role as either Zomo or Wild Cow. Initially – in order to model the task clearly for the children – Aidan asked children to give him suggestions, which he then repeated for the class in role. The following dialogue shows how he did this and supported the children in understanding of the appropriate form and tone at the same time. In other words he was able to help the children to select language that was appropriately structured and conveyed the required voice for the text they were creating.

I'd like you to have a little think. If you wanted to tease Wild Cow, to taunt Wild Cow, to make Wild Cow angry, what would you choose to say to her? It can be a little bit rude, not too rude because it's a book for children remember.

A child offers his example.

'Your nose is too big?' (Repeats it in taunting voice.) 'Your nose is too big! I don't think Wild Cow would like that at all. Well done, that's a really good insult.'

Another child struggles to form a sentence in which he wants to say that Wild Cow's milk is made of grass as his insult. Teacher says: 'Well, how could we say that? How about, "Your milk is all grassy"?'
One child goes too far and presents a rather lavatorial example.

'Oh, that's a bit on the rude side, I don't think we'll use that one. It's important to know what to do here, because you want to be a little bit rude, but you don't want to be too rude. Can you see that?' (Child acknowledges.)

The above dialogue is an example of how Aidan combined high expectations with encouragement in order to foster confidence in the children's use of language. He expected them to understand how to be rude enough to make the text of a children's book funny but to understand where the boundaries were. Furthermore, he was introducing them to differences in tone and register with which they might not have been familiar. Bearing in mind that these children were among the least fluent in English, it was interesting to see how many children had managed to assimilate formulaic phrases and apply them in this context. For example, one child creating a return insult from Wild Cow exclaimed, 'I'm going to get you Zomo!' This perhaps demonstrates how this teacher's investment in talk with the children had allowed them to develop the understanding of the nuances of the English language that Cameron and Besser (2004) found weaker in children with EAL.

As the great fun involved in the role-play carpet session ended, Aidan gave very brief but precise instructions for what the children were to do in their groups. At their tables, the children had each been given a large speech bubble on which to write their insults for Zomo and Wild Cow. Having modelled this for them, by writing onto a large speech bubble as an example, Aidan needed to spend very little time explaining the main activity. The children had all the input they needed from their engagement with the shared reading and writing introduction; minimal time was lost at the transition to tables and pupil motivation drove the success of their output.

GUIDED WRITING

During the guided writing activity, Aidan worked with the least able group. These children had some fluency and were able to write some of their words correctly. The emphasis was on finding the best expression in relation to the plot and the characters, rather than on the mechanics of writing. Children were encouraged to write down what they thought the spellings were, rather than worry about accurate spelling at this point. Nevertheless, where their teacher knew they were well rehearsed in writing conventions, for example in relation to accurate punctuation, he prompted them to compose properly. Through this we see how an experienced teacher has the confidence and knowledge of his pupils to identify which parts of composition are easily incorporated during the drafting process, but where those which require more thought are given less emphasis at the drafting stage in order not to inhibit the pupils' flow of thoughts. Furthermore, because the text being produced was very short, and the children had had maximum opportunity to talk about what they wanted to write, the activity provided a good opportunity to reinforce the range of sentence-level objectives already understood by the class.

Interaction was characterised by constant supporting dialogue with individuals in order to help them write a sentence of speech. This included reference to the spelling strategies used during the word-level work session. For example, one child felt unable to spell a word at all and was encouraged to 'say it like a robot'. The focus on the success of writing a speech bubble was kept by the teacher drawing children's attention to information such as 'we don't need to write "said", because we know that the character is speaking when his words are in a speech bubble.' Children were highly motivated as they were allowed to write insults but retained the sense of appropriate language modelled during the shared-text introduction. This needed further modelling for one child with Aidan again showing how the practitioner can gently guide a child to understanding appropriate language in context: 'Have you ever heard anyone say that? It's a bit nasty. I don't like that. Let's try something else. How about "your horns are like fishes?" Yes, I really like that.'

THE PLENARY

In the plenary to Lesson 2 Aidan took time to read the children's work and explain why the recorded dialogue was appropriate and clever. It was significant, in this plenary, that the children's written responses from the group work, those writing with an adult or independently, showed that they had assimilated the teaching from the shared-text introduction and had written

Aidan, lesson 2

Sequence of multisensory
activities.
Long, 2002

Use of
systematic
phonics
programme,
Stuart, 2004

Section focus	Objective	Activity
Word Level	*Final phoneme -ll*	•Do it like a robot •Phoneme counting •Two letters one sound •Writing words using –ll ending
Text and sentence level	*To prepare and re-tell stories individually and through role-play in groups, using dialogue and narrative from text.(Year 2, term 2, T7)*	Shared text *Zomo the Rabbit* (part read) Role-play in character Creating spoken sentences in speech bubbles
Independent and Guided groups	*To prepare and re-tell stories individually and through role-play in groups, using dialogue and narrative from text.(Year 2, term 2, T7) (Used in writing)*	Writing insults from Zomo to Wild Cow on to speech bubbles
Plenary	As above	Performing dialogue between Zomo and Wild Cow Discussion of effective dialogue Introduction to homework, words with –ll ending

The text is already
known.
Work starts with the
familiar.
 The task is in a
meaningful context,
Wray *et al*. 2002

ombining
ading and
iting skills
ildren
pported in
aking the
ks through
e of one
y objective.
all &
arding 2003

Extensive use of talk
for writing, Verhoeven,
1994
Kotler, A., Wegerif, R.
& Le Voi, M. 2001

Match of introduction
and main activity,
Wray *et al*. 2002

Consolidation, and learning made explicit
Black & Wiliam
2003, Topping and Ferguson, 2005

Figure 7.2 Aidan, Lesson 2.

uccessful, insulting dialogue. Role-play during the introduction had showed hat some children did not understand the role of dialogue in fiction but by he end of the lesson these same children had made tangible progress. Others, vho had understood the task fully in the earlier part of the lesson, demonstrated more sophisticated responses; for example, one had Wild Cow shout t Zomo, 'I will not forget this Zomo.' Another had written, 'You will pay for his Zomo, you will be sorry for this.' These responses further demonstrate his class's absorption of the formulaic phrases in the English language. Considering that these were among the least fluent and that they had worked ndependently, such high-quality output was impressive.

LESSON 3 (TABLE 7.3)

n Lesson 3 we observe some departure from the standard Literacy Hour ormat. We have previously mentioned that this teacher planned according to he number of adults present in his classroom; on this occasion he was the ole teacher. In order that the content was manageable and motivating for all 9 children, with their very considerable range of variance in fluency levels, or this lesson Aidan omitted any work on phonics. Thus he showed that

Table 7.3 Aidan, Lesson 3

Section focus	Objective	Activity
Text and sentence level Stimulus *The Magic Box*, Kit Wright	*To use structures from poems as a basis for writing by extending or substituting elements, inventing own lines and verses (Year 2, term 2, T 15)*	Review of progress so far with part written poems Discussion of effective feature of writing so far Discussion in pairs, related to next section of the poem – what the box is made from and where it will be kept
Paired writing	*To use structures from poems as a basis for writing by extending or substituting elements, inventing own lines and verses (Year 2, term 2, T 15)*	Composition of remaining parts of poem
Plenary		Review of successful work, discussion of vocabulary choice Reading two new poems

teachers must adapt their lessons in order to suit both the objectives and daily changes in circumstance. At the time this was indicative of an ease with use of the NLS that was not common (Earl *et al.*, 2003). Instead he worked with the whole class on one activity, which the children had been working on for the previous 2 days.

This lesson had a poetry focus, with the specific objective being 'to use structures from poems as a basis for writing by extending or substituting elements, inventing own lines and verses' (NLS, Year 2, term 2, T 15). Again we see him concentrating on just one objective; this is something we will also observe in Bridget's teaching. Aidan used Kit Wright's *The Magic Box* (Wright, 1982); a poem in which Wright has placed all manner of beautiful things into an imaginary box.

For this sequence of lessons, of which Lesson 3 was the third, the children had been using the structures in the poem to write their own antithetical poem entitled *The Bad Box*. Into their bad boxes they put things that disgusted or frightened them. Note that there was just one objective for this lesson that goes across word-, sentence- and text-level work. At the time of observation this was a confident use of the NLS. In many ways this lesson looked more like a pre-NLS poetry composition lesson, although we must not underestimate the extent to which this teacher's understanding of his pupils' learning needs, particularly in relation to writing, drove the decisions he made about choice of objectives and pedagogy.

In the two lessons prior to this one, the children had worked in writing pairs and had composed parts of the poem. As they wrote each section, Aidan had drawn their attention to the equivalent section in Kit Wright's poem and had concentrated on how the poet had used language for effect. Starting with a repeated opening phrase 'In our box we will put . . .', each pair had written about those things that they wanted to lock away. They had then been given time to word-process their first two verses – or their teacher had done this for them – so that by this lesson they had a part-composed poem that looked well presented and had some space left below for them to complete their creation. This is a further example of Aidan's attention to the quality of the resources the children were given to work with and the celebration of their effort as they generated well considered text.

INTRODUCTION

In this lesson Aidan taught the whole class. In common with all of us who teach he had to adapt to changing levels of support. His interaction with the children was notably less conversational than in other lessons. He maintained the same high quality modelling and explanation but gave less time to pupil response in the whole-class introduction. In this way he maintained the pace and kept children focused on their objective.

Several children had been absent for the two previous days. In order that they were not excluded from what had gone before, Aidan used an example of one writing pair's work. This was an interesting choice. He might have gone back to the original and explained how those absent were to change it. In doing this he would have lost the attention of the other pupils and lowered their chances of making progress in that lesson. Instead he took the opportunity to review progress and to model the expected writing process for those having to start afresh that day; he was also able to celebrate one particularly good example.

In *The Magic Box*, Kit Wright describes a box in terms of its structure and appearance and puts into it things that are precious. Aidan wanted the children to write poems using the same structure but which contained things that they disliked or were afraid of. The following is an example of how the two 7 year olds, with English as an additional language, had responded to the stimulus:

The Bad Box

In our box we will put cheese coleslaw
A bad dream of scary films that are real
Dragons with blood on their nose and
The bad smell of breaths of dragons.

In our box we will put when my brother hits me
When my sisters don't let me play PlayStation 2
A Japanese uncle from a cartoon

In our box we will put
When people put bombs around the world
And bad guys go inside poor people's houses and steal their jewels.

Through this part-finished poem we can see that the children had understood how to create stanzas, how to use a repeated opening sentence as a poetic device and that they had absorbed a sense of appropriate stanza length and line length. They had also started to use figurative language in order to express their feelings clearly through the text.

As the introduction progressed Aidan first drew the children's attention to the finer details of line length in a poem:

> When you write a story you just carry on writing, but with a song or a poem, you need more time to breathe. You do it a bit slower and so what you need to do to show people that you do that, you start new lines. You show people that they can take a little breath.
>
> So see how the poem is shaped – new line, new line, and new line – and there's even a space to show a longer breath.
>
> So you use the way you put it on the page to help people know they can take their time, and read it really slowly and carefully. At the end of the line there's a comma; it's a bit like a full stop, but it's just half a full stop. It tells you that you can take just a little breath.

Then he read the poem accentuating when he was stopping for line breaks and punctuation.

In previous days the input had focused on choices of word and on potential figurative language. In this lesson, input on shape of the text added to the children's understanding of how poetry differs from prose. Again we see how this teacher was able to plan for an incremental buildup of knowledge and understanding as the children wrote. This meant that any finished product was likely to be of a much higher quality than something generated during one lesson; it also gives us evidence of how Aidan understood the need for children to be deeply embedded in their text production in the same way that Derewianka's (1990) pupils were with their information writing.

Following on from the recap and discussion of line breaks, Aidan turned his attention to supporting the children with composition of the final verse of their poem. For this they would have to describe for the reader what the box looked like and how it locked, as well as where they might put their box.

Having taken the children through unfamiliar vocabulary such as the meaning of 'hinge', Aidan went on to produce a number of different boxes made from different materials. His teacher-talk focused on how they were made, how they locked and how they operated generally. In this way he was able to feed in the vocabulary that the children needed in order to write the lines that would match those in the original.

PAIRED WRITING

Talk for writing

At this point Aidan could have chosen to keep children on the carpet and discuss their possible responses to their task. Mindful of his lack of support, however, and in order to maintain pace and motivation, he moved children in their writing pairs to their tables with their part-finished poems. Division of the introduction into a 'carpet time' and a 'desk time' served to break up the amount of time for which children were listening and ensured that they were comfortable when it came to actually thinking about their composition. Still commanding full-class attention, Aidan set the children a series of talk-based tasks and broke for discussion between each one. Note that there was *no writing* in the first instance. The teacher was aware that he had dominated the conversation while on the carpet and that he needed to give the children time to express their ideas orally before writing them.

The children first had to think what their box was made of. Interestingly several children came up with the idea of glass; this was in neither the original poem nor in the suggestions put forward by the teacher in the introduction. The children explained that they would be able to see the things in their bad box if it were made of glass; perhaps being able to see their fears, knowing they could not get out, was more comforting than concealing them completely. As one pair spoke with Aidan he asked them a series of questions to make them develop their idea further: 'Is it see-through glass? No? It's thick glass. Does it have a colour?'

By asking them to think further about the material he was encouraging them to provide detail that would lift the quality of descriptive and figurative language in the poem.

During this task, it was notable that the least fluent children were given time to articulate their ideas while other children listened patiently. The atmosphere of respect was crucial to their growth in confidence, as was the use of more fluent children to model their more sophisticated ideas. Here we see an example of how the children's needs were nurtured in ways beyond the academic. Critics of the NLS and of more recent pedagogy generally, might despair of the loss of the child as central to the educative process; teaching has become objective driven rather than child centred. In schools where respect and the maintenance of self-esteem are part of the fabric of teacher–pupil response, this is perhaps less likely to happen.

Moving from talk about the material to talk about the hinges, Aidan summarised before setting the second task:

Don't just say glass, say more about the glass. Is it heavy glass, is it shiny, is it thick or thin? Is it strong glass? You will want to think about the hinges. Did anyone think about how they will shut their box? I'll give you a moment to think about that with your partner.

Following discussion about hinges, the children had to work out what sort of lock and key their box would have. Again, Aidan demanded that they concentrated on detail in their language:

I would like to know some of your ways of keeping your box shut – that's if you want to keep it shut. Please don't just say 'lock' to me, tell me and tell the people you are writing the poem for a little bit about what it's like, so I can get a picture of it in my head.

As with their choice of material for the box, children were creative in their ideas for the lock and key. Observe how this is evident in the following dialogue and also how Aidan insists on clarity in the description:

One child talking about his lock: 'Do you know the treasure box? It has a keyhole. Do you know at the top of the hole? I would imagine if there was a gap and there was a card then you could put it in the gap and magically it would open straight away.'
Aidan (child's responses in brackets): 'So it's got a card that opens it. Do you mean like a piece of card?' ('A blue card.') 'Like a card that you take to the bank or just a piece of card like this?' ('A bank card.') 'Ahh, a blue bank card. So has it got something electrical in it, or is it magic?' ('No, it's electrical.') 'That's very interesting, Thank you. I liked the way you said "I would imagine" – that's a really good way of saying it.'

This dialogue about the nature of the various parts of the box lasted for some time and was characterised throughout by responses such as those illustrated above. As the children turned to the task of writing they were effectively scaffolded in their attempts at composition as they had experienced the original model, which gave them a structure, time to put together their ideas through shared talk, conversation about their ideas with their teacher (which further developed their vocabulary use) and the opportunity to hear the ideas of their classmates. This rich layering of experiences meant that the majority of the children were able to write unassisted while their teacher gave his attention to the children who were starting from the beginning and to those who might find the writing process hardest.

Writing

Children worked noisily. They were allowed to carry on verbalising their responses and ideas, but well on-task. Noise level, and its relationship to work, is something that student teachers and NQTs find a constant worry. They might assume that, once chatting, the children are off-task and they, the teachers, have lost an element of control over their classroom. Take comfort in the knowledge that noise can be a feature of an effective working environment; it is whether the noise is productive that matters.

As they worked Aidan spent his time scribing for and supporting his group. As he worked other children came to him for support and he gave them his attention. This was different from the other two lessons observed where children were able to work in smaller groups. In these lessons Aidan had given almost undivided attention to one group at a time. Necessarily we have to make decisions about the best use of our time in relation to pupil progress, depending on the resources available to us.

It was notable that the language use by the group working with Aidan was less sophisticated than that heard in the example read out in the introduction. These children became fixated on stereotypical horror-type images and on using quite repetitive vocabulary: 'In our box we will put works with blood on them, in our box we will put vampires eating blood . . .' This is significant because it potentially demonstrates several things. Firstly, it is perhaps the case that children writing in any language have differing abilities in expressing themselves well. Secondly, those who had not had the chance to develop their ideas for the start of the poem while a part of the class and its layers of rich teacher-led scaffolding were less able to write creatively.

PLENARY

In the plenary we see evidence of how well the children were able to write following their talk-based introduction. Despite their chatter, the majority of the class had finished their poems in the quite short writing time available and had moved on to performing them for each other in preparation for a forthcoming assembly. One pair was asked to read out their poem, although Aidan was careful to praise all the children for their excellent efforts:

In our box we will put the smell of pigs
The dreams of scary stories

In our box we will put different countries like Iraq and America having a war
And killing each other with guns

In our box we will put
Getting told off by the teacher for no reason.

Our box will be made of plastic
That opens magically and closes magically

Our box will be in the woods under the ground
In the woods there will be witches and ghosts and goblins
And under the box there will be trolls.

The following example is taken from work collected from pupils after the lesson:

In our box we will put
Tomatoes in a sandwich
Swimming by ourselves in our dreams
The smell of sour milk

In our box we will put
When people bomb another country,
When my little, baby brother drags me and pulls me and moans at me,
When other people kick us.

Our lock is made out of strong glass
And it is small
Our key is made out of glass and when you turn it it glows.

Our box is made out of strong glass and it has silver patterns on it
And (name) and I are going on a rocket and we're going to leave it on Venus.

The ideas in this second example show evidence of the children's understanding of the structure, but they require fine tuning. However, a fourth lesson on this same poem might have stretched the children's interest. Thus the editing was due to happen when the children were next in the ICT suite.

Aidan, lesson 3

Children organised taking account of available resources, Hay McBer, 2000

Introduction planned according to the needs of the developing writer,Berninger & Swanson 1994

Section focus	Objective	Activity
Text and sentence level Stimulus *The Magic Box*, Kit Wright	*To use structures from poems as a basis for writing by extending or substituting elements, inventing own lines and verses (Year 2, Term 2, T 15)*	Review of progress so far with part written poems Discussion of effective features of writing Discussion in pairs, related to next section of the poem – what the box is made from and where it will be kept
Paired Writing	*To use structures from poems as a basis for writing by extending or substituting elements, inventing own lines and verses (Year 2, Term 2, T 15)*	Composition of remaining parts of poem
Plenary		Review of successful work, discussion of vocabulary choice Reading two new poems

Flexibility with content of introduction, combining reading with writing.Wray *et al.* 2002, Hall & Harding, 2003

Focus on a single objective to scaffold success; learning intentions clear to children. Black *et al.* 2003, Topping & Ferguson, 2005

Discussion grows from high expectations Hay McBer, 2000

Talk for writing, Verhoeven, 1994 Kotler, A., Wegerif, R. & Le Voi, M., 2001

Text given three days to develop, Derewianka, 1990

Consolidation, introducing more stimuli to motivate, OfSTED, 2002a, Berninger & Swanson, 1994

Figure 7.3 Aidan, Lesson 3.

In this way Aidan would be able both to maintain interest in the poem and to revise their skills of editing using a word-processor. The next Literacy Hour would introduce a new poem.

To finish his plenary, Aidan switched attention completely to what seemed like two quite different poems. He and one of the children performed the first, taken from *Please Mrs Butler* by Allan Ahlberg. Although different from *The Magic Box*, this poem uses repetition as a device. The second poem was *Life Doesn't Frighten Me At All*, a poem by Maya Angelou. This text explores potentially frightening things that don't frighten its author. In presenting these two poems Aidan was reinforcing poetic language with one and demonstrating an alternative to locking away fear with the other. The choices looked very different on the surface but actually demonstrate how with careful planning a teacher can maintain interest with what looks like something new and at the same time support learning for a current objective. There was no overt reference to how these two poems worked in this way but to the trained observer their choice was an interesting one.

CONCLUSION

Aidan's strengths as a teacher of literacy have been mentioned throughout this chapter. To summarise, his teaching was characterised by the following features. He kept a very tight focus on his objectives while he was teaching; activities were also very closely matched to the intended outcomes for the lesson. In particular, he ensured that the introductory activities effectively scaffolded success in the independent activities. Aidan knew his children well and carefully used his supporting staff to provide a teaching and learning environment that maximised potential pupil progress. He understood the crucial place of oracy in developing the children's writing skills, in developing their spoken English and in supporting them with their ability to read for inference. Most importantly, he had the confidence to use the NLS in the way he knew suited the needs of his pupils. Thus, although his lessons bore quite a close relation to the prescribed pedagogy for the NLS, they were driven by self-reliance and informed choices that transcended printed guidance.

8 Bridget

BACKGROUND

Bridget had been teaching for 28 years and had only recently moved to Ballard Primary where she had taught for 2 years. She had a degree in English and a PGCE in secondary teaching. During the past 5 years she had taught every year group in Key Stages 1 and 2 apart from Year 4. Bridget's training was originally as an English teacher at secondary school level. After 6 years of secondary school teaching she moved to teach in primary schools because she was interested in why pupils came to her with so little motivation for writing. She worked, during the early 1980s, in a 'progressive' primary school and said that this experience, and the influence of its headteacher, remained a profound and positive effect on her current practice.

Bridget was the science coordinator but had held posts of responsibility for English and as deputy headteacher in previous primary schools. She was attracted to working at Ballard Primary because she wanted to see how the school managed to achieve such very good results in literacy considering its intake.

There were 30 in her class, which reflected the ethnic mix of the school as a whole: approximately 70 % Bengali, with the remaining percentage being mostly white indigenous children and a small number of Somali children. The children were considered the higher achievers in the year group and all were predicted to attain Level 2B or above at the SAT in 2003. Thus, although the majority were bilingual, they differed from the class in Anderson Primary where more pupils had beginner levels of fluency. This difference is apparent in the content and progress of the lessons. Placed together, the two teachers provide a very valuable insight into how pedagogy changes for increased fluency and ability.

Bridget was generally positive in her opinion of the NLS. Its aims were clear to her and she felt that it had enhanced her teaching skills. This was particularly interesting given that, of the three teachers studied in this book, her practice conformed least to the model that the NLS prescribes. In discussion it emerged that Bridget liked the division of word-, sentence- and text-level objectives in the NLS but felt free to teach these in ways she would have used prior to the implementation of the NLS.

She was much less positive about the planning requirements for NLS and felt that the amount of paperwork teachers are expected to produce inhibits progress of the NLS generally. She disagreed that the NLS had led to increased attainment in reading in her class, and was unsure about its impact on writing. Moreover she was concerned by the effect of whole-class interactive sessions on children who are difficult to motivate and felt that the NLS had done little to engage unmotivated pupils. This response was based on her experience of delivering the NLS in two schools.

Bridget felt that her delivery of teaching for reading and writing changed when the NLS was implemented in 1998, but had evolved and returned to where it was pre-NLS. She enjoyed the teaching of specific genres of reading and writing but felt that creativity may have been sacrificed in order to teach children more technical aspects of language. In common with Aidan, she was sceptical about the importance of teaching children about parts of speech when the emphasis should be on the fun aspects of writing. In common with Aidan again, she was also less interested in focusing on so much nonfiction writing such as writing instructions. Ideally she would spend more time on story writing in order to enthuse children about both reading and writing fiction.

Like Aidan she felt that she had a sound knowledge of how to teach reading and writing but was aware that there is always room for improvement. Her responses indicated that her strength is built, to an extent, on her awareness of what she does and does not know. Earl *et al.* (2003) talk of the problem of teachers 'who don't know how much they don't know'. Bridget highlighted a range of issues related to the teaching of reading that she felt she could fine-tune further. These included classroom organisation for teaching reading and making teaching explicit to perceived weaknesses in reading. Her most successful training recently, she considered, had been a course on creative writing with children and training in the use of the Accelerated Learning Programme (Smith and Call, 1999). However, she considered that her teaching strategies were most affected by her own experience with children and their work. In other words, she started with the children and matched her pedagogy to their needs rather than to external guidance.

Bridget produced fortnightly crosscurricular plans in which she varied the amount of literacy covered depending on the overall topic. For example, she would plan to teach some technical aspects of language in a unit that has a history topic like famous people. In these fortnights she would teach fewer literacy lessons because there would be coverage of literacy in the learning for history. At other times, for example where the unit had a specific fiction focus, she would devote more time to literacy in order to build up children's understanding of that written genre. Choices were made all the time about which objectives were most important. Thus objectives were grouped together into units and those considered less useful to the children's current needs might be given less time or not covered.

Planning was largely carried out alone – as Bridget had the only straight Year 2 class – but involved dialogue with a range of other staff. Conversations with the teaching assistant took place daily after school. Further dialogue with the SENCO, IT co-coordinator and assessment coordinator was used as needed. Planning for the teaching assistant was varied according to the demands of the objective and the needs of the children. Bridget also used her teaching assistant for IT support where she felt less confident. All classes in Ballard Primary used interactive whiteboards as part of their teaching.

Phonics was planned for outside the Literacy Hour using a software program called OILS (Open Integrated Learning System, SuccessMaker by RM, 2002, see School Resources, p. 221). This took place during a half-hour slot each day and was used throughout the school, explaining the lack of any phonics teaching in Bridget's lessons. Speaking and listening were explicitly planned for in order to develop the English-speaking skills of the 70 % EAL children and the white UK children who came to school with poor speaking and listening skills and in order to incorporate talk for writing. Reading was planned for both during and outside the Literacy Hour and both for groups and individuals. Writing was taught as part of an extended writing session as well as during the Literacy Hour. Bridget considered that the Literacy Hour was more useful for teaching technical aspects of writing, or for short writing sessions such as the speedwriting observed in Lessons 2 and 3.

Bridget used a wide range of commercial resources for her literacy lessons. These include the *Cornerstones* literacy materials published by Cambridge University Press. Resources from this scheme include the picture for the story in Lesson 2 and the audio story for Lesson 3.

The use of other adults was not a key feature of Bridget's practice. There was a teaching assistant in the classroom in every lesson but he was relatively new to the job and was described as 'in training by me' by the class teacher. This does not mean that Bridget did not use her classroom assistant effectively – he was engaged with children during all parts of the lesson or creating resources when she preferred to teach children alone on the carpet. Nevertheless, the impact of the teaching assistant was qualitatively different from the other classes observed because the relative 'newness' of the teacher–assistant relationship meant that there was less of a pattern to the support the classroom assistant might offer.

Bridget used a range of summative assessments that were part of the school's system for monitoring pupil performance. Targets for children were not expected by the headteacher, Ms Bradshaw, at whole-school level; however, Bridget had individual targets for children 'in her head'. Targets were not written down but she felt she was aware all the time of where the children needed to go next and how they might best work towards this. She shared this ongoing, informal but highly informed system with Aidan. This is an important example of how experienced teachers, when left to make their professional judgements of children's needs, are able to plan effectively without recourse to time-consuming paperwork.

Reading books went home regularly and were changed either by the children or by the teacher. For her lower ability children Bridget used the commercial scheme Oxford Reading Tree (Hunt, 2003a). Homework was set weekly and parents were supportive with it. The class had about a 70 % return rate on homework, which was marked on Monday during class time.

Bridget considered that the key to success in raising literacy standards in her school lay largely with the leadership of the headteacher. She described her as a 'hands-on head' who took a detailed interest in the precise nature of how literacy was being delivered in school. A significant amount of money was spent on staff training; some of this was to enhance teachers' subject knowledge while other training was targeted to individuals specifically to 'give them a lift'. This careful investment in staff's personal and professional development had led to a strong and experienced staff team, which had not moved away.

Bridget also cited success as coming from the shared values and ethos that extended to the ancillary, peripatetic and even supply staff. An enriched curriculum that did not react to initiatives but assimilated them as needed was, she considered, vital to fostering and sustaining the motivation that led to sound learning in the school. Many experiences were built into the school year in order to replace what the children did not have at home. Bridget attributed further success to the combined experience of many members of staff who had been at the school for a long time. Freedom to teach using the most appropriate pedagogy, comparative freedom from paperwork and an investment in staff morale had meant that the school had a core of teachers who shared a collective ethos about learning and that these values were transferred to all newly arrived staff. Her comments remind us of the findings related to successful schools and to schools where the NLS was launched successfully; these schools were characterised by strong leadership and shared ethos that fostered confidence in using national guidance in ways that they saw fit.

THE LESSONS

Bridget considered that effective behaviour management was fundamental to the success of any learning. Her school had a strong emphasis on personal control of behaviour and spent time discussing and modelling positive behaviour with the children in PSHE lessons. Children knew their boundaries and were expected to control their own behaviour appropriately. For example, during lessons this teacher would refer to the most effective behaviours for learning with the expectation that children understood this.

Before lessons started Bridget always provided children with a reading or writing activity – at their tables – which they began as soon as they came into the room and worked at while she was taking the register. The activity usually reflected the lesson from the previous day and built on it to give children an insight into the current day's lesson objectives. It is particularly useful for a beginning teacher to observe how she incorporated these starter activities into her daily plan.

Also of interest to the developing practitioner is the fact that, on the whole, children in this class were not grouped for ability other than when supported by the teaching assistant who worked mainly with those children needing additional help. Children frequently worked in pairs, desk arrangements were fluid, and desks were not set in the traditional six-pupils-per-table groupings that have become common in primary classrooms. This showed the extent to which Bridget had already moved away from the guidance in the NLS, which assumed ability grouping for most lessons. Of the three teachers studied, she took least account of the 'clockface' approach.

As we observe Bridget, note how her lessons carry the same incremental buildup of knowledge that Aidan used to scaffold his pupils' learning. Note also that the expectations for these pupils are very high and that this teacher engages her class in some highly sophisticated discussions about their work and the reasons for their work. Her carefully focused teacher-talk, demonstrated in various transcripts throughout this chapter, was a particular feature of the success of her classroom.

LESSON 1 (TABLE 8.1)

The overview for this lesson immediately gives us evidence of how Bridget combined the objectives for NLS with what she knew of how her children would learn best. It is therefore not always the case that the objectives are taken straight from the guidance. This is true particularly of the word-level work where Bridget simply wanted to develop the children's vocabulary to support their poetry composition. In order to do this she concentrated on the children identifying adjectives; the fact that this is one of the technical terms given over to the Year 3 objectives is evidence both of her high expectations and of her confidence to select objectives that fitted the purpose of the lesson. The word-level objective on her plan for this lesson was one of the more generic and ongoing objectives related to children using their graphic and phonic knowledge in spelling.

In this lesson the overall plan was to target the same poetry objective we have just seen taught by Aidan in his third lesson; 'to use structures from poems as a basis for writing by extending or substituting elements, inventing own lines and verses' (NLS, Year 2, term 2, T 15). Thus, the children were to start with one poem and use it to help them in writing their own poetry. Aidan chose to focus very clearly on structures when he did this whereas Bridget planned for her pupils to write a new section to an existing poem. It is important to stop and analyse this difference.

The choice of approaches indicates a difference in interpretation of the objective, with neither being less valuable than the other. Looking at the

Table 8.1 Bridget, Lesson 1

Section focus	Objective	Activity
Prelesson activity	*To identify adjectives in preparation for poetry composition*	Thinking of words to describe a lion's movement, teeth and eyes
Word level introduction	*To identify adjectives in preparation for poetry composition* *Through shared and guided reading, apply phonic and graphic knowledge and sight vocabulary to spell accurately*	Review words from prelesson activity Discussion related to appropriate adjectives – fitness for purpose
Shared text *If You Want to See an Alligator,* Grace Nicholls	*To use structures from poems as a basis for writing by extending or substituting elements, inventing own lines and verses (Year 2, term 2, T 15)* *To identify and discuss patterns of rhythm, rhyme and other features of sound in different poems (Year 2, term 2, T 9)*	Reading the poem, discussing its features, rhyme pattern, stanza length etc. Looking for key adjectives describing the alligator
Independent work and guided writing	*To use structures from poems as a basis for writing by extending or substituting elements, inventing own lines and verses (Year 2, term 2, T 15)*	Identifying adjectives for the alligator's movement, jaws and eyes Creating a new stanza for the poem using these adjectives
Plenary		Performance of the poem with the addition of the stanza composed by three children in the guided writing group

objective it is in fact multifaceted. An experienced teacher can take an objective like this and identify the part through which he or she can best deliver learning. Conversely, new teachers may become bewildered by so many alternatives and feel that they have to teach the objective in all its manifestations in order to feel that they have 'done it correctly'. What both of these teachers show is that it may in fact be what is *not* written in the objective that matters most; what matters is that children can use the poetry of others to support them in writing their own poetry well. Furthermore, what matters is that children are encouraged to love and enjoy poetry – reading and writing it. The enjoyment that Bridget fostered in her children during this lesson and the way in which she delivered the steps towards writing is of much greater benefit to the creative process than the way in which she had chosen to read this particular objective.

PRELESSON ACTIVITY

We found Bridget's use of the prelesson activity as 'warm-up' particularly interesting. Use of a task during registration, which was directly linked to the plan for the day, meant that children were engaged with thinking about literacy from the moment they came into class. All three teachers had their children working at a literacy activity but in Bridget's case this was highly developed.

The overall aim for the fortnight was the production of a poem about a fierce creature. The task for this lesson was going to be looking for words to use in a poem about an alligator. As a precursor to this, the children had to look for words that would describe a lion. In order to help them with this task the children had a thesaurus to work from (thus covering a different objective in a meaningful way) and a printed word tree onto which they could write words they had found to describe the lion's eyes, jaws and movement. They were to fill these in and bring them to the word-level introduction.

A further interesting interchange came during this lesson preamble. Bridget spoke to the children about some work they had done the previous afternoon on Florence Nightingale. In his answer, one child recalled key facts about her but also made reference to his understanding of her importance because of what they were learning in science about nutrition. In praising him Bridget made reference to his answer being excellent because 'good learning is about making connections.' The way in which this school planned was already richly crosscurricular. Furthermore, Campbell Primary was already teaching its children to think in this way too. This is illustrative of the fact that, while we are looking only at what these teachers and their schools did with literacy, we must remember that they had a bigger picture in view all the time when they taught. They were driven by the need for their children to learn well and to understand and enjoy their own learning, rather than a need to fulfil the requirements of any particular guidance.

WORD-LEVEL INTRODUCTION

Of all the lessons taught by Bridget this conformed most closely to the traditional structure of the hour. This is because, in terms of this objective, a word-level introduction was appropriate. In an aside to us as she taught she said 'What I'm doing is getting some vocabulary into them. You can't write poetry without vocabulary.' As you read on, however, note that this word-level introduction was combined seamlessly with the shared reading so that children would have been unaware of the 'two-part' introduction.

Children brought their lion word lists from their prelesson task to the carpet to share in the introduction. Before starting, Bridget gave one of her characteristically detailed explanations which gave the children a sense of purpose for their work:

> 'Very quickly, I want us to share some of those words that we've been looking up. The next step is going to be that we'll read a poem together about a different creature and we're going to plan our work for it in the same way as this afterwards. So this is the model – this is the example for what you're going to do again when I introduce this new creature to you. So this work is important for getting ready for some work I'm going to ask you to do.'

As teachers we may well plan in this much detail in our heads. We know why we have ordered tasks in a given way. What we perhaps don't do is tell the children why. Bridget's explanation involved the children in understanding their learning in a much deeper way than they otherwise might have. This is important for all children but would have been particularly beneficial to those children with EAL who would have been working harder at understanding the task as presented in their additional language. Given a context for the task, their understanding was clearly supported further and they had a greater chance of success.

Discussion about appropriate words for the way in which a lion moves ensued. In the following extract we see another insight into how Bridget made the process of learning sit overtly on the surface of her delivery. She is listing the children's words on a whiteboard, and one child has given her the word 'glide' to describe the lion's movement:

> 'I think we'll leave glide off, because it's more about how something moves through the water.' Then she changes her mind and says: 'No, maybe when they first move towards something. Yes, I can see how we would use that. I'll put it into our list.'

She changes her mind in front of the children and shares her reasons for doing so. By doing this she is giving them a model for their own thinking in the creative process and demonstrating that her own decisions can be changed. Furthermore, she is accepting that the child who offered this word has had a different insight into how the lion moves, which is equal with the teacher's ideas. We will see later in the lesson that Bridget did not accept weak answers but the above example demonstrates the detailed level at which she was thinking all the time and the high expectations she had of the children in their word choices.

Following this initial discussion Bridget picked up the pace and moved on to words for the lion's eyes. As children came up with suggestions she would ponder them in the same way and give immediate feedback as to why they were more or less effective as choices. It was noticeable that she gave children time to articulate their ideas fully. Those children who were less fluent in English, or who did not understand the meaning of some of the words they had found in the thesaurus, needed time to explain in sentence form what they thought about the lion's features. Alternatively, where children were giving one-word answers, Bridget would encourage them to extend this to a descriptive phrase or sentence using the word.

SHARED TEXT

Moving on from the word-level discussion, Bridget read the children a lively poem entitled *The Alligator* by Grace Nichols (1994, see School Resources, p. 221). As they listened the children were enthralled by this teacher's dramatic and exciting delivery. As an aside at this point, we must never forget that – regardless of the objective – it is our role to entertain and inspire young children with our classroom performance. The 'on-stage' quality of the effective primary school teacher was highly apparent in all the teachers observed.

As the poem reached its climax the words 'RUN FOR YOUR LIFE!' were printed in capitals and the children were unable to resist joining in. They shouted this last line and then applauded excitedly at the end of a poem that they had found very enjoyable. They responded with comments such as 'I think it's wonderful!' and 'It's a genius poem!' Bridget responded enthusiastically with 'Yes, I think it's wonderful as well!' Interestingly, to the child who referred repeatedly to the poem as 'cool' she gave no response. Thus, in her behaviour she sent out the tacit message that formal and appropriate adjectives were worthy of a conversation but that slang was not part of the standard English accepted in the classroom.

At this point Bridget drew the children's attention to some features of this poem. Using an acetate sheet placed over the text, she identified where the verses began and ended. At one point a line stood alone that described the alligator rising up out of the water and it was here that children were to add their own lines later. This conversation about the poem's structure was characterised by Bridget's common feature of encouraging the children to respond confidently and to accept different responses. Thus, she explained that the single line could be seen as a verse and that it was fine to disagree as long as they understood what a verse was. 'This poet is kind of playing around with what a verse is.'

The conversation about the structure of the poem was full of technical words related to poetry writing such as couplet, triplet, rhyming, repetition and pattern. The children had already been introduced to all of these terms in earlier work on poetry and were expected to use them accurately. As they identified the verses they also noted the arrangement of three lines in sets with a repeated first line. Finally, Bridget focused on finding key words in the poem that described the alligator – these being 'big', 'wild', 'fierce' and 'mean'. This brought her neatly to her explanation of the task for the independent work.

INDEPENDENT WORK AND GUIDED WRITING

All of the children worked on the same task for this section of the lesson. In fact, Bridget always worked in this way. Expectations were high, although support was targeted where necessary for those who found reading and writing more of a challenge. The children were given a new word tree, onto which they were to write words that described the alligator's eyes, jaws and movement. They were given some starter words for each and had to find two more words using the thesaurus. The goal was to have words that would go into three sentences to create an extra verse for the poem they had just read. As they had already done this word-research exercise for the lion, minimal explanation was needed and transition to tables for working, mostly in pairs, was minimal. This reminds us of the very close match of introduction and main activity that characterised Aidan's delivery. In both cases learning time was maximised because children were so very clear about what they had to do.

Further evidence of Bridget's high expectations can be observed in the way in which she allowed children to leave to start their work. If she felt that they had not been listening she would ask them to tell her what they were about to do. If they could not, they had to return to the carpet. Also she prompted others with 'If you are walking away thinking, "I need to ask somebody", then don't move.' In addition to this safety measure, that ensured on-task activity during the group work, Bridget had a five-point dial on the wall at which she set the accepted noise level for the children: 'I want the noise level around one or two – that's quiet conversation about the work.'

To encourage the children really to think about their word choice Bridget explained, 'You are looking for the best words, just like Grace Nicholls. We're going to start to build the poem. We'll be playing around with the words.' Working with a group of six, she started by revising the use of the thesaurus with them. Then, as they each looked up one of her starter words, she was able to check individual understanding of alphabetical order when searching a long list.

The use of the thesaurus was not without its problems. On several occasions children went to look up words such as 'gnash' and 'gleaming', which were used for the alligator's teeth, and they were not listed with their alternatives. One child wanted to use the word 'slowly' in relation to the alligator's movement. Bridget encouraged her to look for something more poetic but the thesaurus presented her with 'gradually'. The teacher and pupil discussed whether a word that meant 'little by little' would accurately describe an alligator's movement. Having agreed that it wouldn't they decided together to use 'slowly' after all. This hitch in her planning – that the thesaurus was rather limited – could have been a problem. Instead, Bridget turned it into an opportunity to discuss word choice with the children further. She explained that sometimes our first choices for words are good enough and that the thesaurus does not necessarily present us with something better. Thus the children were given the idea that the thesaurus was a useful tool rather than something that would always provide a 'better' answer. This taught them to be discerning when making word choices for their poem.

Bridget also encouraged the children to think about word order. One child had chosen 'wicked and sinful' for the words describing the alligator's eyes. His teacher asked him to consider whether it should be the other way around. Having played around with these words he stuck with his first decision. Earlier in their conversation they had mentioned that the word 'wicked' in slang terms could mean quite the opposite of its original meaning. Bridget explained to this child that his choice was a good one because by writing 'wicked and sinful' there would be no confusion for the reader about the meaning of the word in this context.

Consider how sophisticated this seems as a conversation to have with 6 or 7 year olds writing in their second or third language. Such high expectations might be absent even in a monolingual classroom and stand as an example of just how high a confident and experienced teacher might take her pupils. It is not that she engages them with adult-level conversation where vocabulary and concepts are unfamiliar but that she has built up a sophisticated vocabulary with the children, which she uses systematically with them. They also understand how to question their own thinking. Through this they are able to converse with their teacher in a way that allows them to make connections in their learning.

Towards the end of this 20-minute section, Bridget encouraged her group to start forming sentences from their chosen words. She identified three children who would create a sentence for either the alligator's jaws, eyes or movement and they wrote these down to share as part of the poem in the plenary. This took her group beyond the work of the rest of the class, and allowed her to present a model of children's work that would support the following day's writing.

PLENARY

This was a brief plenary but in it Bridget managed to recap, reinforce and further enhance children's learning through the use of the writing model. This highly efficient use of the smallest of time slots was a characteristic of all three teachers. They all used the plenary effectively, even if only for 3 or 4 minutes. Before moving into the poetry performance she explained the shortcomings of the thesaurus so that the whole class would understand the point she had made with her group:

> 'We've had a very busy 20 minutes because we were looking up six words, trying to find interesting ones. Some of the words when we looked them up, like "slow", didn't have anything else in the thesaurus better to use, so we went back and we used slow. You get used to the fact that sometimes you find a good word and sometimes you stick with the word you already know.
>
> 'What we've come up with, because we're resilient and we just kept going even though it was a bit tricky, is three sentences to fit in here' (points to part of text where one line sits alone). 'So first of all we need your help to read up to here, and then we're going to have these three to read their sentences.'

The class then read the poem together and the three children from Bridget's group added their very impressive lines:

> 'The alligator's eyes are wicked and sinful.'
> 'The alligator's jaws are savagely powerful.'
> 'He moves, blundering and awkward.'

The longer term objective was for the children to write their own poems about fierce creatures. This lesson ensured that they understood a great deal about how to work on ideas, how to incorporate their ideas into sentences, how poetry differs from prose and how to use effective poetry writing techniques. Their success was further supported by the fact that they were not expected to move straight to writing a finished product. Even as the lesson finished and children were tidying away, Bridget showed a group her holiday pictures of a 'muddy, slushy river', which had featured in the alligator poem.

Note how the children's writing is of a very high quality – just as the poetry was in Aidan's class. This provides us with another example of how, when children are given a small amount of text to produce, they can concentrate on well chosen words. In this way they learn to use language well and to make good choices in vocabulary usage and in sentence structure. Rather than having to produce a whole poem in one session, something that might have been characteristic of early interpretations of the Literacy Hour, they are given time to build up their text incrementally. Thus they potentially learn more from creating one high-quality piece of text over a week or a fortnight than churning out more on a daily basis. Moreover, they even come to enjoy it and feel a huge sense of satisfaction. Remember the role of motivation in Berninger's model (Berninger and Swanson, 1994) and for Derewianka's (1990) pupils? This teacher, and Aidan, show us, in their different interpretation of one objective, how motivation and enjoyment provide a master key for success.

Bridget, Lesson 1

Preparing for writing with choice of vocabulary, Derewianka, 1990

	Section focus	Objective	Activity	
Objectives not from NLS. Fit for purpose. Eclectic mix. Hall & Harding 2003	**Pre-lesson activity**	*To identify adjectives in preparation for poetry composition*	Thinking of words to describe a lion's movement, teeth and eyes	Planning use of vocabulary, Berninger, 1994
	Word level introduction	*To identify adjectives in preparation for poetry composition*	Review words from pre-lesson activity Discussion related to appropriate adjectives – fitness for purpose	Clarifying meaning, Cameron & Besser, 2004
Objectives relate to speaking, writing and reading. Share common purpose to support effective composition. Wray *et al.* 2000	**Shared Text** *If You Want to See an Alligator* Grace Nicholls	*To use structures from poems as a basis for writing by extending or substituting elements, inventing own lines and verses (Year 2, Term 2, T 15).* *To identify and discuss patterns of rhythm, rhyme and other features of sound in different poems (Year 2, Term 2, T 9)*	Reading the poem, discussing its features, rhyme pattern, stanza length etc. Looking for key adjectives describing the alligator	Direct teaching of conventions of written English for poetry, Cameron & Besser, 2004 Activity repeated to support well-chosen vocab.
	Independent work and guided writing	*To use structures from poems as a basis for writing by extending or substituting elements, inventing own lines and verses (Year 2, Term 2, T 15).*	Identifying adjectives for the alligator's movement, jaws and eyes Creating a new stanza for the poem using these adjectives	More repetition to ensure success for writing, Long, 2002
	Plenary		Performance of the poem with the addition of the stanza composed by three children in the guided writing group	Limited amount of writing. Concentration on quality and language

Children see purpose for writing, motivation enhanced , Berninger & Swanson,1994, Derewianka, 1990

Figure 8.1 Bridget, Lesson 1.

LESSON 2 (TABLE 8.2)

The objective for this lesson had been adapted from the NLS objective showing how this teacher had the confidence to offer children experiences that she felt were valuable rather than following the guidance rigidly. In the NLS the objective for fiction writing reads 'to use story settings from reading e.g. re-describe, use in own writing, write a different story in the same setting. Bridget had decided simply to ask the children to write a story using a familiar setting. This choice was supportive of the many EAL children in her class because they were likely to have visited a park and therefore more likely to be familiar with the vocabulary of the park. As she well knew, without talk there would be no writing. However, in addition to this, the writing activity lent itself to writing dialogue, as did the role-play beforehand. Therefore, the lesson also covered the objective 'to prepare and re-tell stories individually and through role-play in groups, using dialogue and narrative from text' (Year 2, term 2, reading objective 7). Interestingly, Bridget, like Aidan, had chosen to tackle this objective through speaking and writing rather than through reading.

Overall, this lesson showed a clear move away from the Literacy Hour common structure and demonstrated creativity in using the objectives.

Table 8.2 Bridget, Lesson 2

Section focus	Objective	Activity
Prelesson activity	*To identify vocabulary related to the park*	Using word maps, the children thought of words relating to events, feelings, sounds and activities in the park
Picture stimulus introduction – a busy park scene	*To use story settings from reading; e.g. redescribe, use in own writing, write a different story in the same setting (Year 2, term 2, T 13)* *To prepare and retell stories individually and through role-play in groups, using dialogue and narrative from text (Year 2, term 2, T 7)*	Talking about the activity in the picture Choosing cameos and predicting what the characters are saying or what might happen to them Role-play in pairs, using starter sentences, to think of dialogue between characters and to imagine events
Speedwriting	*To use story settings from reading; e.g. redescribe, use in own writing, write a different story in the same setting (Year 2, term 2, T 13)*	Writing some lines of the mid-point of a story from a given starter sentence
Plenary		Reading of some stories Discussion related to vocabulary choices Indication of how today's work will feed the next few lessons' story composition

PRELESSON ACTIVITY

As in Lesson 1, this lesson was preceded by an activity during registration that allowed the children to consider some of the vocabulary they might need for their stories. Using a format similar to the word-tree used for identifying fierce creature vocabulary, the children worked on word maps that asked for vocabulary related to the events, feelings, sounds and activities there might be in a park.

This particular lesson took place the day after Eid-ul-Fitr. This is a very important Muslim festival that celebrates the end of fasting for Ramadan. As a result many of the children were away and several of those who were in – including the Muslim classroom assistant – were tired. In order that the weary children could relax into their lesson more easily, Bridget was happy to let them just write about their Eid celebration to share later, rather than insisting on the prelesson task.

INTRODUCTION

During Lesson 2 Bridget's interaction with the pupils showed more use of one-to-one interaction and of role-play. Explanatory talk was less evident than in Lesson 1, although it was still significant, because the children were working chiefly through discussion and role-play to build up their understanding of how to use dialogue in a story. Word-, sentence- and text-level work were interwoven with the lesson moving further away from a traditional Literacy Hour structure. For this reason the analysis of the introductory section could not be split into two clear sections and it does not conform to separate sections for word-, sentence- or text-level work. The purpose of the introduction was for the children to use role-play to enable them to play with language and feelings that they might use in their story. Bridget felt passionate about the children having the opportunity to write stories and shared this excitement with the children.

Starting the lesson, Bridget referred to the craft of the storyteller and gave a characteristically detailed account of what they were going to do and why they were going to do it. She used a large and attractive poster of a busy park scene that was to be the stimulus for the children's story writing.

> Now we're going to look at this park, and this park could be the setting for our story. This is called Paradise Park. I've chosen this setting for our story because so many things can happen in a park.
>
> Remember when we write we have to do lots of choosing. We've spoken about this before, that you have lots of stories in your head. The thing that you need to do when it comes to writing a story is a lot of choosing. It really doesn't matter what you write – it matters how you write it – but what you write is up to you and you've got to do so much choosing, because all those treasures are in your head already.
>
> All those times you've been to a park, all those things that you've done in a park, all those things you can imagine doing in a park, they're all there in your head already. The business of the storywriter is to choose some of those things to write down to make something interesting that other people might like to read – and that you will be pleased with yourself; making something out of all those experiences that you've had. If you are sitting there thinking, 'I don't know a park', that doesn't matter. You can look at this picture and take all those things that you might do in the playground with your friends, and put them into a park setting – all those events, all those people, can just be in the park.

To start the children thinking about their park story Bridget got them to tell her what they most enjoyed at the park. If they offered one-word answers she would engage them in a dialogue that demanded more complex sentences. Where they had difficulty expressing themselves she would model the sentence for them. For example one child wanted to tell her two things but was unable to string them together coherently. Bridget, in saying to him, 'I would

ke to get some ice cream first and then I would like to go for a swim in the
ool,' was demonstrating for him the use of ordinal language and of simple
onnectives. As we discussed in the chapter on EAL, it is those small, 'every-
ay' type words that provide a sizeable obstacle to fluency in a new language.
n this instance the teacher was also giving the child support for his sentence
rmation in the same way that a parent might for a child when learning his
rst language.

Turning to the picture, Bridget asked the children to describe what they
uld see. As each answered she asked them for more information. 'The slide?
Go on, say a bit more about the slide.' The focus of her input throughout
is lesson was on using enough words to make a clear picture of something
nd on choosing the right words; in other words her focus was to enhance the
ildren's use of language in their writing.

Her next task was to ask one child to choose one very small detail in the
cture for the children to discuss. For this she had a coloured acetate sheet,
ith a hole in, which she could place over the larger picture in order to make
'peephole' onto the smaller picture. A scene was chosen with two children
n a seesaw and what may have been a mother watching. Bridget insisted that
e child be precise in exactly which parts of the scene she wanted on show.
e explained to the child that the picture would tell a different story depend-
g on who was in the cameo. The child chose to show only one of the children
n the seesaw – a girl up high in the air – and the mother standing beside her
t looking at the seesaw child not in the peephole. The rest of the class then
d to imagine the 'story' behind the mother and the girl high up on the
esaw. Observe how this was handled:

'So, what we've got is a little girl up high on the seesaw, and there's a lady. She's
not looking at her child, she's looking at the other child and there's some red on
her cheeks. If you are sitting close by you can see that she's got a certain look on
her face. Her mouth is turning down. What does she look like?' (A child looks
and decides that she's cross.)
    'Yes, I think she's cross.' (Another child says, 'I wonder why she's cross?') 'Yes,
I wonder why she's cross. If you could ask her you would say, "why are you cross?"
And what do you think she'd say?'
    Child: 'I'm cross because, the child's mum says, "Let's go home and buy an ice
cream." But the child said, "I want to stay on the see-saw."'

Notice here how the child speaking finds it hard to say what the Mum is
ying; she describes the situation instead. She has also described what the
other is saying to the child who is not in the picture. Bridget picks this up:

Teacher: 'Is she cross with this child here?' (pointing to the child on the seesaw).
'There's only one child in the picture which (name) chose and Mum's not looking
at this girl. What you are doing is you are imagining something that's happening

out of this picture. That's because you've got lots of stories in your head but we want to try and find the story that's for this picture. That was very good, the reason why she is cross, but have a think. She's not looking at this child so she's not telling her to go home, is she?'

In order to counteract both the problem the children were having in thinking of dialogue and the problem of them straying outside the picture in terms of plot, Bridget moved the children on to role-play. She asked them to work in pairs where one was the Mum and the other was the little girl. The children were then able to create dialogue but made the same error in describing a plot that involved the unseen child. Bridget moved the peephole, in order to include the boy at ground level on the seesaw, and allowed the children to work with a part of the picture that made their story-telling flow more readily.

This peephole process was repeated with a second cameo from the larger picture. This time it showed a woman sitting on a park bench eating her sandwiches, but a flock of birds was pestering her by sitting on her head and shoulders. In this part of the introduction, Bridget focused very closely on the appropriate use of adjectives the children might use to describe events in their story. She asked the children how they felt that the woman was feeling about the birds. One child thought that she might be 'terrified'.

Bridget: 'Do you think this lady is feeling terrified?'
Child: 'Yes, she's feeling hungry and the birds won't let her eat so she's feeling terrified.'
Bridget: 'OK, let's think about terrified. Just for a moment, imagine that some birds come and land on your head and your shoulders and you're terrified. What do you do? Quick! Act it. The birds are landing on you – show me terrified.'
Child acts.
Bridget: 'No, you look slightly annoyed. Who can show me terrified?'
Another child comes up.
Bridget: 'That's a terror face, but you still don't look as scared as terrified.
    'If she's terrified let's turn on a sound. Make a sound of being terrified.' (Children scream.) 'Yes, there would be some kind of shrieking going on. What sort of movement would there be? Show me with your hands, and then show me with your legs.'
    'Do you know the first thing I would do if I was terrified would be that I would jump up off that bench. None of you have jumped up so I suggest you aren't terrified; I suggest you are a bit annoyed because the birds are eating your packed lunch. Terrified, we would have a shriek and jump up – that's terror.'

Here we see the attention to detail and the demanding expectations of the teacher. Rather than being pleased that a child with EAL knows an adjective like 'terrified', she pursues its use and persuades the class to see it as inap propriate. Practice of this kind will have been the cornerstone of this school's very high SAT results. Children were not taught so much to pass the test but to write well and to really think about their vocabulary choices and their meaning. These children were thinking in highly sophisticated ways about their use of language. Interestingly, in several of the lessons observed they were able to produce much higher quality written output than their spoken English suggested they were capable of producing. These children were unlikely to mature with the disadvantages in their writing observed by Cameron and Besser (2004) among Key Stage 2 EAL pupils. Teacher–pupil dialogue in this lesson shows how the teacher can take account of children's problems with prepositions and other 'small words', their use of formulaic words and their choice of figurative language.

SPEEDWRITING

'Speedwriting' was a technique for teaching writing that Bridget had learned from one of her recent courses in literacy; a course that was independent of any NLS training. It was simple, but unusual in the context of the classroom practice for literacy at the time. For one thing, it did not involve ability grouping of any kind, and for another, it did not last the required 20 to 25 minutes of the Literacy Strategy's proposed arrangement for independent work. Children simply wrote independently, mostly in silence and for a very short period of time – perhaps 10 minutes. The idea behind it was to allow children to write down their thoughts without interruption straight after their role-play and discussion. This meant that thoughts emerging from the speaking and listening period could be committed straight to paper. The writing was only over a small amount of text – in this case, part of the story following on from a starter sentence – and children were encouraged to focus on their choice of language rather than worrying about spelling or punctuation. This tight focus on producing high-quality text, following talk for writing, mirrors the practice of Aidan in his second lesson where children were also writing dialogue. It also demonstrates a deep understanding of the full range of processes involved in text production, thus working towards some aspects of Berninger's model of developing writing (Berninger and Swanson, 1994).

The children were given the starter sentence 'Suddenly I heard . . .' They were to carry on from this line and to write some story related to the scenes they had just been exploring in the park picture. Some wrote about the birds eating their sandwiches while others moved into new plot lines. Bridget and her teaching assistant moved between the children supporting as necessary. As she spoke with the children her commentary would be related to word, sentence and text levels. She was ensuring that the children were connecting all the different parts of their learning as they wrote, rather than narrowly focusing on the objectives of setting or of using dialogue. As we have said before, her aim was for her children to write well and in order to do this she knew that they needed to see the coherence between features of written text. This capacity to make connections for children when teaching reading and writing was recognised by Wray, Medwell, Poulson and Fox (2002) as they distilled the key features of effective teachers of literacy. The extracts below – each one made to a different child about his or her work – demonstrate this in action:

'Excellent, well done, very exciting language there. You haven't just said the sound, you've said what type if sound it was.'

'No, you haven't finished you're only in the middle. You can't just wake up and it's the end. Are you the man sitting on the bench? OK, so you wake up and what is it you see when you open your eyes? Remember we talked about the birds all around him?'

Reading a child's work, Bridget noticed that she had written something about the bird eating the children and asked for clarification:

Teacher: 'Do you mean the children's lunch or the actual children?'
Child: 'He ate the children's head.'
Teacher (in overawed whisper): 'That's terrible! That is truly terrifying!'
Child: 'And then they called the ambulance.'
Teacher: 'So do you mean they just had a peck at the child's head? Because there's no point calling the ambulance if the child's head is gone is there? Well done, that's a good start, you keep going.'

'That's very well organised writing, well done. Remembering to put your full stops in is a good idea. We need to think where the sentences might be even if we're not worried about the spellings.'

'What noises tell us that something or somebody is frightened? What do people do when they are frightened? What noise would you make? Just tell me first of all, you don't need to write it down.' (Child responds with 'Go away birds.') 'So would that just be in a normal voice? How would a frightened person say that? Let's look in the thesaurus for words other than "talk" – we need a word that's going to take you further.'

Notice how all of the above differ. Although Bridget has a focus on setting as her objective she knows that the children are automatically considering setting as the introductory activity and nature of the writing task have done that for her. Thus she is able to concentrate on the quality of the whole text according to individual need rather than worrying about whether the setting is clear. To a trainee teacher the NLS objective for story setting might well seem to indicate feedback during the independent activity related to setting. She might feel that this is the only aspect of the story on which she should comment. Observe, then, how this experienced teacher has decided that the setting is not such an important feature that it need dominate her input for the children. By the time the children write, it is a given. This is a particularly stark example of how this teacher was able to use the NLS as a framework, but to move away from an objective and towards something much more creative, when the objective was not important for individual progress.

PLENARY

Again the plenary was very brief, but an important opportunity for children to share their work and for their teacher to further discuss language choice in relation to dialogue. Her opening talk makes her intentions for the lesson, and for subsequent lessons, clear:

> It doesn't matter if it's not finished because we're just concentrating on a little bit of the story today. We didn't want to start with 'One day we went to the park . . .' because that would have been boring. This is going to be much more exciting. If you've written anything then well done because it's not easy. You've made some choices and you've written them down.

Note how she refers again to the craft of the storyteller and is able to excite children by giving them a sense of themselves as part of the rich history of storytelling. Now observe the writing of one 6 year old, whose home language was Sylhetti/Bengali, during the 10 minutes of speedwriting:

> Suddenly I heard a crack, it was an earthquake,
>   'Hurry up children it's an earthquake!', Mum yelled.
>   'We are coming Mum.'
>   We quickly jumped in to the car. Dad was already in the car.
>   'Quick Mum, get in the car, its coming towards us,' the children screamed
>   Luckily we drove away in time.

After the child had read aloud Bridget explained that she and this child had worked on some of his word choices but she also praised him for his use of 'luckily', which was spontaneous. The teacher explained to her class how the use of the verbs 'yelled' and 'screamed' had been better choices than 'said' or even 'shouted', as they sounded urgent and panic stricken. In this way she provided the model for children who were to continue writing the next day. Thus, a 4-minute plenary contained the essential recap (the craft of story writing), celebration of children's work (three children read theirs aloud) and movement towards future work with a modelled example as scaffold. This serves to underline the crucial importance of the plenary, however brief, in synthesising the lesson's objective into outcomes.

Bridget, Lesson 2   Exploration of language before
                                                         writing, Verhoeven, 1994

Use of own
objective.
Combining NLS
reading and
writing
text level
objectives,
Hall &
Harding,
2003

Section focus	Objective	Activity
Pre-lesson activity	*To identify vocabulary related to the park*	Using word maps, the children thought of words relating to events, feelings, sounds and activities in the park
Picture stimulus introduction – a busy park scene	*To use story settings from reading; e.g. re-describe, use in own writing, write a different story in the same setting. (Year 2, term 2, T 13)* *To prepare and re-tell stories individually and through role-play in groups, using dialogue and narrative from text (Year 2, term 2, T 7)*	Talking about the activity in the picture Choosing cameos and predicting what the characters are saying or what might happen to them Role-play in pairs, using starter sentences, to think of dialogue between characters and to imagine events
Speedwriting	*To use story settings from reading; e.g. re-describe, use in own writing, write a different story in the same setting. (Year 2, term 2, T 13)*	Writing some lines of the mid-point of a story from a given starter sentence
Plenary		Reading of some stories Discussion related to vocabukary choices Indication of how today's work will feed the next few lessons' story composition

Extensive use of
talk for writing,

Verhoeven, 1994,
Kotler, A.,
Wegerif, R. & Le
Voi, M. 2001

High expectations
in discussion of
word choice,
Cameron &
Besser, 2004

Appropriate
scaffolding
ensures
focus on the
objective
Black *et al*, 2003

Plenary consolidates learning. Purpose of activities
made explicit in wider context of week's
Work, OfSTED,2002a, Black *et al*, 2003

Figure 8.2 Bridget, Lesson 2.

LESSON 3 (TABLE 8.3)

This lesson was the first in a 2-week series of lessons during which the childre
would produce their own story based on a traditional tale. There were som
similarities between Lessons 2 and 3 in that both dealt with different aspect
of story setting. Lesson 3 was an introduction to stories from other culture
and involved the children listening to the story of *Unanana and the Enormou
One Tusked Elephant* (Mayo, 2002, see School Resources, p. 221). This lesso
departed so far from the standard clockface approach that it is meaningles
to break it down into separate sections for commentary – it being more
series of activities that built towards another speedwriting slot. There wer
clear word-, sentence- and text-level objectives to the lesson but they wer
interwoven across the activities so that children made connections across thei
learning throughout. The 'introductory' activities spanned 40 minutes; th
writing activity was 10 minutes of independent speedwriting and the plenar
lasted 5 minutes.

In this African story, Unanana, a strong-minded woman with two beautifu
children, builds a house, against the advice of others, in the road along whic
elephants travel through the forest. Teacher-talk was quite different from th
time spent on each interaction type in Lessons 1 and 2. There was a reductio
in the time spent on one-to-one dialogue and a greater percentage of tim

Table 8.3 Bridget, Lesson 3

Section focus	Objective	Activity
Prelesson activity	*To use story settings from reading; e.g. redescribe, use in own writing, write a different story in the same setting (Year 2, term 2, T 13) (Year 2 range for fiction includes reading stories from other cultures)*	Reading a précis of the story to be heard in shared reading
Introduction Text – *Unanana and the Enormous One-Tusked Elephant*	*To use story settings from reading; e.g. redescribe, use in own writing, write a different story in the same setting (Year 2, term 2, T 13)*	Listening to the story twice; recording adjectives and predicting what will happen next Talking partners ×2
Speedwriting	*Ditto*	Writing what happens next in the story
Plenary		Choosing one well-formed sentence to read aloud Discussion of what makes the children's text interesting

pent on interaction with pairs. This is because Bridget used paired work everal times during the lesson in order to encourage discussion about possible plot development. Overall there was less teacher-talk in this lesson than in the others because Bridget gave children time to explore the plot on their own and, noticeably, left them largely to their own devices during the independent writing. This demonstrates a progression in her expectations of the children's abilities as writers. During Lesson 2 speedwriting was perhaps a new technique, which required some teacher management. By Lesson 3, a month later and closer to the SATs, Bridget was able to leave the children to work largely unassisted but to produce the same high-quality work. Note, however, that she had not reduced the amount of time given over for talk for writing. In fact, this had increased.

INTRODUCTION

Observation of the introduction for this lesson reveals Bridget in characteristic mode; she used very detailed explanations of how the lesson was going to progress so that children had a sense of purpose from the outset:

We're going to carefully listen to the story and then I'm going to stop it. At this point we are going to try and predict how the story might continue and that is going to turn into a writing task today. Don't worry about it, because what you are going to do is you are going to talk with someone else about how you and that other person might think the story will carry on and when you've done that you're going to change partners and talk with someone else. So, before you start writing, you're going to have had a lot of talking about what could happen. Not with me, but with each other. Not only will you have your own ideas but also you'll have the ideas of two other people to whom you will have talked for a few minutes. Then you are going to have a short writing task. I'll give you a writing frame, which will have the starting sentence on it for you and then you'll carry on to write for about 10 or 15 minutes.

She introduced the task related to the story listening thus:

Along the way of listening, there's something specific I want you to listen for, and that's adjectives. Because we've been doing some work about adjectives and what adjectives are; how they can improve your writing by making it more interesting. As you listen to this story, you'll notice some very interesting language being used in the description of certain of the characters who are animals. So to help you record your adjectives very quickly I've prepared a sheet of paper. If you don't get all the adjectives please don't worry. If you get just one that will be good. Don't worry too much about the spelling; the main thing for you is to notice that adjectives are being used and to spot where.

This was a lot to introduce all at once. The children had to remember to listen carefully so that they could predict the next part of the plot and to write down adjectives as they heard them. A teacher with a different style might choose to separate the tasks and still teach this successfully. Indeed, a teacher in training might be advised not to overload children's working memories in this way. However, by challenging her children to think of both at once Bridget was in fact encouraging them to explore the relationship between words, sentences and the text. In order that their working memories were not put on overdrive the children were supported with writing frames during the introduction and again for the speedwriting. The children's written output read at the plenary will demonstrate that this was successful.

LISTENING TO THE STORY

During their first listening children had to concentrate so that they could predict what might happen next. During the second listening they had to write down adjectives related to the characters that the storyteller used. The two activities combined meant that children had the plot well rehearsed in their heads and that they would be able to continue writing using the same language as the storyteller for their model. They had clear task frames that supported their success with the complex dual assignment of listening and responding simultaneously. Bridget indicated that she knew how difficult this was and gave them ideas for managing their tasks based on her own rehearsal of the activity the previous weekend. This was an interesting comment as it gave us an insight into the fact that, with nearly 30 years' experience, this teacher still gave her planning the level of detailed forethought a newly qualified teacher might need. Thus we have evidence of the fact that some aspects of teaching always remain high-maintenance if we are to deliver successful and well prepared lessons. Paperwork was not particularly detailed but consideration of and preparation of well-matched resources, a feature shared with Aidan, was pivotal to success.

Interestingly, the children did not record much in writing while they were listening but in the subsequent elicitation of their ideas by the teacher their recall of plot and descriptive vocabulary was good. They had understood and carried out the task albeit without a recorded outcome. While she was talking to the children about their adjectives some children gave incorrect responses, which were verbs or descriptive phrases. In common with the other teachers observed, Bridget maintained children's self-esteem through careful praise of effort but equally careful correction of misconceptions. She went on to explain why the adjectives were important: 'These words are important as you should be getting a picture of the animal in your head. For example, "a shy, gentle-eyed antelope", "a bold, yellow-eyed leopard".' Through this the children were given more information as to why the adjectives were important to the reader – to foster a visual image. Furthermore, this work drew on other word-level work they had covered in the previous week and for homework. This continuity of learning experience for the children meant that they were given several opportunities to deepen their understanding and assimilate this particular writing convention.

TALKING PARTNERS

In listening to the story the children have learned that, following the building of her house, Unanana had left her two children in the care of 'big cousin'. The enormous one-tusked elephant had come along and, made angry by the house on his path, had eaten the children and terrorised 'big cousin' who had scurried back into the house. Moving on quickly from the task looking at adjectives, Bridget paired the children up and asked them to discuss the next part of the plot with each other using a starter sentence 'When Unanana came back and found out what had happened . . .' At this point she did not invite children to share their ideas with the class first, they talked in pairs and possible plot lines were not shared until the end. This was a useful decision as it meant that children were engaged with their work for more of the time and less likely to lose motivation from having to listen any longer.

As the children talked, Bridget moved between pairs and intervened as necessary. Some were having trouble starting so she would offer them additional questions as 'warm-up': 'What would your mum do, if she came home and found you'd been swallowed by an elephant? What would Unanana do to get her children back?' Others were too quick to move the plot along and their teacher was equally quick to ensure that they adopted a more thorough approach to plot development. Observe the following conversation between Bridget and one of the pairs of children.

Bridget: 'So, she's just come back to the house, and she's sees big cousin looking . . .'

Child 1: 'He's hiding under the bed.'

Teacher: 'OK, so there's big cousin under the bed, what will she say?'

Child 1: 'Where are my children?'

Teacher: 'And what will big cousin say?'

Child: 'I tried to save them but they were gobbled up with the elephant.'

Teacher: 'What would she say then?'

Child 2: 'She would chop the elephant's neck!'

Teacher: 'Hang on, hang on, you've jumped there. She's still in the house with big cousin. The elephant's gone off – she's got to find him first. You don't want a big jump in your story.'

Child 2: 'She gets a big knife and then she goes and looks for the elephant . . .'

Child 1: 'She kills the elephant . . .'

Teacher: 'No, we've got to get her to where the elephant is first. How are we going to do that?'

There are several opportunities in this story for the children to end the plot quickly but they are not allowed to do so by their teacher. Notice that she does not correct their non-standard English for the moment as the thinking about plot progression is much more important. These microdecisions are part of the fabric of the effective teacher's repertoire when fostering good use of English in her pupils.

As this section of the lesson drew to a close, Bridget brought the class' attention to some successful use of English by describing the work of one of the pupils. 'I'm very pleased with D, because when he was explaining to me what Unanana would say when she returned to the house he said "Where are my beautiful children?" That's good because D is using the language of the story.' This served as a useful example for the children as to how they might unite their ideas for plot development with the language of storytelling. Perhaps a little too useful because by the plenary many children had reused this one example, but it is through the reuse of the effective model that children can start to be more inventive with later composition.

SPEEDWRITING

Observation of the speedwriting rendered far less for commentary than the same session in Lesson 2. For this section children were genuinely left alone to write for 10 minutes, other than where they were really stuck. Before they wrote Bridget explained that they would be able to use everything that they had developed during the introductory activities. In this way the fluency of her planning became clear to the children and they were automatically supported in starting their composition.

In order to start their writing the pupils were given another writing frame, which had the same starter sentence used for dialogue in the talk pairs. This allowed them to start quickly as they had only to think of committing their own thoughts to paper, rather than having to spell out the first words unnecessarily. This sheet was to become part of a collection of ideas that they would keep in a folder over the 2 weeks. This folder would be the collection of their thinking as they built up their full story. Thus, the children were introduced to the craft of storytelling as one where ideas might be stored but later discarded or revised; not one where stories were planned and written as a finished product in an unrealistically brief time. Perhaps, then, it comes as no surprise that the headteacher described some of the older children in the school as 'really gifted storytellers.'

As children sat thinking, Bridget gave them some help with additional questions and with the following observation:

> You've got to think about what kind of woman Unanana is. She's the kind of woman who would build her house in the middle of an elephant's road and take no notice of the advice so she's a strong woman. She's a strong, confident woman, but she will be very upset; possibly angry too.

This helped the children to think of both plot and character. Furthermore, Bridget ensured that children kept a realistic hold on the setting they were writing in. One child asked her what sort of 'gadgets' Unanana had:

> Not too many gadgets where she lives. Which gadget? Radar? I don't think so. These traditional stories tend to be set in times or places where they don't have gadgets. Think of all the animals she has got, and they can talk to her – we know that because they already have.

PLENARY

The following three extracts were the sentences produced by three children during their 10 minutes of writing alone. They indicate the progress made not just in this lesson but also in the combination of lessons leading up to this point. There is evidence of the thoughtful use of dialogue fostered during Lesson 2, as well as consideration of plot and setting that was the focus for this lesson:

Child 1: 'When Unanana came back and found out what had happened, she went to the big elephant. "Why have you eaten my beautiful children?" The big elephant said, "why were they playing in the middle of my road?" Unanana ran back and ran towards the big elephant, and hit the big elephant, with her one tusk . . .'

Child 2: 'She asked, "where are my beautiful children Big Cousin?" He said "they are gobbled up by an enormous elephant." "Whaat!" cried Unanana.'

Child 3: 'When Unanana came back and found out what had happened, she was fuming with anger. She nearly wrecked the house. Unanana was going to hunt down the elephant.'

In example 1 we see clever use of dialogue with the elephant's question as a retort to Unanana's question. Also note the sophisticated final phrases where the child uses commas in clauses to remind us of the elephant's one tusk – this is a classic example of the child mastering the genre. In example 2 there is evidence of the work carried out in Lesson 2 where the children had used thesauruses to find more exciting descriptors for their verbs – in this case the child has used 'cried'. Then in example 3 we see good use of story-telling language; this child has chosen to say not just that Unanana 'hunted'

Bridget, Lesson 3 Children given the opportunity to read the story, hear the story and identify vocabulary related to character, plot and setting, before being asked to write. In this way they develop knowledge of the type of language they are likely to need to use in order to write appropriately for the genre and setting. Derewianka, 1990, Berninger & Swanson, 1994

Choice of objective is from NLS, but lesson covers all aspects of writing development children will need for their independent writing. Lesson structure only very loosely matched to 'clock face', Hall & Harding, 2003

Section focus	Objective	Activity	
Pre-lesson activity	*To use story settings from reading; e.g. re-describe, use in own writing, write a different story in the same setting (Year 2, term 2, T 13)* *(Year 2 range for fiction includes reading stories from other cultures)*	Reading a précis of the story to be heard in shared reading	
Introduction Text– *Unanana and the Enormous One-Tusked Elephant*	*To use story settings from reading; e.g. re-describe, use in own writing, write a different story in the same setting (Year 2, term 2, T 13)*	Listening to the story twice; recording adjectives and predicting what will happen next Talking partners x 2	Language development through talk for writing. Verhoeven, 1994
Speed-writing	*Ditto*	Writing what happens next in the story	Small amount of text production. Focus on high-quality text and appropriate choice for vocabulary. Cameron & Besser 2004
Plenary		Choosing one well-formed sentence to read aloud Discussion of what makes the children's text interesting	

One objective used which is the tight focus for each part of the lesson. Activities very closely related across lesson sections. Plenary consolidates and develops Black *et al* 2003

Figure 8.3 Bridget, Lesson 3.

the elephant but that she was going to 'hunt him down'. This gives his story an altogether more interesting and menacing feel.

CONCLUSION

We have referred repeatedly to the fact that Bridget's lessons were the least like the standard pedagogy encourages for the Literacy Hour in 2003. However, the above analyses show that actually her thinking and planning used the *Framework for Teaching* really quite rigorously. Nevertheless, the lessons bear much more resemblance to the kind of creative teaching heralded by *Excellence and Enjoyment* than to the mundane rote-adoption of the teaching for reading and writing common in other schools at the time (Earl *et al.*, 2003).

Her lessons were successful because word, sentence and text level were closely interwoven to provide the connections children need to make in order to understand how to read and write. She also introduced and consolidated knowledge in incremental steps; this being in common with Aidan. There was a buildup of knowledge and understanding across the lesson, matched to creativity in the activities provided, which motivated children to work, so that the end product was of a very high quality and closely matched the desired learning outcomes for the lesson. She adapted her practice and interaction according to her objectives – as demonstrated by the change in emphasis of teacher–pupil interaction for Lesson 3. Her practice bore the hallmark of the confidently eclectic practitioners described by Hall and Harding (2003).

9 Clare

BACKGROUND

With 11 years' teaching experience, Clare was the most recently trained of the three teachers observed. She had a BEd in primary education and took French as her specialist subject. She was both Key Stage 1 coordinator and English coordinator, and held the post of assistant headteacher. During the previous 5 years she had taught all year groups from reception to Year 6; although she may have had her own class of Key Stage 1 children during that time, she was used on a continuing basis as a leading literacy teacher in the school. She was also involved with literacy projects at LEA level. Clare had received more literacy training than Aidan and Bridget – 12.5 days since the NLS was launched. At the time of observation she was more involved in delivering training than in receiving it. Of the three teachers her practice was perhaps closest to the prescribed Literacy Hour, however she felt she had the freedom to teach literacy in a style that suited her pupils.

Clare's class of 30 was as mixed ethnically and in terms of language need as the pupil profile of the school; an altogether more complex mix than that of the pupils in the other two schools. Predictions made in September 2002 estimated that 86 % of the pupils would achieve level 2C or above in both reading and writing at the Key Stage 1 SAT. During observations, the three Year 2 classes were set for teaching. This meant that the class observed was from the middle-ability set for Year 2 and was made up from three separate classes. This made no apparent difference to the success of each lesson because the pupil set had a good relationship with Clare and she was aware of the individual progress of each.

In common with both Aidan and Bridget, Clare agreed that the aims of the NLS were clear to her and that the NLS had probably enhanced her own classroom practice. Also in common with the others observed she was undecided about whether it had directly impacted on pupil attainment and pupil motivation. Furthermore she was undecided about whether the benefits of the NLS outweighed the costs in terms of teacher time and effort required to implement it. Her ambivalence towards the initiative is particularly interesting because she had had the most NLS-based training of the three teachers and was involved in delivering INSET for literacy both in her own school and others in her LEA.

This teacher, who had been a literacy coordinator since 1994, was critical of training provided by NLS consultants when the NLS first emerged. She was also aware that the training she delivered to her own staff at the time had the same 'staid' quality. She had ensured that more recent training had focused on aspects of teaching literacy that were more creative than that associated with the NLS. The school was involved in an arts and drama project with an outside team. This had led to story writing through art and drama, the use of guided drama prior to guided writing. It had supported the school's move to a much more crosscurricular approach to planning and delivery.

Clare felt that she and other teachers in her school had 'moved on' and that their use of, for example, *Progression in Phonics* (DfES, 2000a) or *Developing Early Writing* (DfES, 2000b) was likely to differ from the pre-scribed use of the examples given. She was critical of what she described as the NLS's tendency to 'presume ignorance'. In other words, she resented the assumption that schools were not already using the ideas presented in the above guidance when delivering word- and sentence-level work, prior to their publication.

Nevertheless, her criticism was tempered by recognition of where the NLS had affected her practice positively. Clare described the ways in which the NLS had made her adapt her classroom practice in the following terms:

> It has made it more specific, especially for word- and sentence-level work. I feel my approach is more balanced than it was before when I might have covered a lot more text level. However, I still have to make judgements about some things. It comes down to initiative. If the class don't understand an objective like 'compound words' I'll just leave it, but if it's something important like a particular phoneme then I'll give it more time.

The above demonstrates a common finding among the three teachers: they had the confidence to leave out objectives that they considered less important for developing children's skills as readers and writers. Clare went on to say that she had noticed how the NQTs she mentored did not have the trust in their own judgement, or the confidence of subject knowledge, to move on from an objective that might be relatively unimportant. It is just this dilemma that Earl *et al.* (2003) describe in their report; that those teachers who have suffi-cient subject knowledge can use the framework wisely but that less confident practitioners deliver a much less successful version of the objectives.

In common with Aidan, Clare spent part of each year team-teaching with colleagues who had either an EAL or an SEN focus. Other adults were famil-iarised with the plans at the start of the week and had set routines so that none of their time was wasted during the lesson. Clare felt that, with a good range of quality activities planned and targeted use of additional adults, chil-dren with SEN and EAL should not be excluded from making progress during the Literacy Hour. In order to promote the needs of children with EAL Clare planned specifically for speaking and listening using guided speaking and listening activities. This also supported white, indigenous children with poor language skills. Her interest and training in 'philosophy for children' informed some of this planning, and planning for guided reading. Through this children were taught to develop their use of questioning, their inferencing skills and their emotional literacy.

Teaching assistants were very much a feature of the success of Clare's lessons. Two other adults worked regularly in the lessons and were present for all three observations. One was a trainee teacher on a graduate teacher programme; the other was an experienced classroom assistant with a well established working relationship with the class teacher. The roles of each were clear before every lesson and they were engaged in supporting pupils through all parts of the lesson. Unlike Aidan's classroom, where additional adults worked in separate groups with their children, the other adults in Clare's classroom worked alongside the teacher during carpet and group times. They were noticeably engaged with children as soon as they entered the classroom, when, in common with the other classes studied, literacy activities started immediately and carried on during the register.

Of the three teachers studied, Clare's planning was the most detailed and used a standard NLS weekly planning format that the school had adapted for its own use. Remember that this school had only recently emerged from special measures and had therefore had to conform with planning and pedagogy in ways to ensure success in the eyes of the inspectorate. However, all weekly plans were stored on computer and used year on year. Thus, although planning was detailed, time spent creating plans was limited to annotating revisions to suit that year's cohort. Planning meetings were more about *how* the children would learn best, rather than what they would learn.

Reading was planned for both during and outside the Literacy Hour. Children were targeted for individual reading as needed – particularly boys whose achievement lagged behind that of girls. Clare also planned for paired reading with children from a Year 5 class. Planning for writing combined an hour's extended writing each week with the skills of editing and redrafting, which were delivered through the Literacy Hour along with other technical features of text production. Practice for the SAT was planned overtly and children were made aware of what they are doing. Weekly lessons, such as that for Lesson 2, taught comprehension skills for the SAT.

Individual target setting – particularly for writing – was very much part of Clare's practice, as it was for the school as a whole. As evidenced from Lesson 2, children had their own targets and they were referred to at the end of each guided writing session. The targets were very specific to the child. Clare felt that they motivated children because they represented small steps of incremental progress, which the child could achieve relatively easily. This differs from the practice of the other two teachers studied and is interesting because it highlights the fact that successful teachers may have very different ideas about effective pedagogy. These views will have grown from personal convictions based on experience, the needs of the children and the recent history of the school. Thus it is not surprising that attempts at generalising practice to a single model such as the NLS were automatically subject to differences in interpretation.

Children in this teacher's class took home their books three times a week. The choice was limited to those within a certain band that matched the child's current level of ability. Parental support was variable but the school worked hard at raising it by running reading clubs for parents, opening the library after school for parents to visit with their children and running projects such as 'Dads and Reading' which was led by the male deputy headteacher. Homework was set and tied to the class activities of the week but, again, return rate was variable and parental support was mixed. Clare felt in some ways that, although homework can contribute positively to children's progress, maintaining a flow of meaningful activities and finding the time to follow up the homework in class could present planning difficulties.

Clare identified a range of areas that may have led to the school's success in raising standards in literacy. One of these was the school's 'assessment literacy' (Black *et al.*, 2003; Earl *et al.*, 2003); SAT analysis was very detailed and led to very precise target setting. Highly developed use of teaching assistants who had a clear view of their role with individuals, groups and the class meant that the pupil–adult ratio was managed as effectively as possible. Crosscurricular planning through which the children were able to make links in their learning had supported a rise in attainment, as had additional phonics tuition and the use of extended writing sessions.

She considered that her school's success in teaching literacy had been rooted to a significant extent in the emphasis the school placed on the teaching of reading. This was particularly true of the time invested in developing their approach to guided reading – one of the weakest areas of Literacy Hour delivery nationally (OfSTED, 2002a, 2004). The school had modified its interpretation of the NLS guidance and moved forwards with it in the way that Earl *et al.* (2003) consider crucial if the NLS is to continue to have an impact nationally.

THE LESSONS

Behaviour generally was not an issue for Clare who used a considerable amount of praise during lessons. Expectations were clear in her class and throughout the school. She was keenly aware of their fundamental influence on effective learning. Referring to her mentoring of NQTs, she had noticed how fears about behaviour management could hamper creativity in the delivery of any lesson. Worried that the children might be too noisy or distracted if given stimulating tasks that required independence, newer teachers might opt for low-risk strategies and less creative lessons.

An interesting feature of Clare's practice was her constant reference to expected learning outcomes. In some ways this matched Bridget's focus on what effective behaviour for learning might look like. The children had sets of established expectations for a range of activities such as how to be a good listener or how to write a good sentence. At certain points within each lesson Clare would refer to these and consolidate children's understanding of them with concrete examples from their own work. Her very detailed attention to explanation and modelling in her introductions will become apparent as we observe her three lessons. Note how, although there were a greater number of white, monolingual English speaking children in Clare's class, her practice demonstrated the same clarity and combined word-, sentence- and text-level work that our other effective teachers have shown. This common ground serves as evidence to support our assertion that good literacy practice with EAL pupils is a highly valuable model for good practice with all pupils.

PRELESSON ACTIVITIES

In common with the other teachers observed for this book, Clare's pupils were engaged in a literacy activity before their lesson started. As she took the register and before the class split into sets with the other classes in the year group, children would have a task to do. This task would differ according to the day of the week and other work being covered in literacy. For example, children might be reading their graded reading scheme books or they might be engaged in learning new spellings using the 'look, say, cover, write, check' method. At all times, the children were kept on-task with teaching input from any other adult in the room that day. In this way both the children and the additional adults were engaged in the learning process from the moment they arrived in the classroom.

LESSON 1 (TABLE 9.1)

In Lesson 1 Clare's objective was to teach the children to identify story settings – both in the shared text introduction and during guided and independent work. This lesson therefore provides us with a comparison with both Aidan and Bridget who had covered a similar objective related to writing. For Clare, working with the reading objective, the interpretation of the understanding of story setting is much more literal and focused on the wording of the NLS objective. Aidan and Bridget had introduced stories from a range of settings and had discussed these settings in order to provide a stimulus for writing; their approaches were quite diverse.

This serves to illustrate how some separate objectives in the NLS are interlinked and need to work together. Clare's class was to tie its work from this

Table 9.1 Clare, Lesson 1

Section focus	Objective	Activity
Word level	*Phoneme /air/ and its common graphemic representation –are (Year 2, term 2, W 2)*	• Phoneme segmentation and counting • Reading in different voices • I-spy • Recoding following segmentation • Writing words
Text level *This is the Bear and the Scary Night*	*To discuss story settings; to compare differences; to locate key words and phrases in the text (Year 2, term 2, T 5)*	Reading the story and identifying words related to setting
Group work	*To discuss story settings; to compare differences; to locate key words and phrases in the text (Year 2, term 2, T 5)*	Range of activities relating to shared text. Matching settings with pictures, describing settings
Guided reading ORT – *Max Makes Breakfast*	*To discuss story settings; to compare differences; to locate key words and phrases in the text (Year 2, term 2, T 5)*	Identifying and describing setting details
Plenary		Working with one group, picking one well-constructed sentence. Discussing why the sentences were 'good' or 'very good' sentences.

lesson to writing that had a focus on story setting later in the week. The NLS's habit of filleting text comprehension and production into 'reading' and 'writing' does not always serve the inexperienced teacher well. These three teachers had made the links for their children instinctively.

WORD LEVEL

Word-level work in Lesson 1 consisted of a range of activities consolidating the children's understanding of the long vowel air (/ɛə/) phoneme /air/ and its common graphemic representation -are as in 'care' and 'stare'. A range of well-organised and attractive resources supported games that included reading words in different voices, an I-spy game, separating the words into onset and rime, and writing /ɛə/ words onto whiteboards. This rapidly changing activity-filled session (transcript below) kept children motivated and on-task and was successful because of the amount of explanatory detail that Clare included before each activity change, without losing pace.

'The trigraph we are looking at is this one' (shows -are) 'which is the /air/ sound. There are lots of ways to make the /air/ sound, and later in the week we are going to find out others. But today, we are going to concentrate on this one.

'I've got a list of -are words here. What we are going to do is break it down and then say the whole word. I'm going to demonstrate, and then when you think you can, you can join in.

'C-are, care; D-are, dare; H-are, hare. Now that kind of hare isn't the type on your head, it's the one that looks like a rabbit.

'Now, how many phonemes are in this word. S-t-are, stare? S-p-are, spare. S-c-are, scare.

'This time we are going to see if we can read the whole list of words from the top to the bottom without breaking them down. We're going to read them in a very posh voice, and I want to hear you pronounce the letters very carefully. Care, Dare, Hare, Stare, Spare, Scare. Oh Excellent, Jolly Good!' (Said with an affected accent.)

'This time we're going to do it in a grumpy voice and we're going start from the bottom and go to the top. Scare . . . [etc.] Very good and what really pleased me was some of you were looking at the words when I was pointing to them.' (All said in a grumpy voice.)

'This time we're going to do it in a happy voice and this time I'm going to point to any word I like in any order.' (This time children have to read alone.)

'OK, you're too good at that. I'm going to see if I can trick you in a game of I-spy. It's got to be one of the words on here.'

'I spy with my little eye a word beginning with h-. I spy with my little eye a word beginning with s-c-.' (As she did this she sounded out the initial phonemes rather than saying them, using carefully accurate pronunciation of sounds.)

'I still can't trick you out. Try this. This time I'm going to break the word so I might say something like h-are and I want you to all call back to me which word I'm saying.

'Excellent. I'm going to make it even harder. This time I'm going to call a word out and I want you to break it down into phonemes. Take care! – words like care have got two phonemes, but some of them have got three. Stair.' (Children call back s-t-air, etc.)

'We're going to do one last thing. Have a good look at those words. I'm going to give out the whiteboards and I'm going to turn the sheet with the words over to see how many you can write. I know you can read them but I also want to know if you can write them and spell them properly with a-r-e. What sound does this a-r-e make? (Child answers 'care'.) 'No, on its own it's "-are". It looks like "are" (as in "we are") doesn't it, which is even more confusing. When it's in these words it makes the -are sound.

'It doesn't matter if you don't remember them all, it's spelling them correctly that matters to me.'

Passes out whiteboards one between two. Helps pairs on the carpet as they try to write their list.

Noticing one child who has written a word with a different representation of the trigraph. 'Ah, now tell me that at the end, because "tear" is spelt a little bit differently.'

'Oh, very good. I'm going to write some of these up on the board, they are so good.

'That's a good one. You've got two that weren't actually on the list.

'Let's look at these words on the board. Let's see if we've spelt them correctly. How about this one, h-are, thumbs up or thumbs down? Yes, I'm going to give that one a big tick. What about this one? H-e-? No, there's something wrong with that word. I need to check through my work and correct this one, can you help me?' (Children give her correct spelling.) 'Let's read it now. H-are. Is that right? Yes, I'm really pleased that I've checked through my work and corrected it.

'What about this one? I think it's meant to say dare. Thumbs up or down? Down. What could we do to make it better?' (Child says, take that 'e' out, it shouldn't be -ere.) 'That's right because we're looking at the -are trigraph.'

As this word-level session progressed children were kept engaged by the rapid change in the type of activity presented. At times individuals were asked questions, but in the main the whole group was kept occupied with an intense focus on the trigraph for that day. Added to this, the two other adults in the room worked with predetermined individuals to support their needs. The use of the multiple spelling games approach and the focused use of other adults is reminiscent of the practice of Aidan. Consider also how Clare had not chosen to take phonic work out of her lessons; firstly, the children were 'set' so she knew that she could pitch work according to the ability of the majority and, secondly, she knew the importance of phonic work given the wide range of linguistic fluency in her class. In other lessons we will see evidence of Clare's flexibility in her planning for the Literacy Hour, as she did not always devote the first part of her lesson to phonics.

SHARED TEXT

Moving on swiftly from her word-level introduction – the pace was always tight and children were rarely given opportunities to lose concentration – Clare introduced the shared text for that day. With her objective of looking at story settings she had deliberately chosen a text that was simple to read but had multiple changes in setting – *This is the Bear* (Hayes, 1994). Thus, we see a recurring feature among our teachers; that they take great care in choosing the most appropriate resources to suit their objectives.

Starting her introduction Clare ascertained firstly that the children understood what a setting was – one child was able to explain this accurately to the rest of the group – and then asked them to predict what the setting of the text might be from clues on the front cover. Having started the children thinking about setting she introduced a task for them to do while she read; they were to put their hands on their heads every time the story changed. She read slowly and with much expression in order to bring the simple text to life and to give the children time to notice vocabulary related to the setting. As their hands went up to their heads she targeted questions to individuals that made the scene changes apparent for those who had not noticed them. In addition to this she uncovered words written up earlier onto her flipchart; these words were those related to the story settings so that, by the end of the reading, there was a list of setting types on display beside the text. This is another example of the attention to fine detail that will scaffold children's understanding during delivery.

INDEPENDENT WORK

As the reading ended, Clare moved swiftly onto the process of grouping children for the independent work. Here was quite a major difference between this teacher and those observed in earlier chapters. Unlike Aidan and Bridget, who most commonly gave children the same activity, Clare usually planned for a range of activities during independent work. The rationale was similar to her counterparts – in that activities related to the other adults in the room and the ability of the groups they were working with – but the difference in activities was marked.

For this lesson two groups had to match a set of mismatched pictures of settings from *This is the Bear* to written captions describing the settings. A third group had to match a sentence of their own to the pictures of the settings and another group, working unassisted, had to draw pictures in response to written descriptions it was given. A fifth group worked as a guided reading group with Clare, where input was also related to story setting. Through this description of the activities we can see that they were closely related to each other and to the objective. Subtle differences in the nature of the task were planned to take account of differing ability within the set and the availability of adults.

This was not the much-criticised carousel model adopted in the early days of the Literacy Strategy, where teachers provided one set of activities for the week and groups came to them on different days. The activities were not to be repeated because they were for that day only and for those groups only. This was differentiation at a very detailed level, which would allow children to make progress against the objective dependent on their stage of understanding and on whether they were working independently or with another adult. It also made sure that Clare was able to give her guided reading group the undivided attention that they needed. Differentiation of this quality came from a detailed understanding of her pupils that in turn grew from the assessment-literate culture of this school.

GUIDED READING

The children read a reading-scheme text titled *Max Makes Breakfast* (Hunt, 2003b). They read the text with approximately 90 % accuracy – showing the close match of text to reading ability required for guided reading. However, in common with Aidan, Clare's practice for guided reading was not that proposed by the NLS. Rather than have all the children reading simultaneously, children read one after the other and the teacher picked up teaching points and asked questions about the setting between readers. Those children who were not reading at any given time were asked to put up their hands if they wanted to say something about the setting. In this way her learning objective - to teach the children about story setting – was given prominence in the reading session and tied the reading activity to the writing activity carried out by the independent groups. Notice also that the task for the shared reading session, to indicate when setting changed, had acted as a precise model for how children were to work in the guided reading session, thus minimising the time needed for explanation and maximising teaching time.

Clare's characteristically detailed modelling for the children continued through the guided reading session. After reading the first page, where a girl was wrapping a present for her grandfather at the breakfast table, Clare asked the group to describe the setting. Having insisted on full sentences for answers and having given the children the opportunity to respond as fully as they could, she went on to expand an example for them in order to show them what level of detail could be possible:

Child 1: 'She's in the kitchen.'
Child 2: ' She's wrapping her Grandad's present.'
Clare: 'I'm going to say something. I'm going to say that you can see the leftover breakfast on the table and the plates haven't been cleared away. There's a clock on the wall so I know it's quite early in the morning – it's five past seven. There's a calendar and it's open at the month of June.

'So, do you know, if I was writing this story I might write some more details to make it interesting. I might say, "Kerry was wrapping up the present she had bought. She pushed all the breakfast things to one side. She opened the drawer behind her to get some sellotape and scissors. She looked at the clock on the wall and thought "oops, it's five past seven, I need to get a move on."'

Notice that her storytelling goes well beyond setting description and alludes to plot and character; in this way she shows us that her apparently literal interpretation of the objective is more fluid that it might have seemed at first. She is well aware of the limitations of a blinkered approach to producing narrative that tries to exclude all features other than the one in the objective.

The session continued and it was evident that the children were noticing more and more detail about the setting in each picture. One child, a pupil with EAL, drew his teacher's attention to the floor pattern and was praised not only for his observation but also for using the technical vocabulary appropriately. Clare commented:

> He's noticed some more detail about the kitchen, that it's got black and white tiles on the floor in a pattern, and he was using all the right words to describe it to me like 'setting' – he wasn't just saying the place he was saying 'the setting has changed'.

By emphasising why this child's contribution was a good one, Clare was giving other children an insight into how they might perform better. This commentary on how to learn effectively was particularly characteristic of Clare's and Bridget's pedagogic style but we will also remember examples of Aidan explaining why some children's use of English was good. This serves to underline how these three teachers understood that it was their job to enhance not just the children's learning, but their learning about their learning – their linguistic metacognition.

As the guided reading session came close to its conclusion, Clare, who at this point had worked uninterrupted with her group for 20 minutes, turned to the rest of the class and gave a demonstration of how her high expectations drove the pupils to succeed:

> You've got two minutes left for your work. By the time we finish I'll be expecting groups 1 and 2 to have finished sticking your pictures in neatly. Group 3, I'll be expecting you to have finished your pictures and I'll be looking at them to see lots of detail. Group 4, I'll be looking for lots of detail in your sentences as well. Lots of words to tell me where they are. If you have finished you should still be working quietly so that I can hear the readers, and you should be looking at your work to see how many setting words you can find.

As children came to the carpet for the plenary it was obvious that they had worked well on-task, had understood their tasks and had made tangible progress.

THE PLENARY

In common with Aidan and Bridget, Clare always ran a plenary. Like her counterparts these were usually no more than 5 minutes but were organised in such a way that the time was used very effectively to recap, to reinforce and to identify future work for the children.

One of the groups had been writing sentences to match scenes from the text used in the shared reading session. They were asked to find what they considered their best sentence to read aloud. In order to select this sentence they had to use the criteria for writing good sentences that their teacher had reminded them of during the introduction to their activity: that it had a capital letter, a full stop and that it made sense. In this way she was activating self-assessment in the children's responses to their own work. Furthermore, she used peer-assessment once the sentences were shared. Observe the following dialogue, which demonstrates this:

> Reads a child's work: ' "This is the owl who dragged the bear in the twinkly stars." Tell me why that is a good sentence.' (Child response: 'It makes sense.') 'That's right, it makes sense. If it made sense it would be a good sentence but this is a very good sentence – what makes it a very good sentence?' (Child response: 'She didn't say stars, she said twinkly stars.') 'That's right, she used an adjective. I think I'm going to use that in my stories, because if the stars are out at night time I can just picture them in my head, and that makes it more interesting to read about the setting. Well done.'

In this class, where children were trained to think analytically about their work, Clare was able to engage in self- and peer-assessment frequently. This allowed her to see just how much the children had understood because, Clarke (1998) informs us, we know that children 'know it' when they can explain things to us. This expectation that children could explain things was in fact a thread that ran throughout Clare's lessons from the introduction, where she would ask children to extrapolate the objective, through to showing their understanding of their tasks and finally to assessing how well they and their

Clare, Lesson 1   Use of systematic phonics training, Stuart, 1999, 2004

Section Focus	Objective	Activity	Multisensory spelling games, Long 2002
Word Level	*Phoneme /air/ and its common graphemic representation –are (Year 2, term 2, W 2)*	• Phoneme segmentation and counting • Reading in different voices • I-spy • Recoding following segmentation • Writing words	
Text level *This is the Bear and the Scary Night*	*To dicuss story settings, to compare differences; to locate key words and phrases in the text. (Year 2, term 2, T 5)*	Reading the story and identifying words related to setting	
Group work	*To dicuss story settings, to compare differences; to locate key words and phrases in the text. (Year 2, term 2, T 5)*	Range of activities relating to shared text. Matching settings with pictures, describing settings	
Guided Reading *Max Makes Breakfast*	*To discuss story settings, to compare differences; to locate key words and phrases in the text. (Year 2, term 2, T 5)*	Identifying and describing setting details	
Plenary		Working with one group, picking one well-constructed sentence. Discussing why the sentences were 'good' or 'very good' sentences	

Use of one objective across lesson sections for coherence.

Wray et al. 2002

Hall & Harding, 2003

Close match of intro and main activities. Reading and writing objective combined, Wray et al. 2002

Developing children's metalinguistic awareness, focus on small piece of text and effective vocabulary choice, Cameron & Besser, 2004

Figure 9.1 Clare, Lesson 1.

peers had done. Literacy standards in this school had been raised by a culture of high expectation that had melted into the fabric of classroom practice, as demonstrated by this teacher.

LESSON 2 (TABLE 9.2)

Lesson 2 started with a sentence-level focus – past tense -*ed* ending. Shared text and independent work then focused on writing character profiles. However, all sections of the lesson were related by the use of one text (*Kipper's Birthday,* Inkpen, 1994) which was common to the word-level introduction, the work on character profiles and to the independent work. Only the guided writing group had a modified task. Thus, in common with Lesson

Table 9.2 Overview of Clare, Lesson 2

Section focus	Objective	Activity
Sentence level	*To use verb tenses with increasing accuracy in speaking and writing, and to use past tense consistently for narration (Year 2, term 2, S 5)*	Reading *Kipper's Birthday* with past tense endings covered up. Considering what is wrong with the words that have been changed and what their common feature is
Text level *Kipper's Birthday*	*To identify and describe characters (Year 2, term 2, T 6)*	Adding to a list of key words that describe Kipper's character. Looking for evidence in the text to justify choices
Group work	*To identify and describe characters (Year 2, term 2, T 6)*	Comprehension questions related to shared text (SAT practice). Answers require increasingly higher order comprehension skills
Guided writing	*To identify and describe characters (Year 2, term 2, T 6)* *To use verb tenses with increasing accuracy in writing (Year 2, term 2, S 5)*	Task to describe their teachers in a way that someone reading the character portrait would know who they were speaking about
Plenary		Revision of difficulties with answering comprehension questions

1, sections of the NLS Literacy Hour were clear but objectives and activities were carefully interwoven to produce a coherent lesson where children were able to make connections across their learning.

It is important to note here that a key teaching point arising from this lesson does not appear as an objective. During the text-level introduction and during the group activity Clare was training her children to use their inferencing skills when answering questions. She encouraged them to look beyond the text in order to draw conclusions about Kipper's character and for the reasons for his actions. As the children were soon to sit their SAT comprehension paper, this was an important skill for them to learn in order that they could attain the higher National Curriculum levels. It is interesting, then, that although our children are tested for this skill, it does not appear overtly as an objective. Training and newly qualified teachers need very much to be aware of the difference between asking literal and higher order questions of children during reading comprehension and this example lesson provides a useful insight into how this might work.

SENTENCE-LEVEL INTRODUCTION

Clare's intention for sentence-level work on her weekly plan had been different from the one observed. In days previous to this lesson Clare had noted that many children were habitually leaving off the -ed ending from verbs in the past tense so that they remained in the present tense. Thus she chose to adapt her planning and to focus on this very important feature of the children's writing, which affected grammatical agreement in their sentences.

Changes like this require confidence in the practitioner. Those new to teaching might worry that they should ensure coverage of the objectives and they are not wrong to do so. However, such 'coverage' cannot be at the expense of the children's understanding. At interview, all three teachers observed referred to the fact that they felt comfortable with a greater focus on some objectives than on others and were motivated more by the desire to develop good readers and writers among their children than by a need to tick off lists of objectives. So, for example, it mattered to Clare that her children paid attention to tense as they wrote because use of the wrong tense profoundly affects the sense and impact of written text. The preplanned activity, which was discarded, was related to grammatical agreement but less embedded in the children's current work and therefore less likely to be of value.

The activity used the shared text from the previous day – *Kipper's Birthday* – and was very different from the phonic work seen in Lesson 1. This capacity to provide a varied range of interesting activities that held children's interest was a common feature observed across these classrooms. Clare had gone through the text beforehand and had covered up all of the -ed endings. Rather than share the objective with the children – as she normally did – she simply asked them to read the story with her and to wave their hands at her when they read something that they felt was wrong. Children correctly identified the missing -ed endings as they questioned the sense of each sentence where present tense was used erroneously. For some children the verb agreement was clearly still confusing; they tried to insert the -ing ending for example. Thus it became obvious that the teaching point was well matched to the children's current learning needs.

As the story ended one child was able to identify the common problem with all of the words the children had identified – that they were missing their -ed endings. In order to reinforce the point, Clare then asked the children to articulate what they thought her objective had been. The conversation with the 6 and 7 year olds looked like this:

Teacher: 'Who could be really clever and think about what we have just learned? What could our learning objective have been?'

Child 1: 'To be able to know -ed.'

Teacher: 'That's really clever, you used language that I usually use.'

Child 2: 'To be able to use -ed in our words.'

Teacher: 'How about we say, "to remember to use -ed in our words when we are writing about the past." I will know if you know it by reading your stories and seeing if you remember to put -ed in.'

The school was encouraging this exploration of learning among its pupils at the time and it continues to do so. The rationale for unpicking objectives in such detail was to foster a sense of deeper understanding in the children about their learning. It was already widely acknowledged that sharing learning objectives with children enhanced progress during the lesson because children understood the purpose for their activities (Black *et al.*, 2003). The conversation above shows this taken a stage further: the children have to be able to describe not only what they have learned but also what they are learning and why they are learning it.

TEXT-LEVEL INTRODUCTION

The use of a separate heading here gives the impression of an introduction where the children were very clearly aware of two parts. In fact, by using the same text, Clare moved seamlessly onto her text-level objective where children were learning to put together character profiles from the text. Thus we are aware, as practitioners, of a move to a different level of input but the children were left to absorb the word and text level together so that they could make connections between the two when producing their own writing later. The teacher must be aware of where these differences lie and of how to use the NLS *Framework for Teaching* as the highly valuable tool that identifies those differences but the children need to be supported in learning through a connected sequence of activities such as those demonstrated in this lesson.

In the previous day's lesson, the children had identified some aspects of Kipper's character and these had been recorded in a class list: 'he likes doing new things, he tries hard with spellings and cooking and he's friendly'. In this lesson they revisited the text with the task of finding out more. This proved quite difficult as the features that had been identified in the previous lesson were very obvious from the pictures, plot and text. Finding out more required going deeper into the text and using their inferencing skills. Clare was hoping to develop inferencing skills in the children when answering questions for their forthcoming SATs; this skill is a higher order reading skill and one that we have already noted may be lacking in children reading English as an additional language. It is also lacking in children who generally have underdeveloped speaking and listening skills and this deficiency prevents attainment at the higher levels for both Key Stages 1 and 2. Thus, it is a skill that needs explicit teaching in the way that the following transcript illustrates. Note how the children are having genuine difficulty to start with, and that Clare actually needs to model for them how she can develop meaning from the text:

Teacher: 'Yesterday we made this list about Kipper and we had found out all of this about him. We said he likes doing new things, he tries hard with spellings and cooking, and he's friendly. Today I want to see if we can add anything else to that list. This time when we read it, we're thinking about what we already know about Kipper.' (Reads one page.)

Teacher: 'Now, can anyone tell me something else that we've found out about Kipper? Don't tell me what he did, but tell me what he's like.'

Child: 'He's got big ears.'

Teacher: 'Is that something we can find out from this bit of the story?'

Child 2: 'He's friendly, because he's writing an invitation to Tiger.'

Teacher: 'We know he's friendly, but now we've got even more evidence. Well done.'

Child 3: 'He enjoys writing invitations.'

Teacher: 'I think we already knew that he writes invitations. Do we really know if he enjoys it? I'm going to read you a bit of the text and show you what I think I know about Kipper from it.' (Reads.) '"That one's yours, these are for the others," he panted. "Can't stop, balloons."'

Teacher: 'I think I've found out something new because it's got "rushed" here and "panted" here. What else might we know about him?'

Child 4: 'He's very busy.'

Teacher: 'Yes, I think he's very busy and he's always in a rush. I'm going to add that to our list.'

Following this model, Clare read on with the children for while. They came to a part of the story where Kipper had made a birthday cake for himself, eaten it all and fallen asleep. At this point children were able to make new observations about his character: 'he's sleepy', 'he likes cherries', 'he's greedy'.

The final observation, that he was greedy, had required genuine inference because the child had deduced it from Kipper's huge appetite for the cake. Appropriately, the pupil was praised for his efforts and thus the pupil's success was used to further support the children in understanding how they might infer meaning from the text.

The above example illustrates clearly how, within a very short section of the lesson, children can be brought forward from vague understanding to a much clearer understanding of the objective through the careful use of modelling. This modelling has to grow from an ongoing assessment of pupils through identification of misconceptions; from active use of assessment for learning. Clare excelled at this and used modelling to clarify misconceptions and to good effect throughout her lessons.

Further time was spent on ensuring that the children could write sentences about Kipper's character, which would prepare them for their group activities. Having read for a long time Clare switched to a paired writing activity using whiteboards. Before setting the children off on their task she referred them back to their objective which was 'to describe characters' and explained that she was going to make the objective a little harder by adding to it 'to describe characters in sentences'. Characteristically for her, she proceeded to model a sentence before asking the children to do theirs:

> I'm just going to write two words down here, 'hungry' and 'greedy'. How can I put those into a sentence?
>
> I'm going to think it first. 'He was so hungry that he ate the whole cake greedily.' So I've thought it, now I'm going to write it. Can you help me? What will I put at the beginning? What will I put at the end? Now, am I just going to leave it? No, I'm going to check it. So I've thought it, I've written it, now I'm going to check it.

In modelling her sentence she not only gave children ideas for how they might put their sentences together from the preidentified list of Kipper's character features; she also rehearsed the class's mantra for producing sentences in their writing. The children wrote busily in pairs and produced sentences such as the following:

'Kipper was busy making his invitations.'
'Kipper was in a rush.'
'Kipper was very hungry and he was rushed.'

In some sentences there were errors, which were used carefully as teaching points. For example, one sentence said 'He like cherries.' Clare read this out and posed the question, 'He like cherries or he likes cherries?' By articulating the difference she gave this pupil a chance to hear his error and identify it. She was also able to make a reference to the importance of endings on verbs which had been picked up earlier in the word-level work.

GROUP ACTIVITIES

The transition to group activities was managed with same well-paced efficiency that characterised Aidan's practice. The introductory activity matched
the main activity very closely and the paperwork needed was already out on
the children's tables. In her introduction to the activities, Clare explained
what the children were to do, modelled the first of their comprehension questions for them and gave them further information as to how today's work built
on the previous day's SAT practice:

> Teacher: 'On your desks you have got sheets with questions on and you have
>   also got a little bit of the Kipper book which you will need to share. I've put
>   the book there because – what did we talk about yesterday when you were
>   answering a question, what do you have to do? – that's right, you read the
>   question three times, you find the bit in the story that answers it three times,
>   then you write your answer and then you check it. I'm going to model the first
>   one for you. My question is, "What did Kipper think of when he woke up?
>   What did Kipper think of when he woke up?" I'm not going to try and
>   remember it, I'm going to find the bit in the story that answers this question.'
>   (Peruses text and finds it.) 'His first thought was balloons.' (Repeats this and
>   explains.) 'I found that really quickly. You might need to take longer, but
>   that's all right. So what did Kipper think of when he woke up? Answer it in
>   a sentence.'
> Child: 'The first thing Kipper thought of was balloons.'
> Teacher: (Repeats this.) 'Excellent. I'm going to write this and check it. So we're
>   putting together the work we did in SATs practice yesterday and the work we've
>   done on Kipper today. You can do this but you need to do this carefully. I'd rather
>   you answered four questions really well, than answered all of them and rushed
>   them and didn't look for the answers in your booklet.'

Groups were set to work either independently or with another adult. This
time they all had the same task – an interesting difference from Lesson 1
where the children had incrementally different tasks. The choice was appropriate given that, in the SAT, all the children are presented with the same
task. The questions became harder as they progressed and gradually required
more in terms either of inference or prediction; this mirrors the way in which
questions of reading comprehension in the SAT require increasingly higher
order reading skills. Table 9.3 shows the questions and an analysis of which
skills children would use in order to answer them.

GUIDED WRITING GROUP

As was common in her practice, Clare worked consistently with one group
during the group activities. This guided writing group was given a task that

Table 9.3 Reading comprehension questions

Question	Comprehension skill required
What did Kipper think of when he woke up?	Here the answer can be lifted from within a sentence in the text. This means that the child can answer this using recall or simply by reading the text and matching the words in the question to provide an answer sentence. The danger with too many questions of this type is that children's lack of comprehension can be disguised
Where did he rush?	Ditto
Who did he give the invitations to?	Ditto
What did it say on the invitations?	This is a little trickier because the children have to form a sentence using the invitation wording; they can't take it straight from the text
What did Kipper do at 12 o'clock?	This was also difficult because the text for it was a little way in to the children's booklet and required them to have understood all that went before it
How do we know that Kipper is looking forward to his birthday?	This requires children to put together a range of evidence from the text that may not be all in one place
Is Kipper greedy?	This requires both inference and for the child to form an opinion. They may decide that he is greedy because he has eaten all of his cake or they think that he was justified in eating all of his cake when his guests had not appeared
Why do you think Kipper dreamed about cake?	A clear example of inference. The author does not say why, but it is clear that he has Kipper dream of cake because he has just eaten a whole one
Who do you think is at the door?	This demands that the child is able to infer meaning and that he can remember a lot of the plot. He needs to remember who Kipper invited, why they were not there the previous day, and why they might now be knocking at the door
What do you think will happen next?	This requires prediction and reasoning based on a full understanding of the text

matched the objective – to write character profiles – but which did not rehearse them for the SAT. This choice is interesting because it shows that greater importance was given to teaching writing effectively than to training for the test. Clare knew that children would receive sufficient practice in other ways and chose to use her literacy lesson for teaching necessary writing skills. These writing skills would, of course, be of automatic benefit to the SAT.

The task set for this group was that they had to describe a teacher in their year group without naming her. The description was to be good enough for anyone reading it to be able to recognise the teacher described. The children were given a series of starter sentences, which they had to turn into a paragraph of prose in their books. For example: 'My teacher is . . . and . . .'; 'I think she is . . . years old.' 'She likes . . . , but she dislikes . . .' By giving the children so much detail in the structure of the sentences Clare was ensuring that they focused only on characteristics rather than becoming sidetracked by the mechanics of whole sentence writing. This meant that they were able to produce more text – a full character profile – and it freed their teacher to concentrate additionally on good sentence structure and verb agreement. Thus, with careful identification of what she wanted from the task, this teacher set her pupils an activity that matched the lesson objectives closely and was unlikely to be undermined by the myriad other tasks involved in text production. This shows how her attention to detail was driven more by an understanding of the writing process than by the NLS guidance that served only to set a suitably age-appropriate objective.

Interaction with the children during the first parts of the lesson was heavily dominated by Clare's modelling. During the guided session this switched exclusively to one-to-one dialogue with the children as they wrote their sentences. Some of the feedback focused on encouraging the children to check their sentences for errors:

'My teacher is kind and smart.' That's a good first sentence. Remember your full stop. Your next sentence is 'I think she is . . . years old.' If you're writing about me you better not write 90.
Is that the beginning of a sentence, or is it a name? Do you need that capital letter near the end?
'My teacher is kind and she is 33 year old.' Years old?
'My teacher beautiful and kind? My teacher *is* beautiful and kind.' Oh, it's a good job we checked it through.

Other feedback was used to encourage better sentence structure:

'She often looks good.' Who are you writing about? Could you say something else so that it gives me more information and I know who you are talking about?
Well done, do you know why I really like yours? Because you have used the word 'helpful' and nobody else has used that, so that's really good.

'She likes people who are on the good listener's lists, because they sit nicely on the carpet.' Why is that a good sentence? Yes, that's right, it's a good description and she said 'because' so she's given a reason. That's a really good sentence.

Further feedback was given towards the end of the session where progress was mapped against the pupils' individual targets. Of the three teachers observed, Clare was the only one to use targets in this very overt way; this was in part because the school had recently emerged from multiple HMI visits as it grew away from special measures but, perhaps more importantly, because this practice sat naturally with the school's focus on encouraging children to understanding more about their learning. Observe how this happened:

A., your target was to put full stops at the end of sentences. Wow! You have done that beautifully. 'My teacher is lovely and kind, full stop. I think she is 33 years old, full stop. She often looks good with her skirt and her jumper, full stop. She likes people who do neat work, full stop.' I'm going to write in your book 'good, you have achieved your target of working in sentences. Next time I want you to try and do that without me sitting next to you.

M., your target was to improve your presentation, do you think it's better? Yes, I think so too. In fact, since you started this new book it's started getting better. Look, this is much better than that one. Well done.

B., your target was to check through your writing, so read it and check it through now.

This kind of target-related feedback is powerful for many reasons identified by Black *et al.* (2003). It is linked directly to an individual child's stage of learning and is therefore closely matched to each child's needs. It recognises attainment in a small-step way that raises self-esteem and promotes frequent success. It also provides the next step towards written fluency – we see this particularly in the first example. Given the range of languages in the class and the differences in the children's level of fluency, this detailed attention to assessment was a highly effective tool for raising attainment.

PLENARY

During the plenary, teacher-talk was dominated almost exclusively by a return to teacher modelling. Rather than asking for answers to her questions, she used a far more telling question. She asked the children to let her know which questions they had found it difficult to answer. This allowed Clare to analyse what the children had found difficult in answering their comprehension questions and to further explain to them how to make the text work for them in finding answers.

The first child had experienced difficulty with 'What did Kipper do at 12 o'clock?' Her teacher responded thus:

'What did Kipper do at 12 o'clock?' Right, I'm going to see if I can answer that one. Do you know what, I'm going to look for 12 o'clock and see if that helps me. I'm going to read it quickly, I'm going to skim it and . . . I've found it, it's not on the first page. I'm going to read where it is. 'At 12 o'clock, Kipper carefully placed his cake on the table.' I think that answers the question. 'At 12 o'clock, Kipper carefully placed his cake on the table.' Does that answer the question? Have I said what he does at 12 o'clock? Yes, so it might not be on the first page, you might have to turn over.

A second example of how Clare modelled the answering of the questions is given in the following. The question to which she is responding is 'What did it say on the invitation?'

' "What did it say on the invitation?" Which word do you think I should look out for?' (Child: 'Invitation.') 'Yes, and that word appears quite a few times doesn't it? Is that bit there the bit that it says on the invitation?' (Points to the page.) 'So what you could do is find the bit that's in slightly different writing, because that's the bit from the invitation. Did you find it in the end? You didn't, so did you go on to the next one instead? Well done, you didn't give up, you kept looking. But remember that if you have trouble finding one answer you can go on to the next one and then come back.'

Here she responds with some further questioning that allows her to focus on what to do when questions are tricky. In this way, she doesn't repeat the teaching of her first point, which was how to form a clear sentence. This maximised the opportunities in this plenary for supporting effective comprehension technique.

A third child asked her for help with one of the questions requiring inference:

'Why do you think that Kipper dreamt about cake?' Ahh, that's a 'why question'. Those are always the hardest because you've got to give your own reasons and the answer isn't always in the story. Why do you think he dreamt about cake?

For this much more demanding question Clare has done two things. Firstly she has explained to the children that this is a difficult question. She identifies for them that the place of 'why' in the question structure makes it tougher than the earlier questions. In this way she simultaneously puts them at their ease by allowing them to feel more challenged by the question. Secondly she has started to give them a clue as to how they might be expected to answer this question: they will need to give a reason. Furthermore, in helping them to answer the question she has given it back to them. With the earlier, more literal questions, she has modelled the answers or the answering technique. Notice how with the more demanding question she asks more of the children. By the end of this short but teaching-filled plenary, children had put

Clare, Lesson 2   Two objectives chosen that are combined in taught input throughout lesson, Wray *et al.* 2002

Objective chosen after assessment of children's needs.

Black *et al.* 2003

Introductory activities support both reading and writing in group work,

Wray *et al.* 2002

SAT revision in a meaningful context Wray *et al.* 2002

Section Focus	Objective	Activity
Word Level	*To use verb tenses with increasing accuracy in speaking and writing, and to use past tense consistently for narration. (Year 2, term 2, S 5)*	Reading *Kipper's Birthday* with past tense endings covered up. Considering what is wrong with the words that have been changed and what their common feature is
Text Level *Kipper's Birthday,* Mick Inkpen	*To identify and describe characters (Year 2, term 2, T 6)*	Adding to a list of key words that describe Kipper's character. Looking for evidence in the text to justify choices
Group work	*To identify and describe characters (Year 2, term 2, T 6)*	Comprehension questions related to shared text. (SAT practice) Answers require increasingly higher order comprehension skills
Guided Writing	*To identify and describe characters (Year 2, term 2, T 6)* *To use verb tenses with increasing accuracy in writing, (Year 2, term 2, S 5)*	Task to describe their teachers in a way that someone reading the character portrait would know who they were speaking about
Plenary		Revision of difficulties with answering comprehension questions

Word level input supports later text level output in guided writing. Wray *et al.* 2002

Building on previous day's activity, but raised expectations requiring inference. Hutchinson *et al.* 2003

Direct teaching of inference for reading Oakhill 1996, Hutchinson *et al.* 2003

Consolidation and identification of misconceptions, OfSTED, 2002, Black *et al.* 2003

Figure 9.2 Clare, Lesson 2.

forward several acceptable answers that demonstrated their capacity to see beyond the printed text. In nurturing this understanding in her class, Clare demonstrated both her understanding of how to teach high-order reading skills and her understanding of their crucial place in teaching deep comprehension.

LESSON 3 (TABLE 9.4)

The conduct of Lesson 3 was qualitatively different from Lessons 1 and 2 in that text-level objectives dominated the introduction. Arguably, the focus was on individual words within a text but Clare's teaching objective was for the children to learn how to use a glossary for a nonfiction text. Despite this apparent difference in planned delivery, the nature of Clare's interaction with the pupils continued in a similar vein to her other two lessons; a dominance of precise and detailed modelling in her explanatory talk. This was accompanied by a great deal of questioning as she asked the children to explain their understanding of, for example, alphabetical order to her during all parts of the lesson.

Clare was using this lesson as a vehicle to promote children's understanding against the objectives but she also had an opportunity to teach the children

Table 9.4 Overview of Clare, Lesson 3

Section focus	Objective	Activity
Text level *Elephants*	*To understand that dictionaries and glossaries give definitions and explanations (Year 2, term 2, T 17)* *To use dictionaries and glossaries to locate words by initial letter (Year 2, term 2, T 16)* *To recognise a range of ways of presenting text (Year 2, term 2, S 7)*	Labelling different parts of a non-fiction text including the glossary. Justifying why we think this is an information book Identifying words in the text in bold type. Using the glossary to find their definitions
Group work	*To understand that dictionaries and glossaries give definitions and explanations* *To make class dictionaries and glossaries of special interest words (Year 2, term 2, T 20)*	Creating own glossary of elephant words from a list of mixed-up words and definitions
Guided reading	*To recognise a range of ways of presenting text (Year 2, term 2, S 7)*	Reading an information text and identifying its features Discussion around the book's use of key words in bold but lack of a glossary
Plenary	*To use dictionaries and glossaries to locate words by initial letter (Year 2, term 2, T 16)*	Putting a range of words into alphabetical order using first or second letter

about more than the basic use of glossaries in nonfiction texts. This teacher was using them to give the children the capacity to read information texts with understanding. In order to do this she paired several objectives from the text-level list with one from the sentence-level work for that term. Yet again, we observe how our effective teachers made use of the objectives but taught them creatively in order to establish both lasting understanding and pupil motivation. There are, seemingly, more objectives for this lesson than for Lesson 2 but they work so closely together that the children are given understanding of all of them through the use of one text. This is another example of how Clare chose resources very carefully so that they would precisely deliver her objectives.

INTRODUCTION

Before this lesson started and before the children from other classes joined hers to make up this middle-ability set, Clare shared some photos of a holiday she had taken in Botswana. She did this in order to feed in some background knowledge about the sorts of animals they were to see in that day's shared text. This is reminiscent of Bridget's conversation with the children following their poetry composition about the muddy, slushy river. Tiny details like this give us an insight into how many teachers consider how they will resource the briefest of moments during the school day in order to enhance the children's educational experience. This is the sort of intuitive practice that does not appear in printed guidance but which can engage and motivate pupils so very effectively at the start of a lesson:

> Teacher: 'I went to a country in Africa called Botswana so I've brought in some photos. Those are wildebeest – we'll be finding out about those in the book. I've got pictures of grasslands too. Lots of zebra and giraffes. That animal is called a hyena. When we look at this book perhaps you'll be able to spot some more elephants.'
>
> Child: 'How long did it take you to get there?'
>
> Teacher: 'I think it was about 10 hours, but we stopped in South Africa on the way. It was overnight so we slept for most of it.'
>
> Child: 'What does the pilot do?'
>
> Teacher: 'You know, I've wondered before what the pilot does because he has to stay awake for a long time. I think he probably slept beforehand and I think they have two pilots as well.'
>
> Child: 'If they fall asleep, yeah, the aeroplane can fly itself.'
>
> Teacher: 'Yes, it's very clever, they have something they can put on – I don't know what you call it.'

Her dialogue with the children was informal and yet informative. She responded with interest to their questions and encouraged their curiosity.

As the lesson started for the whole group, Clare introduced the new text with questions; she wanted the children to decide whether they thought the book was a storybook or a nonfiction text that would give them information. In order to answer they had to give her not just their opinion but they had to give her a reason as well. This insistence on developing an argument was a noticeable part of her teaching throughout the three lessons observed. Children had to articulate 'why' and were encouraged to ask questions all the time about what they were reading. In this way not only were their comprehension skills enhanced but they would be better placed to put forward arguments in their writing having been given the opportunity to think aloud first. Observe how this genuine dialogue, which fostered the children's thinking, began:

Teacher: 'Today, we're looking at a new book. Have a look at this book and try and decide if you think it's going to be a fiction book or an information book – a nonfiction book. Hands up if you think it's going to be a storybook. Hands up if you think it's going to be an information book. OK. Now put your hand up and tell me why.'

Child: 'Because it's an information book and tells you all about animals.'

Teacher: 'How do you know that?'

Child: 'Because there are three animals and the title "Elephants".'

Teacher: 'So there are three photos and the title Elephants – does that sound like fiction or nonfiction?'

Child: 'Nonfiction.'

Not content with one argument for the book being nonfiction, Clare had created a game for the children that would give them a series of clues as to the book's nature. She had a set of cards with book features written on them and, one by one, children came up to her and stuck them on to the relevant parts of the book:

Teacher: 'OK, what we're going to do is label the different parts of the book, and then afterwards I want you to tell me if you still think it's an information book, or if you have changed your mind and you think it's a story book instead. We're going to be a bit like detectives and find out what it is. I'm going to need your help, I need to someone to pick a card.'

(Child picks a card saying 'front cover'.)

Teacher: 'Would you like to stick that on the front cover?'

(Another child picks 'back cover'.)

Teacher: 'Would you like to stick that on the back cover? Have we got any clues really yet as to whether it's fiction or nonfiction?'

Class: 'No.'

Teacher: 'No, not really. They're both going to have a front cover and a back cover aren't they?'

Child: 'We haven't even got inside the book yet.'

Teacher: 'You're right, we haven't even got inside. I think when we do it's going to be easier to find out what it is.'

It seems likely that Clare had organised the cards in such a way that, when children chose them, they were picking out the least salient clues first. Thus the activity wasn't undermined by a word like 'glossary' appearing early on. Later cards were labels for features that were more likely to yield evidence of the book's genre:

(Child picks the card 'contents'.)

Teacher: 'Do you think you could find the contents page? Do you think it will be at the front or the back?'

Class: 'Front.'

Child: 'Near the front cover.'

Teacher: 'You were right, it is at the front cover. Let's have a look at what the contents are – elephant relatives, where elephants live, elephant families, trunks and tusks, keeping clean, finding food, eating and drinking, babies, growing up, glossary, index. Hands up if you still think it's a storybook now. Hands up if you think it's an information book. Yes. Can anyone give me another reason why they think it's an information book?'

Child: 'It has a contents page.'

Teacher: 'Yes. Though some storybooks have contents pages. But it's more likely to be a nonfiction book. The really exciting thing about nonfiction books is that you don't have to start at the front and read all the way through. You can look down the chapter list and think about what you would like to find out about. So, I want to find out about food. I can look through the contents list and find that on page . . .'

As the features identified became more significant, their teacher gave the children more explanatory detail about them. This highlights an interesting choice for the beginner teacher; in lessons where an effective pace is maintained the teacher is likely to give more attention to those parts of the dialogue with the children that serve to support the specific lesson objective. Conversations regarding less significant parts of the book were kept brief. By the end of this task the children recognised that the book was likely to be nonfiction because it had a contents page, a glossary and photographs rather than pictures. This exploration of the broad features of an information book meant that the class stood more likelihood of understanding the purpose of a glossary, which is what they were introduced to next.

The introduction changed focus, and Clare introduced a new 'word of the week'. During the previous week, when the children had learned how to use dictionaries, the class words had been 'definition' and 'alphabetical order'. For this week the teacher wanted them to remember the word 'information' because they were to spend the week looking at information books. At this point Clare explained to the children that their learning would be useful not just for literacy, but for science where they would be researching using nonfiction texts. Additionally, in ICT, they were going to use an online encyclopaedia.

If we consider the overarching objective for nonfiction for Year 2, term 2 – 'to use dictionaries, glossaries and other alphabetically ordered texts' – it is obvious that it has an application well beyond the literacy lesson. Through her planning, Clare was using the Literacy Hour to give children the skills they needed to use this type of text, but the application of the newly learned skills was given a purpose through other curriculum areas. Perhaps, after the publication of *Excellence and Enjoyment*, such joined-up thinking seems obvious. However, reports at the time and more recently (OfSTED, 2005a indicate that teachers still need help in moving away from a compartmental ised approach to their planning, which doesn't allow children to make these connections in their learning.

Continuing to make the children work hard as they read this shared text, Clare began to draw their attention to the use of bold type in the text. As she read the children were to shout out 'bold!' every time she came to a word that was printed in this way. When they did so, their teacher spent time discussing likely definitions and modelled for them why the glossary was so important:

> Begins reading.
> Teacher: 'African elephants live mainly on the hot, open **grasslands**' (Class: 'Bold!')
>   'of Africa. I don't think I know that word. I think it might mean a land with lots
>   of grass, but I'm not sure what that means, so what can I do?'
> Child: 'Go to the back of the book.'
> Teacher: 'Why should I look at the back of the book?'
> Child: 'Glossary.'
> Teacher: 'The glossary. Here we go. I think I might look near the bottom to find
>   grasslands? No? OK, nearer to the top. A, b, c, d, e, f, g – yes it's going to be
>   quite near the top because "g" is nearer the beginning of the alphabet.' (Reads
>   definition.) 'Well I was almost right; I thought it would be covered with grass,
>   but I didn't know it would be dotted with trees. So I found out a new definition,
>   a new meaning, some new information and I can picture "grasslands" in my head
>   now.'

This activity continued for several pages before Clare turned to sending children away for their independent activities. As always, with this teacher and the others observed for this book, the very close match of introductory activity to group activity meant that the children were able to move to their work quickly and with understanding.

INDEPENDENT ACTIVITY

As in Lesson 2 children worked at the same activity, other than the guided reading group who were working with their teacher. Their activity was to create a glossary of their own. They had to imagine that they were publishers and that they had to put some glossary terms and definitions into alphabetical order. This involved them being given a sheet of wrongly matched words and definitions that they had to rearrange. The task combined the new information given to them in that day's introduction, concerning the nature of a glossary, with the work they had covered on alphabetical order from the previous week. In fact, Clare made this quite clear to them when articulating what she had planned as their learning outcomes:

> At the end of this lesson I want you to have learned two things about glossaries.
> I want you to have learned that the words to be defined are written in bold. The
> second thing I want you to find out is that it is in alphabetical order. You should

be brilliant at this because of your very good dictionary skills. You were very good at putting things about the Fire of London in order on Friday.

Her explanation did not just communicate the learning objective in isolation; it gave the children an illustration of how the objective would look as an outcome. In other words, the children had a carefully defined sense of where they were going and how they might be successful.

GUIDED READING

As in Lesson 1, the activity for the guided reading group bore a close resemblance to the work children had covered during the shared-text introduction. As always, this teacher gave her group a careful introduction to that day's reading with reasons for her choice of text and tasks:

> What we are going to do is look up all the different things there are in a nonfiction book, the different ways information is presented. Later in the week in your writing you might be doing some things in bold. Today we're going to look at some books to give you some ideas.

Having articulated the objectives for the session Clare introduced two books that the children would be reading. Both were information texts and both were linked to the work the children were doing on living things in their science lessons. Prior to reading the book the children were given the task of identifying the features of the first book – *Hedgehogs* – that made it a nonfiction book. After being left for a minute to look the book and discuss it with a partner the following dialogue ensued:

> Child 1: 'It's got photos and it's got an index.'
> Teacher: 'Well done, you were a good listener.'
> Child looking at the index: 'What are these numbers for?'
> Teacher: 'All those numbers are the page numbers you will look at to find things out. Anything else?'
> Child 3: 'It's got a contents page.'
> Teacher: 'Well done, let's read the contents page.'
> Child 3: 'It's got bold writing.'
> Teacher: 'It has got bold writing at the top, well done!'

The conversation was brief but allowed Clare to ascertain that the children had understood the print conventions for nonfiction books. This is a classic example of how this teacher used 'assessment for learning' as an integral part of her practice.

Children read all together, page by page – another departure from the recommended guided reading practice of the NLS. This organisational choice was a good one because it was then easy for the teacher to stop the children where she needed to make a teaching point about text presentation or definitions and thus support her objectives for the lesson. Words in this text were printed in bold, but finding their definitions became problematic when the children discovered that there was no glossary for them to look up the word 'hibernate':

> Teacher: 'Do you think that makes it a good non-fiction book? No, it doesn't really does it? I think we could make this a better book and put a glossary in it, otherwise we've got to use a dictionary or work out what it means on our own. So, does anyone know what hibernate means?'
>
> Child 1: 'It means when it's winter it's very cold so it [the hedgehog] doesn't come out. When it's Spring it comes out because it's sunny and warm.'
>
> Teacher: 'Well done, that was a good explanation. Maybe if we were writing our own glossary for this you could write that in the back. Why do you think then, if this word isn't in the glossary, it's in bold?'
>
> Child 2: 'Because it's in the contents page.'
>
> Teacher: 'No, it's not on the contents page, hibernate isn't on the contents page.'
>
> Child 3: 'It could be that it's an interesting word.'
>
> Teacher: 'I think that's a good point, N. It's using words that are interesting or important words and making them bold.'

This dialogue is a good example of how teachers use guided reading to *teach* reading, rather than to hear reading. As such, it is a powerful model for developing comprehension and book-handling skills as well as simple word recognition. Another example of this strength is illustrated in the following:

> Does anyone notice anything about the way that this is presented? I have noticed a word just here. It's not in bold but it looks a bit different. It says here 'hedgehogs have bright eyes but they cannot see very well.' Can you see that 'cannot' is written in a different way – sort of slanting to one side? That's called italics and that means when you read it you've got to emphasise it, those words are important: it's a bit like saying 'although'. (Reads it with emphasis to model how the meaning is emphasised by the formatting of the text.)

These two examples present us with a valuable insight into the use of guided reading as an objective-based teaching session. The teacher had put as much thought into how she would conduct this group work as she had into the planning of any other part of the lesson. The tasks were scaffolded by what she had covered in the introduction and were given a purpose because the children were to be producing their own nonfiction texts in an extended writing session that afternoon. Thus they would have an understanding of the features of information writing that might potentially enhance the quality of their own composition.

This excellence in the use of the guided reading model – albeit adapted for preference by this teacher – remained unusual long after this observation. A recent OfSTED report into the teaching of reading identified the key differences between successful use of guided reading and where teachers had not understood its nature:

> The successful sessions showed clearly the principles of guided reading in action: drawing pupils' attention to strategies for decoding, making objectives explicit, guiding pupils to apply key strategies in their independent reading, and assessing individuals as they read. However, many teachers taught guided reading ineffectively and it became little more than pupils reading around the group in turn . . . In some instances, particularly in Key Stage 2, pupils were left to their own devices to read silently or share books.
>
> (OfSTED, 2004, p. 22)

Consider just how far Clare's practice was divorced from the weaker model we see OfSTED describing. The children would have left this 20-minute reading session, and that in Lesson 1, with a sound appreciation of a whole range of reading-related knowledge. This thorough approach would have fostered their enjoyment of books and their understanding of the different purposes for reading. Furthermore, as their teacher made frequent reference to how their reading might support their writing, these children were able to think of print in broad terms: as a combination of word-, sentence- and text level features that need to be brought together to produce a meaningful and high quality written or read output.

PLENARY

In common with her other lessons, Clare delivered a brief but purposeful plenary where she concentrated her attention on those children who had not worked with an adult during the independent activities. Rather than review work already covered she provided a game for the children whereby they had to make a correctly ordered glossary by holding up word cards in a line at the front of the class. This allowed her to consolidate the children's learning and to assess their understanding.

As each child came up with a word, Clare engaged the class in discussion about the correct order. This reinforced work from the previous week when the class had looked at dictionaries and set it in the context of a list of words that were associated, as in a glossary. Initially questioning about position of words revealed sound understanding of basic alphabetical order. However, when their teacher raised the complexity of the ordering, she was able to assess that not all children had understood how to order words starting with the same phoneme:

'"Hoofed," H, where's she going to go? Yes, well done; almost in the middle. "Herd"? This is a hard one. Is it going to become before hoofed or after hoofed?' (Child answers 'after'.)

'After? Which comes first – e or o? Yes, e, so you are going to go before "hoofed".

'Last one, "grasslands". What does this begin with? G? OK, g . . . h. Are you going to stand before the h or after the h? a, b, c, d, e, f, g . . . h. You need to go before because g comes before the h. Hold them all up so people can see. Thumbs up if you think they're in alphabetical order. Thumbs down if you think we need to move somebody. Who do you think we need to move, T.? J and B? Can anyone explain to Tommy why we don't need to move J and B? That's right, we need to look at the second letter. There is an e in "herd" that comes before the o in hoofed, so they are in the right place.'

The fluency of this lesson was retained to the very end when Clare referred to work that the class would be doing later in the week. The requirements of Berninger's model for developing writing (Berninger and Swanson, 1994) were met clearly through this sequence of activities; children's later success at writing was assured because they had knowledge about the subject, knowledge of the genre and knowledge of the text features that would aid transcription.

Clare, Lesson 3

Combination of text and sentence level objectives that support overall understanding of the features of an information book. Choice of activities takes this support further, Wray *et al.* 2002, Hall & Harding, 2003

Combination of objectives and activities put together to support children's written composition later in the week. Gradual acquisition of necessary knowledge for writing, Derewianka, 1990

Section focus	Objective	Activity	
Text level Elephants	*To understand that dictionaries and glossaries give definitions and explanations. (Year 2, term 2, T 17)* *To use dictionaries and glossaries to locate words by initial letter. (Year 2, term 2, T 16)* *To recognise a range of ways of presenting text. (Year 2, term 2, S 7)*	Labelling different parts of a non-fiction text including the glossary. Justifying why we think this is an information book Identifying words in the text in bold type. Using the glossary to find their definitions	Direct teaching of conventions of written English, Cameron & Besser, 2004 High expectations of children, Hay McBer, 2000
Group work	*To understand that dictionaries and glossaries give definitions and explanations* *To make class dictionaries and glossaries of special interest words. (Year 2, term 2, T 20)*	Creating own glossary of elephant words from a list of mixed up words and definitions	Discussion closely matched to objective, while also teaching children the need to be discerning as readers, Hall & Harding, 2003
Guided Reading	*To recognise a range of ways of presenting text. (Year 2, term 2, S 7)*	Reading an information text and identifying its features. Discussion around the book's use of key words in bold but lack of a glossary	
Plenary	*To use dictionaries and glossaries to locate words by initial letter. (Year 2, term 2, T 16)*	Putting a range of words in to alphabetical order using first or second letter	

Opportunity taken to identify and correct misconceptions, Black *et al.* 2003

Figure 9.3 Clare, Lesson 3.

CONCLUSION

There are obvious differences between the practice of Clare and the other two teachers observed. You will notice that we have included a great deal more transcripts of her teaching; this is because her teaching was characterised by the use of very detailed modelling that is best observed in transcription. It was in watching Clare's lessons that we came to so clearly understand what was exciting about the practice of effective literacy teachers; that it is *what* teachers *say* in delivery, not just what they *do* with the NLS at the planning stage that makes the difference to children's learning. We have made far fewer references to how Clare's teaching supported the pupils in her class who had EAL. However, it would be wrong to assume that these children were not very well supported indeed. Remember that it was these children who, by the time they reached the end of Key Stage 2, were outperforming their monolingual peers in the SATs.

This teacher's practice grew from her understanding of how effective modelling would support her pupils who came from a wide range of linguistic backgrounds. Thus she engaged less in one-to-one dialogue – although this was still highly prevalent. We also observed more teaching of reading in these lessons, whereas Aidan and Bridget, coincidentally, were observed more in lessons where writing was the key focus. Thus, the three teachers together provide us with a range of teaching guidance that would support all our pupils, as well as being highly effective for our pupils with EAL. Finally, we have already explained that Clare's practice was more closely related to the prescribed pedagogy for the NLS. In this way, she provides us with three very clear examples of how literacy can be brought to life with rigorous yet highly informed use of the *Framework for Teaching*.

10 Conclusion

In this final chapter we report on followup interviews carried out at the three schools in 2005. These interviews show that the schools had continued on their own creative journeys as child and adult learning communities but that the overarching principles that promoted effective learning two years earlier were largely unchanged. To conclude, we map together the findings from research related to children's early literacy development with the elements of successful practice from our case studies.

The research for this book was carried out in 2003 – some 3 years prior to publication. In recognition of the fact that schools are dynamic communities and that change is the natural order for the primary curriculum as successive governments continue in the search for the holy grail of 'best practice', we felt that return visits were necessary. In particular, we were interested to see if the schools had changed anything in their practice or in their philosophies as a result of *Excellence and Enjoyment* (DfES, 2003) and the drive for 'creativity'; this particular agenda had been on the horizon when we first observed the teachers.

Reassuringly we found that the reasons for the schools' excellence remained constant. There had been changes – particularly to the curricular structure in both Ballard and Campbell – but the underlying strengths were recognisably holding firm. These strengths were the leadership of the headteachers and the senior management team; the clarity of each school's vision for children's education and the fact that this was a philosophy shared with all staff; the understanding of the importance of a broad and balanced curriculum and an unwavering focus on learning rather than on teaching. Partnered with this was the sheer creativity and drive of the individual teachers observed and their detailed understanding of how children develop as readers and writers.

You might be tempted to sign off here but stay awhile and have a look at where the schools are now. Through the interviews it became obvious that part of the vision for these schools was their own continual evolution; they were constantly involved in a quest to provide a better learning environment for their children. The ways in which they were changing, as described by their headteachers, serve as examples of how all schools might choose to move on as we walk away from the straightjacketed days of the initial implementation of the NLS.

Only one of our teachers was still in post in her school: Bridget, most recently arrived of the three observed, was still teaching at Ballard Primary. Clare had moved to a deputy headship and Aidan had moved to France to work in an international school. Such upward movement is not surprising given the capabilities of the teachers and is further endorsement of their schools as training grounds for excellence. Thus, the material for the following commentary is taken largely from conversations with the headteachers, but we have also included Bridget and comments from the deputy headteacher at Anderson Primary. Rather than give you individual accounts, we have drawn out common themes from the interviews and discussed them under headings. These shared ideas best illustrate how all schools might choose to interpret the relative freedom with which they may now organise their curriculum, and they reflect activity that is perhaps common to schools across England as they respond to changes in thinking about learning and teaching.

EXCELLENCE AND ENJOYMENT: A POLICY LEVER FOR CHANGING THE NLS?

When asked if *Excellence and Enjoyment* had in any way affected the ways in which they managed their curriculum, all three headteachers answered that it had simply validated what they were already doing. In earlier chapters in this book, which comment on where the schools were in 2003, we surmised this was the case. The schools welcomed the document but saw it only as a natural and necessary progression after the rigour of the NLS. However, all three schools were implementing changes in the way they viewed and planned for literacy as a result of changes in their own thinking that were prompted by other developments in educational theory and new technology.

Some of these changes affected each school's management structures. At Anderson Primary the deputy headteacher commented that they were looking at introducing a more global curriculum structure; one where subjects had less clearly defined boundaries than those fostered by the NLS, NNS and Curriculum 2000. This had led to a change in thinking about the management of subject areas and the structuring of staffing generally. As a result of this the core subject coordinators, accustomed to a key role in curriculum planning and a significant chunk of delivery time being devoted to their subjects, were anxious that their subjects might be downgraded. However, the intention was to revise how the school thought about the curriculum at grass roots level rather than to reduce or increase time for specific subject coverage.

Similarly, Campbell Primary was looking to develop teams that were not necessarily subject based. Ms Chadwick explained that these were more likely to consist of generic posts such as those for *key skills* or for *creativity*. Campbell's governing body was awaiting new funding arrangements due to start in schools in 2006 before making any changes. At the time of interview, however the school had a staff member responsible for literacy in every key stage; thus illustrating that even as thinking changed, the foundations of literacy were underpinned by a safety net of experienced staff. In contrast Ballard Primary had maintained a subject-based structure for staffing, with a newly appointed deputy headteacher leading English. He had been a literacy consultant for the LEA and was highly praised by Ms Bradshaw for bringing a new perspective to the subject. Ballard's maintenance of the status quo for subject leadership was offset by a very radical change in curriculum structure, which is discussed in the next section.

CHANGING THE CURRICULUM STRUCTURE: CREATIVITY IN ACTION

Ballard and Campbell primaries had made quite profound changes to their curriculum structure since we had first observed them. Both had continued to teach a great deal through the arts, and both headteachers maintained a very clear focus on the place of literacy in the curriculum but each had moved forward in response to developments in its vision of what mattered for their children's learning.

At Ballard Primary the staff had adopted the International Primary Curriculum (IPC, 2006, see School Resources p. 221). In essence this meant that they still delivered both the literacy and numeracy strategies but they did not deliver the rest of the National Curriculum as published by the DfES/QCA. The IPC is a theme-based curriculum, cross-matched with the objectives of the National Curriculum, which has been used successfully in British schools abroad and is beginning to appear in some schools in England. Its authors describe it as a curriculum that fosters 'academic and personal development and the development of a global awareness or international-mindedness' (http://www.internationalprimarycurriculum.com). Ballard was already very much a school that followed its own tune in 2003 with great success, borne out by SAT results, so it is perhaps not surprising that it had chosen to adopt a whole new model for curriculum planning. Both Bridget and Ms Bradshaw spoke with great excitement about its introduction; each having taken it on with typical confidence and objectivity as to its strengths or weaknesses.

This quite dramatic change for curriculum planning had grown from an increasing respect for several educational thinkers; among them Daniel Goleman, the man behind developments in understanding emotional intelligence (Goleman, 1996), Howard Gardner whose theory of multiple intelligences (Gardner, 1993) had appealed in particular to Ms Bradshaw's own theories about learning, and Alistair Smith whose work on accelerated learning (Smith and Call, 1999) had been evident at our visits in 2003. Both headteacher and staff liked the way that the IPC gave them a curriculum where links were made across subjects but where the integrity of subjects remained.

Children were taught in theme-based blocks that were mapped by the school onto their morning work in literacy and numeracy. For example, Bridget, now with a Year 1 class, was working on the theme of toys in the afternoons and had linked this to writing a story of a toy's day at school in the morning literacy lessons. Typically for her, the writing was to be produced over a fortnight. She had not lost sight of what the children's needs were in developing their early writing skills but she did say that she now thought less about separate areas of learning. She described IPC as giving 'a feeling of narrative running through the week' because of the way in which it linked thinking and learning across lessons. However, the school was also aware that it had to keep a watching brief on children's development of key skills. Bridget would adapt her planning to include more NLS if she felt that an area, say poetry, had received insufficient coverage.

Campbell Primary had continued on a journey of curriculum change that had been evident when we first visited. Ms Chadwick explained that they were focusing much more on the development of enquiry-based learning; echoing the words of Ms Bradshaw she mentioned influences that included emotional intelligence, multiple intelligences and accelerated learning. To this end the school had abandoned any use of QCA schemes of work and had returned to the more skills-based objectives of the National Curriculum. They were, in fact, developing their own schemes of work that were based around six areas of learning for children: questioning skills, making connections, describing their learning, evaluating their learning, problem solving and personal communication. The school was also part of an arts-based teaching and learning research project with the Gulbenkian Society. Although clearly different from Ballard in its approach to curriculum development, the similarities between the ways in which the two schools were thinking about learning are obvious. This is interesting in the absence of any particular guidance on how schools might develop the 'creativity' demanded by *Excellence and Enjoyment*. It is as if both schools – and Anderson, which was looking at a 'more global curriculum' – had come to their understanding through their analysis of current educational theory. In light of the criticisms of writers around 2003 – that schools had become too mundane in their approach to curriculum delivery – their energy and imagination is further evidence of their shared identity as schools that take responsibility for their own destinies. It is also clear that these schools made the links between theory and practice all the time and were not tied to the printed word or received wisdom.

MAINTAINING A LITERACY FOCUS

Thus, we are beginning to see a picture of three schools where curriculum change had involved considerable removal of subject-based barriers and a clear commitment to a more thematic approach where skills and learning took precedence over content. However, the interviews also revealed that each school had retained its very clear view of how to develop the children's skills as readers and writers. The teachers and headteachers were still very keenly aware of where the children's needs lay and had maintained target-setting and monitoring systems that ensured appropriate progress was made by individuals and groups. Even though the teaching might have become more fluid and the timetable less rigorously carved up into subject areas, the desire to teach literacy that inspired children and was relevant to their needs remained a constant. Perhaps most interestingly, none of the schools had abandoned the NLS, or even spoke negatively of it. The prescribed pedagogy for the hour was mostly gone but the attention to the termly objectives remained.

Anderson Primary had regained confidence in the LEA literacy team and was tackling sentence-level work among staff through training. It had also enlisted the LEA consultant's help in improving writing. Mr Abbott described a very different relationship with the advisory team, which was clearly based more on the school's analysis of where it wanted to go rather than on the very formulaic 'one-size-fits-all' approach of early NLS training. The position of the NLS in the school was, therefore, still strong, although the school's commitment to its broad and balanced curriculum always ensured that the children were learning some of their literacy skills outside English lessons. The deputy headteacher explained that staff were being trained in thinking more broadly about the sorts of literacy they might introduce to the children. For example teachers were being encouraged to use media like art or film when teaching children about fiction. Similarly nonfiction writing might be tackled in lessons other than English. She made an interesting point about the intervention packages to support failing readers – *Early Literacy Support, Additional Literacy Support* and *Further Literacy Support*. Her point was that the very rigid timetabling associated with these intervention strategies and the very precise way in which they demanded support staff time worked against the drive for creativity. Thus, the school had to consider ways in which it could safety-net those at risk from reading failure while moving away from specific NLS guidance.

Campbell Primary had experienced a similar problem and had decided to stop setting its classes as a result. Ms Chadwick said that setting did not sit comfortably with creative teaching and they were looking at other ways of safeguarding progress in literacy such as teaching in single-sex groups. They had already had some measurable success with disaffected Year 5 boys who had improved their reading and writing scores following focused input from the deputy headteacher. Ms Chadwick admitted that there would always be a tension between creativity and the requirements of the SATs. She conceded, in fact, that the standards agenda was not going to change and that schools simply had to find a way of living with it. Nevertheless the school had also developed a strong commitment to allowing the development of oracy before reading and writing. This was evident in the interview with Caitlyn, the EAL coordinator, in Chapter 6. Ms Chadwick was aware that holding firm in their belief in the importance of oracy and resisting teaching children to pass the tests might mean a drop in SAT results in Key Stage 1. Nevertheless she felt, no doubt rightly, that the benefits to her pupils further up the school would be considerable and that this would eventually be borne out by raised results at Key Stage 2. Standing firm in favour of an appropriate literacy curriculum and long-term aims, against the requirement to be seen to improve results all the time in the short term, would take courage. However, all three head-teachers were blessed by a confidence that they could convince an inspection team that their way was the right way.

Campbell, like Anderson and Ballard, was still using the NLS, but had the sense that it was starting to recede into the woodwork as teachers became so familiar with it that the objectives became second nature. In order to ensure that children's literacy needs were met, each year group identified literacy targets and gave them a concentrated 20-minute slot each day. In this way there was no need to include all specific skills-based teaching in a literacy lesson and these lessons could be kept for much more inspiring work. However Ms Chadwick was keen to point out that she felt the NLS and the Literacy Hour still provided a valuable structure for ensuring that a full range of literacy objectives were taught. She felt, like the staff at Ballard Primary, that there would always be a need to keep a check on where coverage was slipping as the school moved to a more crosscurricular approach.

Ballard Primary had retained its unerring commitment to engagement with high-quality texts. Ms Bradshaw was keen to emphasise that this was what literacy teaching in her school had always been about and that this was unchanged. As she put it: 'We were never convinced that the Literacy Hour was the right way to engage with high-quality texts. So our main focus is that – engagement – the highest level of *engagement in the best quality literature that we can provide for the children.*' The school had developed a focus on fostering thinking skills through reading texts. Staff were working on high level deconstruction of good quality texts in order to engage the children in dialogue by looking at dilemma and ambiguity in stories. Ms Bradshaw noted that several prominent children's authors were highly critical of the NLS practice of analysing text for its own sake. Rather than analysing character or deconstructing a sentence, she felt that children need to engage with the messages and worldviews portrayed in literature in order to shape their own views of the world and of themselves.

MAINTAINING STANDARDS IN LITERACY

All three schools had maintained successful SAT results in literacy either regardless of or because of their developing models for teaching literacy and the rest of the curriculum. A feeling that they were able to be more creative with their curriculum input had not in any way led to a reduction in target setting or monitoring of the teaching of literacy. Indeed, it could be said that the curricular developments had enhanced both these areas of practice. At Campbell, as we have already mentioned, year groups were identifying target areas of weakness in literacy and were intensifying support around these by teaching them outside literacy lessons. Anderson had adopted a similar model of focusing on specific areas for additional input.

The headteachers at Ballard and Anderson both welcomed changes to the Key Stage 1 SAT, which now includes a greater emphasis on teacher assessment. Neither identified that changes to the Key Stage 2 English tests had presented a problem. Mr Abbott joked that one of his pupils had decided to write a completely different story from that in the SAT question because he had thought that the set story was too boring. This echoes comments by the children's laureate Michael Morpurgo who has been heavily critical of the ways in which children are tested at 11 in English. Ms Bradshaw commented that she felt her pupils 'bring their own resources to the SAT' and that a change in the question type shouldn't matter if they have learned the skills they need to write well. Taken alongside Ms Chadwick's determination to hold out for oracy even if it meant a drop in SAT results, we see a collective confidence in these schools that underpinned the strength of their vision and success. That is not to say that they disregarded the importance of good performance in the SAT; on the contrary they were keenly aware of the need to take note of the standards agenda but they knew that schools could find their own routes to success.

In order to support maintenance and continuing improvement in standards, each school had further developed its model for training staff. We have already mentioned that Anderson was working closely with the LEA team on specific areas of writing. Campbell pursued a similar model and was focusing on staff's understanding of phonological awareness training and the teaching of spelling. Ballard had decided to move away from its model of sending staff out for days of inspiring literacy training and was providing more inhouse training for staff. Ms Bradshaw still saw a place for days away from school but thought that they were more to feed her staff's morale in terms of giving them a nice day out at a hotel in London. She felt that this served a useful purpose but that the school gained more in the longer term from its systems for coaching and mentoring, induction and reinduction into the values and ideas that were important in Ballard Primary.

SO, TO ANSWER OUR QUESTION...

We started the research that became this book with the intention of finding out what teachers do with the NLS in schools where results are good but where the pupils are disadvantaged socially and linguistically. We have drawn your attention to a wide range of areas where the teachers and their schools demonstrated excellence in their practice and we have often commented in general on the schools and their overall curriculum approach. But the heart of this book is provided by the classroom practice of Aidan, Bridget and Clare, and so it is with them that we shall conclude.

The data collected from the nine lessons observed served to vindicate the headteachers' identification of these three teachers as successful teachers of literacy. All three teachers were experienced professionals who exhibited the qualities identified by Hay McBer (2000) in their study of effective teachers. For example, they were confident, analytical thinkers who exhibited considerable subject knowledge and a willingness to learn more about how their children might learn to read and write. This is not to say that they had a detailed theoretical understanding of literacy development, but that they had an in-depth understanding of how children learn – and how children learn to read and write – and had the confidence to adapt their classroom delivery accordingly. It was also the case that their lessons flowed naturally and that the balance of whole-class, group and individual teaching was tailored to the needs of the learning objectives. Furthermore, their pupils were engaged in focused and on-task behaviour for nearly all of the time in all of the lessons observed.

There was evidence that these effective teachers had considerable confidence and experience with teaching reading and writing and that they were very aware of which pedagogical models worked best for their children (Hall and Harding, 2003). They planned and delivered at a metacognitive level starting from what they wanted the children to learn and working towards the best possible model of how they might teach it. Their planning was based on their knowledge of what worked and why it worked. They were clearly aware of the complex nature of reading and writing and had this concern to the forefront when planning how they might teach each new concept and link it to prior learning.

Their confidence and precise subject knowledge meant that they were not afraid to adapt the prescribed pedagogy for the NLS. They had already analysed its potential weaknesses – a lack of speaking and listening, insufficient time for writing, and possible problems with the proposed model for guided reading – and had adapted their teaching models to circumvent these. They also appreciated its strengths; a concentrated focus on word-level work and a rigour in the termly objectives that enabled them to plan for a wider range of writing opportunities than they might previously have done. Most importantly, their own higher order teaching skills and their understanding of the extent to which their spoken interaction with the children was pivotal to the success of the lesson meant that the potential for learning in any part of the lesson was fully maximised. It is, of course, likely that this excellence in delivery meant that they were good teachers overall, rather than just effective teachers of literacy.

Nevertheless, the three teachers showed that they understood how to teach literacy effectively as their practice was in line with that of Wray, Medwell, Poulson and Fox's (2002) effective teachers of literacy. They matched Wray, Medwell, Poulson and Fox's findings in that their lessons linked the teaching of word-, sentence- and text-level objectives into meaningful experiences for the children. This was the case in all nine lessons observed, even though the objectives and the pedagogy might have varied considerably. A further match was found in the brisk but appropriate pace of the lessons delivered and the extensive use of modelling and explanation in their teacher–pupil interaction. Finally, the three teachers' practice corresponded to Black *et al.*'s (2003) and to Hall and Harding's (2003) findings in that they were assessment literate and shared a belief in the essential role of motivation in teaching children to read and write.

Looking at similarities in classroom practice, these are found on some basic classroom practice levels and in other, deeper ways related to the teachers' understanding of how their own practice affected the learning of their children. At a basic level the teachers engaged the children in literacy activities as soon as they were in the classroom and before the register. This activity was part of the everyday routine for the children and part of the effective classroom management that kept the children on-task. All three teachers planned effectively for the other adults working with them and these adults engaged with the children from the very beginning of the school's day. Routines were clear and children knew what was expected of them at all points in any of the lessons observed.

The most striking, and perhaps the most important, similarity between the teachers' delivery of the Literacy Hour was that they all understood how to create and deliver an interesting, fluent lesson that combined word- and sentence-level objectives into a meaningful text-based experience (Wray, Medwell, Poulson and Fox, 2002; Hall and Harding, 2003). Further to this, they all planned to teach their objectives through a series of lessons that would be linked to extended writing sessions and to other curriculum areas, so that opportunities for writing were maximised. Moreover, the quality of activities designed by all three teachers was creative and stimulating. In other words, their effective teaching may have had more to do with their interpretation of the strategy's objectives than with their use of any prescribed pedagogy. That is, they were basing their practice firmly, albeit unknowingly, on models of effective teaching promoted by Berninger and Swanson (1994) and Cameron and Besser (2004).

Resources were always attractive and very carefully matched to the tasks and to the learning intentions. This attention to detail came from planning what was mostly implicit. As already discussed, planning was not particularly evident from paperwork but there was a wealth of evidence to demonstrate the teachers' thinking prior to the lesson. This thinking had clearly grown from a concentration on *how* best to teach, rather than on *what* to teach.

Furthermore, each teacher knew precisely how to use the resources; this was not the rote adoption of the NLS or commercial resources seen by the OISE team in their final evaluation of the NLS (Earl *et al.*, 2003).

What is interesting is that, despite the crucial similarities identified above, the three teachers delivered their Literacy Hours in quite different ways. Aidan and Clare delivered phonics-type word-level work first when it suited the objectives, whereas Bridget did not use the Literacy Hour for phonics. Aidan and Clare used a range of activities to motivate children during word-level work but the games and activities used were quite different. Aidan and Clare largely used the set sections of the Literacy Hour, whereas Bridget departed from them considerably. Aidan used his additional adults to give children focused input for perhaps an entire lesson, whereas Bridget and Clare used their additional adults to work alongside them. Aidan and Clare mostly taught their children in ability groups whereas Bridget used fluid group and desk arrangements. Clare often worked with a guided reading group during the lesson, while Aidan and Bridget might frequently teach reading outside the hour. All three teachers used a plenary to consolidate learning, but varied its delivery.

The above comments related to difference in classroom delivery and management show, perhaps, that the fact that the teachers understood the crucial role of making connections for children in the lesson, so that word-, sentence- and text-level work were combined, was much more important than the detail of how the objectives were delivered. Nevertheless, if it were the case that confidence in understanding how and what to plan was the only criterion for an effective lesson, then questions around why the NLS had failed to create more effective teachers would not be so much in evidence (OfSTED, 2002a; Earl *et al.*, 2003). Is it perhaps the case that this confidence with planning and subject matter has to be partnered with the understanding of how to talk to children whilst teaching in order to ensure that they make progress? In other words, without an in-depth understanding of how to scaffold learning appropriately, perhaps much of the excellence of the planning would be lost. The findings related to teacher–pupil interaction from these three effective teachers sheds some light on this question.

As we said earlier in the book, we had set out to find out what these teachers *did* with the NLS but we quickly became aware that it was what they *said* during delivery that really lifted the lessons from good to excellent. An aspect of this was the teachers' very confident dialogue with the children – whether at whole-class, group or individual level. Each teacher knew the children very well and was secure in his or her knowledge of lesson content and those lessons related to it. Thus, their pupils were motivated by high-quality questioning and conversation targeted to their group and individual needs. In addition to this, the teachers were always aware of the need to promote understanding for their EAL pupils and this made the children, not the objective, the starting point for delivery.

The excellence of teacher–pupil interaction from all three teachers was a key feature that led to the success of their lessons. Creativity in the activities involved and detailed knowledge of the subject matter and of their children were of paramount importance but they would have been rendered less important if it were not for the quality of each teacher's exposition. It was through this that children were engaged and empowered to make progress during the lesson. This was particularly significant given their status as second-language learners. Through the careful scaffolding of their learning – both in the detail of explanation and the incremental buildup of skills and knowledge over time – the children were supported in making connections for themselves and in having the confidence to make progress while working either with the teacher or independently. The three teachers used the NLS objectives as a useful tool for teaching but their pedagogy was closely allied to the fundamental models of effective teaching described by Vygotsky and Bruner (Wood, 2000) and to the research-based model for teaching writing such as that presented by Berninger and Swanson (1994).

IMPLICATIONS FOR LITERACY PRACTICE IN PRIMARY SCHOOL CLASSROOMS

One of the recurring themes throughout this study of three effective literacy teachers has been the acknowledgement of their deep level of subject knowledge related to literacy. It is as if we see in them the embodiment of what the Kingman Report (DES, 1988) was hoping to foster nearly two decades earlier. This has particular significance for schools as they work toward establishing an identity for literacy teaching in their classrooms that ensures rigour in covering the range of knowledge about language that children need to have in order to read and write successfully. For some schools this knowledge about language may have atrophied into lessons where children are taught the basics of grammar in dry and demotivating ways. Or perhaps, where lessons have the appearance of some creativity but are in fact suffocating children's enjoyment of literature. Take for example, pupils writing their own version of Rudyard Kipling's *If* in order to demonstrate their understanding of the use of conditionals.

What we can learn from our research schools is that teachers do need to teach, for example about genre, grammar for reading and writing and about inference for high-level text comprehension, but that the teaching will be most effective when certain choices are made about how to deliver the learning. What these teachers showed was that fitness for purpose was a much more appropriate method of determining when to teach what than using a set of objectives and a tightly prescribed pedagogy regardless of content. Their subject knowledge was not just what Kingman described, understanding how the English language operates, but it went beyond that to understanding how children best develop as literate individuals. The NLS, as it currently stands, does not take this second and very important strand of knowledge into account. It gives teachers the subject knowledge without the crucial understanding that it is in the delivery that the difference will be made (Willows, 2002). In providing a set pedagogy it perhaps deludes teachers into thinking that they are 'doing it right' while simultaneously undermining their confidence to teach lessons that do not look like a Literacy Hour. Thus, in schools where standards in literacy stagnate and fail to rise, teachers and their senior managers may be forgiven for adopting increasingly formal approaches to the NLS rather than seeing that maybe they need to step outside it in order to motivate and inspire their children to be engaged with literacy.

This problem for schools – that they may not be able to see the need for a greater theoretical understanding among their staff for teaching literacy – is compounded further by the continuing use of the NLS as more-or-less the only tool for teaching English in our schools. As more and more teachers come into the system who have not seen any model other than the NLS and they, in turn, become the hard-working mentors to trainee teachers practising in their classrooms, attempts to move away towards a more flexible approach in teaching literacy become harder for senior managers to implement. It is difficult to take away the security blanket of prescription, and to ask newly qualified teachers to let go of what they know at a time when they are finding their way in a very demanding profession. It also requires that senior managers themselves are confident in their vision for literacy and can see how to support their staff in sharing that vision. If the evidence from the OISE team (Earl *et al.*, 2003) still stands, it seems likely that headship teams are not commonly so clear in their understanding of literacy development as those we met in our research schools.

Nevertheless, before we paint too critical a picture of 'the most ambitious large-scale reform witnessed since the 1960s' (Fullan, 2000, p. 19), we should consider that the national ambivalence towards the use of the NLS, articulated in Chapter 2, is there for a reason. Even given the slowdown in improvement in reading and writing standards in recent years, it is probably the case that it successfully introduced teachers in English primary schools to a richer understanding of the complexities of literacy development than they might otherwise have had. Those of us teaching in the years prior to its introduction will have memories of 'hearing children read' in ways that now seem unfocused and not centred on individual learning need. We will also have very little memory of teaching children the conventions of the English writing system; of introducing them to the wealth of genres through which we communicate effectively in writing. To repeat Stainthorp's (1999) comment, we are unlikely ever to know whether it is the pedagogy of the *Framework for Teaching* that has led to improvements in standards and in teaching. Our problem now is in unpicking which parts of the NLS we might want to retain and which we might cast aside as we develop our teaching into something more personalised and creative.

The key message that Clare, Aidan and Bridget give us is that teachers of literacy should probably retain the *Framework for Teaching* as a very useful and rigorous structure for their planning. However, they must unite their planning with far less tangible aspects of the effective teacher's classroom repertoire. Their excellence, as we have observed repeatedly throughout this book, had very little to do with words on paper. These less visible and very much unprescribed aspects of delivery are the ability to motivate and inspire children with a love of reading and writing, an understanding of how literacy develops and the small steps needed to support that development and, finally, the use of dialogue with the children that precisely targets learning needs by modelling new concepts and engaging children's thinking. Such subtle and higher level teaching skills do not come from reading a well-designed lesson plan; plans are only a starting point. To truly fly, teachers need to engage fully with the psychological processes that will support learning. Only then can they teach in ways that are excellent and which foster enjoyment.

REFERENCES

Adams, M.J. (1990) *Beginning to Read: Thinking and Learning about Print*, MIT Press, Cambridge, MA.

Alexander, R. (2004) Still no pedagogy? Principle, pragmatism and compliance in primary education. *Cambridge Journal of Education*, **34**, 7–33.

Alexander R., Rose, J. and Woodhead, C. (1992) *Curriculum Organisation and Classroom Practice in Primary Schools: A Discussion Paper*, DES, London.

Alexander R., Rose, J. and Woodhead, C. (1993) *Curriculum Organisation and Classroom Practice in Primary Schools: A Follow Up Report*, DES, London.

Baddeley, A. (1985) *Working Memory*, Oxford University Press, Oxford.

Bailey, M. (2002) What does research tell us about how we should be developing written composition? In R. Fisher, G. Brooks and M. Lewis (Eds), *Raising Standards in Literacy*, Routledge Falmer, London.

Barry, C. (1994) Spelling routes (or roots or rutes). In G.D.A. Brown and N.C. Ellis (Eds), *Handbook of Spelling: Theory, Process and Intervention*, John Wiley & Sons, Chichester.

Baumann, J.F. and Kameenui, E.J. (1991) Research on vocabulary instruction: Ode to Voltaire. In J. Flood, J. Jensen, D. Lapp and J.R. Squire (Eds), *Handbook of Research on Teaching the English Language Arts*, Macmillan, New York.

Beard, R. (2000a) *The National Literacy Strategy: Review of Research and other Related Evidence*, DfES, London.

Beard, R. (2000b) Long overdue? Another look at the National Literacy Strategy. *Journal of Research in Reading*, **23**, 245–55.

Beard, R. (2003) Not the whole story of the National Literacy Strategy: a response to Dominic Wyse. *British Educational Research Journal*, **29**, 917–28.

Bereiter, C. and Scardamalia, M. (1987) *The Psychology of Written Composition*, Lawrence Erlbaum Associates, Hillsdale, NJ.

Berninger, V.W. (1999) Coordinating transcription and text generation in working memory during composing. *Learning Disability Quarterly*, **22**, 99–112.

Berninger, V.W., Abbott, R., Whitaker, D., Sylvester, L. and Nolan, S.B. (1995) Integrating low- and high-level skills in instruction protocols for writing disabilities. *Learning Disability Quarterly*, **18**, 293–309.

Berninger, V.W. and Swanson, H.L. (1994) Modifying Hayes and Flower's model of skilled writing to explain beginning and developing writing. In J.S. Carlson (Ed.) (series editor E.C. Butterfield), *Advances in Cognition and Educational Practice*, Vol. 2. *Children's Writing: Towards a Process Theory of the Development of Skilled Writing*, JAI Press, New York.

Berninger, V.W., Yates, C., Cartwright, A., Rutberg, J., Remy, E. and Abbott, R. (1992) Lower-level developmental skills in beginning writing. *Reading and Writing: an Interdisciplinary Journal*, **4**, 257–80.

Bialystock, E. (1997) Effects of bilingualism and biliteracy on children's emerging concepts of print, *Developmental Psychology*, **33**, 429–40.

Black, P., Harrison, C., Lee, C., Marshall, B. and Wiliam, D. (2003) *Assessment for Learning: Putting it into Practice*, Open University Press, Maidenhead.

Black, P. and Wiliam, D. (1998) *Inside the Black Box*, School of Education, Kings College London, London.

Bradley, L. and Bryant, P.E. (1983) Categorizing sounds and learning to read: a causal connection. *Nature*, **301**, 419–21.

Brown, J.S., McDonald, J.L., Brown, T.L. and Carr, T.H. (1988) Adapting to processing demands in discourse production: the case of handwriting. *Journal of Experimental Psychology: Human Perception and Performance*, **14**, 45–59.

Bullock Report (1975) *A Language for Life: Report of the Committee of Inquiry appointed by the Secretary of State for Education and Science under the Chairmanship of Sir Alan Bullock*, HMSO, London.

Byrne, B. and Fielding-Barnsley, R. (1991a) Evaluation of a program to teach phonemic awareness to young children. *Journal of Educational Psychology*, **83**, 451–5.

Byrne, B. and Fielding-Barnsley, R. (1991b) *Sound Foundations*, Peter Leyden Educational Publishers, Sydney.

Byrne, B. and Fielding-Barnsley, R. (1993) Evaluation of a program to teach phonemic awareness to young children: a one-year follow-up. *Journal of Educational Psychology*, **85**, 104–11.

Byrne, B. and Fielding-Barnsley, R. (1995) Evaluation of a program to teach phonemic awareness to young children. A 2- and 3-year follow up and a new preschool trial. *Journal of Educational Psychology*, **87**, 488–503.

Byrne, B., Fielding-Barnsley, R. and Ashley, L. (2000) Effects of preschool phoneme identity after six years: outcome level distinguished from rate of response. *Journal of Educational Psychology*, **92**, 659–67.

Cameron, L. and Besser, S. (2004) *Writing in English as an Additional Language at Key Stage 2, DfES RR 586*, DfES, London.

Cipielewski, J. and Stanovich, K.E. (1992) Predicting growth in reading ability from children's exposure to print. *Journal of Experimental Child Psychology*, **54**, 74–89.

Clarke, S. (1998) *Targeting Assessment in the Primary Classroom*, Hodder & Stoughton, London.

Clarke, S. (2000) *Unlocking Formative Assessment*, Hodder & Stoughton, London.

Clarke, S. (2003) *Enriching Feedback in the Primary Classroom*, Hodder Murray, London.

Coltheart, M., Rastle, K., Perry, C., Langdon, R. and Ziegler, J.C. (2001) DRC: A dual-route cascade model of visual word recognition and reading aloud. *Psychological Review*, **6**, 204–56.

Connelly, V., Dockrell, J.E. and Barnett, J. (2005) Research note: the slow handwriting of undergraduate students constrains overall performance in exam essays. *Educational Psychology*, **25**, 99–107.

Connelly, V. and Hurst, G. (2002) The influence of handwriting fluency on writing quality in later primary and early secondary education. *Handwriting Today*, **2**, 5–57.

Cummins, J. (2000) *Language, Power and Pedagogy: Bilingual Children in the Crossfire*, Multilingual Matters, Clevedon.

Derewianka, B. (1990) Rocks in their head. In R. Carter (Ed.), *Knowledge about Language and the Curriculum: the LINC Reader*, Hodder & Stoughton, London.

DES (1988) *Report of the Committee of Inquiry into the Teaching of English Language* (The Kingman Report), HMSO, London.

DES (1992) *Curriculum Organisation and Classroom Practice in Primary Schools*, HMSO, London.

DfES (2000a) *Progression in Phonics*, DfES, London.

DfES (2000b) *Developing Early Writing*, DfES, London.

DfES (2001) *The National Literacy Strategy; Framework for Teaching*, DfES, London.

DfES (2002) *Supporting Pupils Learning English as an Additional Language*. Revised edition, DfES, London.

DfES (2003) *Excellence and Enjoyment: A Strategy for Primary Schools*, DfES, London.

Dombey, H. (2003) Interactions between teachers, children and texts in three primary classrooms in England. *Journal of Early Childhood Literacy*, **3**, 37–58.

Earl, L., Fullan, M., Leithwood, K., Watson, N., with Jantzi, D., Levin, B. and Torrance, N. (2000) *Watching and Learning 1: OISE/UT Evaluation of the Implementation of the National Literacy and Numeracy Strategies*, DfES, London.

Earl, L., Levin, B., Fullan, M., Leithwood, K., Watson, N., with Jantzi, D., Mascall, B. and Torrance, N. (2001) *Watching and Learning 2: OISE/UT Evaluation of the Implementation of the National Literacy and Numeracy Strategies*, DfES, London.

Earl, L., Watson, N., Levin, B., Leithwood, K., Fullan, M. and Torrance, N. with Jantzi, D., Mascall, B. and Volante, L. (2003) *Watching and Learning 3: OISE/UT Evaluation of the Implementation of the National Literacy and Numeracy Strategies*, DfES, London.

Edwards, V. (1998) *The Power of Babel: Teaching and Learning in Multilingual Classrooms*, Trentham Books, Stoke-on-Trent.

Ehri, L.C. (1995) Phases of development in learning to read words by sight. *Journal of Research in Reading*, **18**, 116–25.

Ehri, L.C. (1997) Learning to read and spell words. In L. Rieben and C.A. Perfetti (Eds), *Learning to Read: Basic Research and its Implications*, Lawrence Erlbaum Associates, Hillsdale, NJ.

Ellis, A.W. (1993) *Reading, Writing and Dyslexia: A Cognitive Analysis*, Lawrence Erlbaum Associates, London.

Fisher, R. (2002) Shared Thinking: metacognitive modelling in the literacy hour. *Reading, Literacy and Language*, **36**, 64–8.

Fisher, R. (2004) Embedding the Literacy Strategy: snapshots of change? *Literacy*, **38**, 134–40.

Fisher, R. and Lewis, M. (2002) Examining teaching in the Literacy Hour: case studies from English classrooms. In R. Fisher, G. Brooks and M. Lewis (Eds), *Raising Standards in Literacy*, Routledge Falmer, London.

Fisher, R., Lewis, M. and Davis, B. (2000) Progress and performance in National Literacy Strategy classrooms. *Journal of Research in Reading*, **23**, 256–66.

French, F. (1998) *Anancy and Mr Drybone*, Frances Lincoln, London.

Frith, U. (1985) Beneath the surface of phonetic dyslexia. In K. Patterson, J. Marshall and M. Coltheart (Eds), *Surface Dyslexia: Neuropsychological and Cognitive Studies of Phonological Reading*, Lawrence Erlbaum Associates, London.

Fullan, M. (2000) The return of large scale reform. *Journal of Educational Change*, **1**, 5–27.

Gardner, H. (1993) *Frames of Mind: the Theory of Multiple Intelligences*, Fontana, London.

Gibbons, P. (1993) *Learning to Learn in a Second Language*, Heinemann, Portsmouth, NH.

Goleman, D. (1996) *Emotional Intelligence: Why it can Matter more than IQ*, Bloomsbury, London.

Goswami, U. and Bryant, P.E. (1990) *Phonological Skills and Learning to Read*, Lawrence Erlbaum, Hove.

Goswami, U. and East, M. (2000) Rhyme and analogy in beginning reading: Conceptual and methodological issues. *Applied Psycholinguistics*, **21**, 63–93.

Gregory, E. (2001) Sisters and brothers as language and literacy teachers: synergy between siblings playing and working together. *Journal of Early Childhood Literacy*, **1**, 301–22.

Hall, K. and Harding, A. (2003) *A Systematic Review of Effective Literacy Teaching in the 4 to 14 Age Range of Mainstream Schooling*. EPPI-Centre, Social Science Research Unit, Institute of Education, University of London, London. Available at http://www.eppi.ioe.ac.uk, accessed 18 January 2006.

Hallam, S., Ireson, J. and Davies, J. (2004) Grouping practices in the primary school: what influences change? *British Educational Research Journal*, **30**, 118–40.

Hannon, P. (1995) *Literacy, Home and School: Research and Practice in Teaching Literacy with Parents*, Falmer Press, London.

Hardman, F., Smith, F. and Wall, K. (2003) Interactive whole class teaching in the National Literacy Strategy. *Cambridge Journal of Education*, **33**, 197–215.

Hargreaves, L., Moyles, J., Merry, R., Paterson, F., Pell, A. and Estarte-Sarries, V. (2003) How do primary school teachers define and implement 'interactive teaching' in the National Literacy Strategy in England? *Research Papers in Education*, **18**, 217–36.

Harris, A. and Chapman, C. (2002) *Democratic Leadership for School Improvement in Challenging Contexts*. Paper presented to the International Congress on School Effectiveness and Improvement, Copenhagen, 2002. Available from www.ncsl.org.uk/mediastore/ICEIPaper.

Hayes, J.R. (1996) A new framework for understanding cognition and affect in writing. In C.M. Levy and S. Ransdell (Eds), *The Science of Writing: Theories, Methods, Individual Differences, and Applications*, Erlbaum, Mahwah, NJ.

Hayes, J.R. and Flower, L.S. (1980) Identifying the organisation of writing processes. In L. Gregg and E.R. Steinberg (Eds), *Cognitive Processes in Writing*, Erlbaum, Hillsdale, NJ.

Hayes, S. (1994) *This is the Bear*, Walker, London.

Hay McBer (2000) *Research into Teacher Effectiveness*, DfEE, London.

Helavaara-Robertson, L. (2002) Parallel literacy classes and hidden strengths: learning to read in English, Urdu and Classical Arabic. *Reading*, **36**, 199–36.

Her Majesty's Inspectorate (HMI) (1991) *English Key Stage 1: a Report by HM Inspectorate on the First Year, 1989–90*, HMSO, London.

Hobsbaum, A. (2003) *Book Bands for Guided Reading: Organising Key Stage One Texts for the Literacy Hour: 3*, Institute of Education, University of London, London.

Hoover, W.A. and Gough, P.B. (1990) The simple view of reading. *Reading and Writing: An Interdisciplinary Journal*, **2**, 127–60.

Hughes, D.M. (1997) *A Longitudinal Study of the Development of Writing in 4–7 Year Old Children*. University of Reading, unpublished PhD thesis.

Hunt, R. (2003a) *The Oxford Reading Tree*, Oxford University Press, Oxford.

Hunt, R. (2003b) *Max Makes Breakfast (The Oxford Reading Tree)*, Oxford University Press, Oxford.

Hutchinson, J., Whiteley, H., Smith, C. and Connors, L. (2003) The developmental progression of comprehension-related skills in children learning EAL. *Journal of Research in Reading*, **26**, 19–32.

Huxford, L. (2002) The implementation of the National Literacy Strategy in England. In R. Fisher, G. Brooks and M. Lewis (Eds), *Raising Standards in Literacy*, Routledge Falmer, London.

Inkpen, M. (1994) *Kipper's Birthday*, Hodder Children's Books, London.

Jackson, N.E. and Coltheart, M. (2000) *Routes to Reading Success and Failure*, Psychology Press, Hove.

Joshi, R.M., Williams, K.A. and Wood, J.R. (1998) Predicting reading comprehension from listening comprehension: is this the answer to the IQ debate? In C. Hulme and R.M. Joshi (Eds), *Reading and Spelling: Development and Disorders*, Lawrence Erlbaum Associates, Mahwah, NJ.

Keeney, T.J., Cannizzo, S.R. and Flavell, J.H. (1967) Spontaneous and induced verbal rehearsal in a recall task. *Child Development*, **38**, 953–66.

Kellogg, R.T. (1996) A model of working memory in writing. In C.M. Levy and S. Ransdell (Eds), *The Science of Writing: Theories, Methods, Individual Differences and Applications*, Erlbaum, Mahwah, NJ.

Kellogg, R.T. (1997) *Cognitive Psychology*, Sage, London.

Kenner, C. and Kress, G. (2003) The multisemiotic resources of biliterate children. *Journal of Early Childhood Literacy*, **3**, 179–202.

Kotler, A., Wegerif, R. and Le Voi, M. (2001) Oracy and the educational achievement of pupils with English as an additional language: the impact of bringing 'Talking partners into Bradford schools'. *International Journal of Bilingual Education and Bilingualism*, **4**, 403–19.

Kress, G. (1996) Writing and learning to write. In D.R. Olson and N. Torrance (Eds), *The Handbook of Education and Human Development*, Blackwell, Oxford.

Kroll, B.M. (1981) Developmental relationships between speaking and writing. In B.M. Kroll and R. Vann (Eds), *Exploring Speaking and Writing Relationships*, National Council of Teachers of English, Urbana, IL.

Lloyd, S. and Wernham, S. (1992) *The Phonics Handbook* (1994 onwards), *Jolly Phonics*, Jolly Learning Ltd, Chigwell.

Long, S. (2002) Tuning in to teacher-talk: a second language learner struggles to comprehend. *Reading*, **36**, 113–18.

Lundberg, I., Frost, J. and Petersen, O.-P. (1988) Effects of an extensive program for stimulating phonological awareness in preschool children. *Reading Research Quarterly*, **23**, 264–84.

Maclean, M., Bryant, P.E. and Bradley, L. (1987) Rhymes, nursery rhymes, and reading in early childhood. *Merrill-Palmer Quarterly*, **33**, 255–82.

Marsh, G., Friedman, M., Welch, V. and Desberg, P.A. (1981) Cognitive-developmental theory of reading acquisition. In G.E. Mackinnon and T.G. Waller (Eds), *Reading Research: Advances in Theory and Practice*, Academic Press, New York.

Mason, J. and Allen, J.B. (1986) A review of emergent literacy with implications for research and practice in reading. *Review of Research in Education*, **13**, 3–47.

McDermot, G. (1996) *Zomo the Rabbit: A Trickster Tale from West Africa*, Voyager Books, London.

Miller, G.A. (1956) The magic number seven, plus-or-minus two: Some limitations on our capacity for processing information. *Psychological Review*, **63**, 81–97.

Morais, J., Cary, L., Alegria, J. and Bertelson, P. (1979) Does awareness of speech as a sequence of phones arise spontaneously? *Cognition*, **7**, 323–31.

Mortimore, P., Sammons, P., Stoll, L., Lewis, D. and Ecob, R. (1988) *School Matters: The Junior Years*, Open Books, London.

Moss, G. (2004) Changing Practice: The National Literacy Strategy and the politics of literacy policy. *Literacy*, **38**, 126–33.

Nagy, W.E., Herman, P. and Anderson, R. (1985) Learning words from context. *Reading Research Quarterly*, **19**, 304–30.

Oakhill, J.V., Yuill, N.M. and Parkin, A.J. (1986) On the nature of the difference between skilled and less-skilled comprehenders. *Journal of Research in Reading*, **9**, 80–91.

OfSTED (1996a) *Subjects and Standards: Issues for School Development arising from OfSTED Inspection Findings 1994–5, Key Stages 1 and 2*, HMSO, London.

OfSTED (1996b) *The Teaching of Reading in 45 Inner London Primary Schools: a Report by Her Majesty's Inspectors in Collaboration with the LEAs of Islington, Southwark and Tower Hamlets*, OfSTED, London.

OfSTED (1998) *The National Literacy Project: An HMI Evaluation*, OfSTED, London.

OfSTED (2000a) *Inspecting Subjects 3–11: Guidance for Inspectors and Schools*, OfSTED, London.

OfSTED (2000b) *Improving City Schools: Strategies to Promote Educational Inclusion*, OfSTED, London.

OfSTED (2000c) *The National Literacy Strategy: the Second Year*, OfSTED, London.

OfSTED (2001a) *The National Literacy Strategy: the Third Year*, OfSTED, London.

OfSTED (2001b) *Teaching of Phonics: A Paper by HMI*, OfSTED, London.

OfSTED (2002a) *The National Literacy Strategy: the First Four Years 1998–2002*, OfSTED, London.

OfSTED (2002b) *Teaching Assistants in Primary Schools: An Evaluation of the Quality and Impact of their Work*, OfSTED, London.

OfSTED (2003) *The National Literacy and Numeracy Strategies and the Primary Curriculum*, OfSTED, London.

OfSTED (2004) *Reading for Purpose and Pleasure: An Evaluation of the Teaching of Reading in Primary Schools*, OfSTED, London.

OfSTED (2005a) *The National Literacy and Numeracy Strategies and the Primary Curriculum*, OfSTED, London.

OfSTED (2005b) *Annual Report of Her Majesty's Chief Inspector of Schools 2003–4*, OfSTED, London.

Paley, V.G. (1990) *The Boy who would be a Helicopter; the Uses of Storytelling in the Classroom*, Harvard University Press, Cambridge, MA.

Parke, T. and Drury, R. (2001) Language development at home and school: gains and losses in young bilinguals. *Early Years*, **21**, 117–27.

Perera, K. (1984) *Children's Writing and Reading: Analysing Classroom Language*, Blackwell, Oxford.

Perfetti, C.A. (1985) *Reading Ability*, Oxford University Press, New York.

PIRLS (2001) *Trends in Children's Reading Literacy Achievement 1991–2001: IEA's Repeat in Nine Countries of the 1991 Reading Literacy Study*, http://isc.bc.edu/pirls2001i/PIRLS2001_Pubs_TrR.html, accessed 20 May 2005.

PISA (2000) *Reading for Change: Performance and Engagement across Countries, Results from PISA 2000*, www.pisa.oecd.org.

Reynolds, D. (1998) Schooling for literacy: a review of research on teacher effectiveness and school effectiveness and its implications for contemporary educational policies. *Educational Review*, **50**, 147–62.

Robbins, C. and Ehri, L.C. (1994) Listening to stories helps kindergartners learn new vocabulary words. *Journal of Educational Psychology*, **86**, 54–64.

Sacks, D (2003) *The Alphabet*, Hutchinson, London.

Sainsbury, M., Schagen, I. and Whetton, C. with Hagues, N. and Minnis, M. (1998) *Evaluation of the National Literacy Project: Cohort 1. 1996–98*, NFER, Slough.

Sammons, P., Hillman, J. and Mortimore, P. (1996) *Key Characteristics of Effective Schools: A Review of School Effectiveness Research*, OfSTED/IOE, London.

Seidenberg, M.S. (2002) Using connectionist models to understand reading and dyslexia. In R. Stainthorp and P. Tomlinson (Eds), *Learning and Teaching Reading*, BPS, Leicester.

Service, E. and Turpeinen, R. (2001) Working memory in spelling: evidence from backward typing. *Memory*, **9**, 395–421.

Seymour, P.H.K., Duncan, L., Mikko, A. and Baillie, S. (2005) *Quantifying the Effects of Orthographic and Phonological Complexity on Foundation Literacy Acquisition: The English–Finnish Contrast*. Paper presented to the XIIth Annual Conference of the Society for the Scientific Study of Reading, Toronto.

Seymour, P.H.K. and Elder, L. (1986) Beginning reading without phonology. *Cognitive Neuropsychology*, **3**, 1–36.

Share, D.L. (1995) Phonological recoding and self-teaching: sine qua non of reading acquisition. *Cognition*, **55**, 151–218.

Simon, B. (1981) Why no pedagogy in England? In B. Simon and W. Taylor (Eds), *Education in the Eighties: The Central Issues*, Batsford, London.

Siraj-Blatchford, I. and Clarke, P. (2000) *Supporting Identity, Diversity and Language in the Early Years*, Open University Press, Maidenhead.

Skidmore, D., Perez-Parent, M. and Arnfield, S. (2003) Teacher–pupil dialogue in the guided reading session. *Reading, Literacy and Language*, **37**, 47–53.

Smith, A. and Call, N. (1999) *The ALPS Approach: Accelerated Learning in Primary Schools*, Network Educational Press Ltd, Stafford.

Stainthorp, R. (1999) The Big National Experiment: Questions about the National Literacy Strategy. *Psychology of Education Review*, **33**, 3–8.

Stainthorp, R. (2004) W(h)ither phonological awareness? Literate trainee teachers' lack of stable knowledge about the sound structure of words. *Educational Psychology*, **24**, 753–66.

Stainthorp, R., Henderson, S., Barnett, A. and Scheib, B. (2006) *Handwriting: Policy and Practice in Primary Schools*, Institute of Education, University of London, London.

Stainthorp, R. and Hughes, D. (2004) What happens to precocious readers' performance by the age of 11 years? *Journal of Research in Reading*, **27**, 357–72.

Stanovich, K.E. (1986) Matthew effects in reading: Some consequences of individual differences in the acquisition of literacy. *Reading Research Quarterly*, **21**, 360–407.

Statham, E. (1993) *Scattered in the Mainstream: Educational Provision for Isolated Bilingual Learners*. Unpublished PhD thesis, University of Southampton.

Stuart, M. (1995) Phonemic analysis and reading development: some current issues. *Journal of Research in Reading*, **28**, 39–49.

Stuart, M. (1999) Getting ready for reading: early phoneme awareness and phonics teaching improves reading and spelling in inner-city second language learners. *British Journal of Educational Psychology*, **69**, 587–605.

Stuart, M. (2004) Getting ready for reading: a follow-up study of inner city second language learners at the end of Key Stage 1. *British Journal of Educational Psychology*, **74**, 15–36.

Stuart, M. and Coltheart, M. (1988) Does reading develop in a sequence of stages? *Cognition*, **30**, 139–81.

Stuart, M., Dixon, M., Masterson, J. and Gray, B. (2003) Children's early reading vocabulary: Description and word frequency lists. *British Journal of Educational Psychology*, **73**, 585–98.

Sulzby, E. and Teale, W. (1991) Emergent literacy. In R. Barr, M.L. Kamil, P.B. Mosenthal and P.D. Pearson (Eds), *Handbook of Reading Research*, Vol. 2, Longman, New York.

Sylva, K., Hurry, J., Mirelmann, H., Burrell, A. and Riley, J. (1999) Evaluation of a focussed literacy teaching programme in Reception and Year 1 Classes: classroom observations. *British Educational Research Journal*, **25**, 617–35.

Tizard, B. (1984) *Young Children Learning: Talking and Thinking at Home and at School*, Fontana, London.

Topping, K. and Ferguson, N. (2005) Effective literacy teaching behaviours. *Journal of Research in Reading*, **28**, 125–43.

Treiman, R. (1992) The role of intrasyllabic units in learning to read and spell. In P.B. Gough, L.C. Ehri and R. Treiman (Eds), *Reading Acquisition*, Erlbaum, Hillsdale, NJ.

Treiman, R., Kessler, B. and Bourassa, D. (2001) Children's own names influence their spelling. *Applied Psycholinguistics*, **22**, 555–70.

Van Kleeck, A. (1990) Emergent literacy: learning about print before learning to read. *Topics in Language Disorders*, **10**, 25–45.

Vellutino, F.R., Scanlon, D.M. and Tanzman, M.S. (1994) Components of reading ability: issues and problems in operationalizing word identification, phonological coding, and orthographic coding. In G.R. Lyon (Ed.), *Frames of Reference for the*

Assessment of Learning Disabilities: New Views on Measurement Issues, Paul H. Brookes Publishing Co., Baltimore, MD.

Verhoeven, L. (1994) Linguistic diversity and literacy development. In L. Verhoeven (Ed.), *Functional Literacy: Theoretical Issues and Educational Implications*, John Benjamins Publishing Company, Amsterdam.

Walley, A.C. (1993) The role of vocabulary development in children's spoken word recognition and segmentation ability. *Developmental Review*, **13**, 286–350.

Watson, J.E. and Johnston, R.S. (1998) Accelerating reading attainment: the effectiveness of synthetic phonics, *Interchange 57*, SOEID, Edinburgh.

West, R.F. and Stanovich, K.E. (1978) Automatic contextual facilitation in readers of three ages. *Child Development*, **49**, 717–27.

Whitburn, J. (2001) Effective classroom organisation in primary schools: mathematics. *Oxford Review of Education*, **27**, 411–28.

Whitehurst, G.J. and Fischel, J.E. (2000) A developmental model of reading and language impairments arising in conditions of economic poverty. In D. Bishop and L. Leonard (Eds), *Speech and Language Impairments in Children: Causes, Characteristics, Intervention and Outcome*, Psychological Press, Hove.

Whitehurst, G.J. and Lonigan, C.J. (1998) Child development and emergent literacy. *Child Development*, **69**, 848–72.

Willows, D. (2002) The balanced literacy diet: using a food pyramid concept to cut through the great debate over phonics vs. whole language. http://www.aasa.org/publications/sa/2002_0`/willows.htm, accessed 20 May 2005.

Wood, D. (2000) *How Children Think and Learn*, Blackwell, Oxford.

Wray, D., Medwell, J., Poulson, L. and Fox, R. (2002) *Teaching Literacy Effectively in the Primary School*, Routledge, London.

Wright, K. (1982) *Hot Dogs and other Poems*, Puffin, London.

Wyse, D. (2003) The National Literacy Strategy: a critical review of empirical evidence. *British Educational Research Journal*, **29**, 903–16.

SCHOOL RESOURCES

Goal plc (2002) *GOAL: Assessment for learning*, www.relearn.com

IPC (2006) *The International Primary Curriculum*, www.internationalprimary-curriculum.com

Mayo, M. (2002) *Unanana and the Enormous One Tusked Elephant*, in Cornerstones for Writing Year 2 Teacher's Book and CD, Cambridge University Press, Cambridge.

Miskin, R. (2000) *Superphonics*, Hodder Children's Books, London.

Nichols, G. (1994) *Give Yourself a Hug*, A & C Black, Cambridge.

Renaisance Learning (2002) *Accelerated Reader*, www.renlearn.com

RM(2002) *Successmaker*, www.rm.com

Author Index

Subject Index